Outreach Library Services for Distance Learners

Editors

Neela Jagannathan
Santosh Panda
Uma Kanjilal

Viva Books Private Limited
New Delhi • Mumbai • Chennai • Kolkata • Bangalore

Viva

First published, 2004

VIVA BOOKS PRIVATE LIMITED

- 4262/3, Ansari Road, Daryaganj, New Delhi 110 002
  E-mail: viva@vivagroupindia.net
- 215-216 New Apollo Estate, 2nd Floor, Mogra Lane, Andheri (E), Mumbai 400 069
  E-mail: vivamumbai@vivagroupindia.net
- 7, Aziz Mulk, Seventh Street, Thousand Lights, Chennai 600 006
  E-mail: vivachennai@vivagroupindia.net
- B-103, Jindal Towers, 21/1A/3 Darga Road, Kolkata 700 017
  E-mail: vivakolkata@vivagroupindia.net
- 7, GF, Sovereign Park Aptts., 56-58, K. R. Road, Basavanagudi, Bangalore 560004
  E-mail: vivabangalore@vivagroupindia.net

Visit us at *www.vivagroupindia.com*

ISBN 81-7649-681-2

Published by Vinod Vasishtha for Viva Books Private Limited, 4262/3 Ansari Road, Daryaganj, New Delhi 110 002.

Printed and bound at Raj Press, New Delhi - 110 012.

Advisory Committee

Professor H. P. Dikshit, Vice Chancellor, Indira Gandhi National Open University, India

Professor S. C. Garg, Pro-Vice Chancellor, Indira Gandhi National Open University, India

Professor Andrew McDonald, Director of Information Services & Professor of Information Management and Strategy, University of Sunderland, UK

Harvey Gover, Assistant Campus Librarian & Head of Reference, Washington State University, USA

Dr. (Mrs.) Neela Jagannathan, Librarian & Information Officer, Library & Documentation Division, Indira Gandhi National Open University, India

Professor Santosh Panda, Professor of Distance Education, Staff Training & Research Institute of Distance Education, Indira Gandhi National Open University, India

Dr. (Mrs.) Uma Kanjilal, Reader, Library & Information Science, School of Social Sciences, Indira Gandhi National Open University, India

Contents

Section Three: Outreach Library Services in Other Asian Countries

Section Four: Outreach Library Services in UK and USA

Foreword

We have witnessed some very dynamic changes in the development of distance education, ranging from the first generation print based correspondence model to the fifth generation intelligent, flexible learning during the last few decades. Seamless access, learner-centeredness, innovativeness, dynamism and capacity to accommodate change are some of the basic characteristics of technology-enabled distance education. Never before, we were able to provide education on demand in real time to reach even sparsely located communities.

The role and importance of library and information services in acquiring new knowledge and propelling advancement of frontiers of knowledge in higher education are well understood by all. However, to ensure cost effectiveness, some open distance learning institutions have developed a false notion that the well-designed and developed course material alone is sufficient for learning through distance mode. We have to realize that often learners in distance education are very motivated and focused in acquiring knowledge and therefore need strong support in the form of library and information services also. It is encouraging to see an emerging dimension of support through the virtual libraries in the form of additional research, review and referral material. Fortunately, the open and distance learning system has assimilated and fruitfully absorbed dynamic developments in information and communication technology and are therefore in a better position today to meet the demands of virtual library services for distance learners. The papers collated in this volume seek to strengthen, support and focus on greater requirements and enhanced needs of library services for distance learners.

There is a general contemporary trend about the realization of the significance, importance and relevance of library services to support the distance learners. Now there is a greater visible focus on providing distance learners with a variety of library services, including document delivery in portable document format (pdf), access to digital libraries, e-mail reference services, virtual reference desks, and online literature searches of databases, etc. Several institutions are engaged in developing learning resource portals for different target groups of learners, with a view to provide area specific web-based information and services to learners, and save their time from browsing the unlimited information available on the Internet. We feel that there is a greater need to develop online resource support, and virtual research environment for the benefit of a fairly large cross section of learners and professionals.

The present volume is an updated, revised, and edited version of the papers presented in the Pre-Conference Seminar of the XV Asian Association of Open Universities (AAOU) organized by the Indira Gandhi National Open University on February 20, 2002 at New Delhi on 'Outreach Library Services for Distance Learners'. The Seminar addressed issues relating to design, development, management, and technology of providing access to quality library and information services to distance learners. The contributors to this volume have presented their ideas, theories and practices with emphasis ranging from local issues to global concerns. An experienced editorial team led by Dr. Neela Jagannathan has accomplished a commendable work in putting the papers together in a framework that would be an important addition to the fast growing literature in this area of vital importance. I am confident that this book will evolve and attract considerable interest in all those who are concerned with the quality of library services for learners, specially in institutions of open, distance, and virtual learning.

H. P. Dikshit

Vice Chancellor, Indira Gandhi National Open University and Chairman, Distance Education Council, New Delhi

Acknowledgements

The mission of the editors in bringing out this book is to share the views presented by the various librarians and distance educators at the Pre-Conference Seminar on 'Outreach Library Services for the Distance Learners' on February 20, 2002 prior to the main conference on 'Access and Equity: Challenges for Open and Distance Learning' of the XV Annual conference of the Asian Association of the Open Universities from February 21–23, 2002. A venture to produce a book of this nature requires support from various individuals.

We express our sincere gratitude to Professor H. P. Dikshit, Vice Chancellor of the Indira Gandhi National Open University (IGNOU) and Chairman of the Distance Education Council for writing the foreword of this book and supporting the Seminar as Chairman of the Organising Committee. We are also indebted to Professor S. C. Garg, Pro-Vice Chancellor, IGNOU for his constant encouragement in our endeavour and suggestions from time to time. We are grateful to them for the valuable advice and timely assistance.

Our sincere appreciation is due to Professor Andrew McDonald, Director of Information Services and Professor of Information Management and Strategy at the University of Sunderland, UK and Mr. Harvey Gover, Assistant Campus Librarian and Head of Reference Section for Washington State University at Tri-Cities, Richland, Washington, USA for agreeing to deliver the Inaugural Address and the Keynote Address and be on the Advisory Committee for the publication of this book.

Our sincere thanks are due to the authors of the chapters. Each one of them has shared their unique experiences, knowledge and research findings on the theme 'the outreach library services to the remote learners'. Their valuable contributions and cooperation have facilitated us in the compilation and editing of this volume.

We also appreciate the assistance provided by Ms. Surekha Mittimani in monitoring day to day work, keeping track of the correspondence with the authors and the publisher as well as for assisting in the preparation of the lists of abbreviations, acronyms, figures, graphs and tables. We would also like to thank Ms. Usha Rani for word processing the papers and updating the editorial corrections.

Last but not the least, our heartfelt thanks are due to Mr. Vinod Vasishtha of the Viva Books Private Limited, New Delhi for making this quality publication a reality in a record time.

List of Abbreviations and Acronyms

A&M	Agricultural and Mechanical
AAOU	Association of Asian Open Universities
ABI	Abstracted Business Information
ACRL	Association of College and Research Libraries
ADAPT	It is a Human Resource Community Initiative funded through the European Social Fund (ESF), with a budget of 333.5 million Euro for the period 1995-2000 in Great Britain. Introduced in 1995, ADAPT supports projects which aim to help the workforce, particularly those employed in SMEs, to adapt to industrial change.
ADB	Asian Development Bank
AFW	ALICE for Windows
ALA	American Library Association
APWI	Indonesian Public Internet Facilities Association
ARIEL	It is Document Transmission System
ASAB	Access with Speech and Braille System
ATiT	It is an audio-visual and information technologies company based in Belgium since January 99 specialising in the field of Education and Culture.
AU	Autonomous Unit
AVEC	Audio Visual Education Centre
BA	Bachelor of Arts
B.Com.	Bachelor of Commerce
B.Ed.	Bachelor of Education
BIDE	Bangladesh Institute of Distance Education
BJMC	Bachelor of Degree in Journalism and Mass Communication
BLDSC	British Library Document Supply Centre
BLIS	Bachelor in Library Science
BOU	Bangladesh Open University
BOUPP	Bangladesh Open University
BRAOU	Dr. B.R. Ambedkar Open University
CATPB	Computer Awareness and Training Programme for Beginners
CBT	Computer Based Training

CCD	Charge Coupled Device
CCRTVU	Central China Radio and Tele-Vision University
CCTV	Closed Circuit Television
CD-ROM	Compact Disk Read Only Memory
CDS/ISIS	Computerized Documentation Services / Integrated Set of Information Systems
CFN	Certificate Course in Food and Nutrition
CODLINK	Commonwealth Open and Distance Learning Knowledge Network
COL	Commonwealth of Learning
CREDIT	Cantonese Reader Electronic Document in Text Format
CRIDAL	Centre for Research in Distance and Adult Learning
CRL	College Research Libraries
D/ENRM	Diploma/Masters in Environmental Sciences and Management
DAO	Dissertation Abstracts Online
DCCT	Diploma Course in Culture & Tourism
DCO	Diploma in Computer in Officer Management
DEC	Distance Education Council
DELNET	Developing Libraries Network
DFID	Department for International Development
DHL	It is a Courier express service under Deutsche Post World Net
DIKTI	Direktorat Jenderal Pendidikan Tinggi (Director General of Higher Education)
DILS	Distance and Instructional Library Services
DLIS	Diploma in Library and Information Science
DLS	Distance Learning Section
DNHE	Diploma in Nutrition and Health Education
DOS	Disk Operating System
DTHM	Diploma in Tourism and Hotel Management
ECIS	European Consortium of Independent Schools
ERIC	Educational Resource Information Centre
ETC	Education Technology Collection
GERC	Graduate Educational Resource Centres

GIF	Graphic Interchange Format
GLOSAS	GLObal Systems Analysis and Simulation Association
GUS	Global University System
HEFCE	Higher Education Funding Council for England
HKBU	Hong Kong Blind Union
HKOU	Hong Kong Open University
HKSAR	Hong Kong Special Administrative Region
HSS	Humanities and Social Sciences
ICDE	International Council for Distance Education
ICDL	International Centre for Distance Learning
ICT	Information and Communications Technologies
IEEE	Institute of Electrical and Electronics Engineers
IET	Institute of Educational Technology
IFLA	International Federation of Library Associations and Institutions
IGNOU	Indira Gandhi National Open University
ILA	Indian Library Association
ILL	Inter Library Loan
ILLiad	Inter Library Loan Internet Accessible Database
ILS	Integrated Library System
INFLIBNET	Information Library Network
INTERNET	Inter-related Networks or a Network of Information Networks
IRC	Information Resource Centre
ISMED	Institute for Science and Mathematics Education Development
ISP	Internet Service Provider
IT	Information Technology
ITB	Institut Teknologi Bandung (Bandung Institute of Technology)
ITS	Integrated Technical Services Workstation
ITU	Information Technology Unit
JAWS	Job Access with Speech for Windows
KOU	Kota Open University

L&DD	Library and Documentation Division
LAN	Local Area Network
LARC	Library and Resource Centre
LC	Learning Centre
LCDL	Library Corners for Distance Learners
LCs	Local Centres
LIS	Library and Information Science
LITA	Library & Information Technology Association
LRITC	Library, Research and Information Technology Centre
MA	Master of Arts
MBA	Master of Business Administration
MITOCW	Massachusetts Institute of Technology Open Course Ware
MJMC	Master of Degree in Journalism and Mass Communication
MLIS	Master in Library Science
NGOs	Non-Governmental Organizations
NICNET	National Informatics Centre Network
NIEMT	National Institute of Educational Media and Technology
NSDL	The National Science Digital Library
NSF	National Science Foundation
NSU	Nova Southeastern University
OCLC	Online Computer Library Centre
ODE	Open and Distance Education
ODI	Office of Documentation and Information
ODL	Open and Distance Learning
OL / DE	Open Learning / Distance Education
OPAC	Online Personal Academic Librarian
OPAL	Online Personal Academic Librarian
OPENET	Open Education Network
OUHK	Open University of Hong Kong
OUSL	Open University of Sri Lanka

PCs	Personal Computers
pdf	Portable Document Format
PGDE	Post Graduate Diploma in Education
PGDFM	P.G. Diploma in Financial Management
PGDHRM	P.G. Diploma in Human Resource Management
PGDLL	P.G. Diploma in Labour Laws Industrial Relations and Personnel Management
PGDMM	P.G. Diploma in Marketing Management
PhD	Doctorate of Philosophy
PIN	Personal Identification Number
PT	Perseroan Terbatas (Company Limited)
PULINET	provincial University Library Network
QAA	Quality Assurance Agency
RC	Regional Centre
RDEC	Regional Distance Education Centres
ROUTES	Resources for Open University Teachers and Students
RRCs	Regional Resource Centres
RRI	Radio Republik Indonesia
SAFARI	Skills in Accessing, Finding and Reviewing Information
SAIDE	South African Institute for Distance Education
SBP	School Broadcasting Programme
SC	Study Centre
SCONUL	Society of College, National and University Libraries
SCONUL	Standing Conference of National and University Librarians
SDI	Selective Dissemination of Information
SEFLIN	Southeast Florida Library Information Network
SMET	Science, Mathematics, Engineering and Technology
SOUL	Software for University Libraries
STOU	Sukhothai Thammathirat Open University
STRIDE	Staff Training and Research in Distance Education
TCs	Tutorial Centres

THAILINET	Thai Library Network-Metropolitan
TV	Television
TVRI	Televisi Republik Indonesia
TVU	Television University
UGC	University Grants Commission
UKOU	United Kingdom Open University
UNESCO	United Nations Educational Scientific & Cultural Organisation
UP	University of Phillippines
UPBJJ	Unit Program Belajar Jarak Jauh (Regional Office Centre)
UPD	University of Philippines Diliman
UPLB	University of Philippines Los Banos
UPOU	UP Open University
URL	Uniform Resource Locater
US	United States
UST	University of Science and Technology
UT	Universitas Terbuka
VCP	Video Cassette Player
VCR	Video Cassette Recorder.
VoIP	Voice over Internet Protocol
VTLS	Virginia Tech Library System
WAIS	Wide Area Information Service
WAN	Wide Area Network
WIN/ISIS	Windows / Integrated Set of Information Systems
WSU	Washington State University
WWW	World Wide Web
XML	Extendable Markup Language
YCMOU	Yashwantrao Chavan Maharashtra Open University

List of Figures and Maps

List of Charts and Graphs

List of Tables

Introduction

Neela Jagannathan and Sanjaya Mishra

Open and Distance Learning (ODL) has made tremendous growth all over the world during the last three decades. The growth in number of distance learning institutions, increase in number of programmes / courses, exponential growth in literature on ODL, increasing number of conferences and the growth in number of distance learners – all these have contributed immensely towards the development and maturation of a strong and sustainable system of education. However, equitable access to Library, Information and Documentation (LID) services is far from satisfactory as compared to their availability to learners at conventional education institutions. In this context, the Pre-conference Seminar on "Outreach Library Services for Distance Learners" was organized on February 20, 2002 by the Library and Documentation Division (L&DD) of the Indira Gandhi National Open University (IGNOU) prior to the XV Annual Conference of the Asian Association of Open Universities (AAOU) on the theme "Access and Equity: Challenges for Open and Distance Learning" from February 21-23, 2002 at New Delhi. The papers in this volume come from the Pre-Conference Seminar.

The term 'outreach' is coined from the verb 'to reach out' meaning extending services to a wider section of the society. According to Harrod's Librarians' Glossary (Ed. 8: 1995) compiled by Ray Prytherch,

> "Outreach is the process whereby a library service investigates the activities of the community it serves and becomes fully involved in supporting community activities, whether or not centred on library premises."

Outreach library services therefore, refers here to the services rendered to the distance learners at their homes or offices outside the premises of the ODL institution.

The phrase "Outreach library services" in the theme of the pre-conference was selected with great care to get information regarding Library and Information services (LIS) provided to Distance Learners (DLs) at the Open Universities of the Asian Region and / or Distance Teaching institutions in various other developed and developing nations. Primarily the focus and objective of organizing this Seminar was to share experiences of rendering LIS to different categories of distance learners particularly women and those who are physically challenged, socio-economically disadvantaged, remote and geographically distributed and migrating population of defense and other mobile employment sectors.

It is evident from the literature available on the subject that Librarians and Information Scientists of the Open Universities (OUs) and Distance Teaching Institutions (DTIs) were very much concerned to provide the LIS services to their new clientele of distance learners. A number of countries have developed guidelines for library services to distance learners. In USA the Association of College and Research Libraries which is the division of the American Library Association, USA devised the first set of guidelines in 1967 and it has since been revised in

1982, 1990, 1998 and 2000 keeping pace with the frequent changes in availability of modern innovative multimedia technologies for providing access to the distance learners. In 1993 Canada developed similar guidelines and is now in the process of revising it. Australia prepared guidelines for library services to external students in 1982. Elizabeth Watson (1992) suggested guidelines for developing countries, especially for the Caribbean Islands. However, it has yet to accept any formal acceptance. The latest venture in this area has been by the Sectional Committee on Distance Education of the Indian Library Association (ILA), Delhi, India. The guidelines have been published by the Distance Education Council, Indira Gandhi National Open University in 2001. Though these guidelines exit, they have not been seriously followed in rendering library services to the distance learners in the developing countries due to several infrastructural constraints.

Number of conferences and seminars on the topic has also been organized so far. In USA, the Central Michigan University, Mt. Pleasant at Missouri started conducting biannual conferences on "Off-Campus Library Services" (OCLS) way back in 1982. Till now, ten OCLS conferences have been successfully organized at St. Louis, Missouri (1st: 1982), Knoxville, Tennessee (2nd: 1985), Reno, Nevada (3rd: 1986), Charleston, South Carolina (4th: 1988), Alburqueque, New Mexico (5th: 1991), Kansas City, Missouri (6th: 1993), San Diego, California (7th: 1995), Providence, Rhode Island (8th: 1998), Portland, Oregon (9th: 2000), Cincinnati, Ohio (10th: 2002) attracting librarians from all over the world to discuss various issues related to the provision of Library Services to Distance Learners and share experiences gained from planning, designing and delivering services to this unique group of learners. The web site of the Off-campus Library Services Conferences at http://ocls.cmich.edu/oclsc2002pubs.htm provide more information about these conferences and their publications.

In the United Kingdom, so far four conferences on "Libraries Without Walls: the Delivery of Library Services to Distance Users" (LWW) have been organized by the Centre for Research in Library and Information Management (CERLIM) at Mytilene, Greece (I-1995 & II-1997), Molyvos, Lesvos, Greece (III-1999 & IV-2001). The fifth LWW will be held at Aegean Island of Lesvos, Greece from September 19-33, 2003. The details regarding these conferences can be viewed at the URL http://www.cerlim.ac.uk/projects/bibdel.html & http://www.cerlim.ac.uk/conf/lwwconfer.html Andrew MacDonald had organized a Seminar on "Library Services to Distance Learners" at the University of Sunderland, Sunderland, U. K. from June 5-9, 2000.

In India, the first National seminar on Distance Education and Library was organized under the joint auspices of the Kerala Library Association and the Quillon Public Library and Research Centre at Quillon from December 2-4, 1988. Later the Indian Distance Education Association (IDEA) had an exclusive session on "Library Support Service in Distance Education" during its IV Annual Conference on "From Learner to Learner – Developing Strategies Towards a Better Student Support Services in Distance Education" from November 22-24, 1996 at the B. R. Ambedkar Open University, Hyderabad.

The Open University of Hong Kong (OUHK) organized the Librarians' Round Table on "Developing Digital Library Resources" in 1998 prior to the XIII Annual Conference of the AAOU at Hong Kong. Later in the subsequent year, the OUHK also organized a meeting of Librarians at the Regional Conference of the International Council of Distance Education (ICDE) in 1999 to debate on this subject.

The Commonwealth of Learning, Vancouver organized a virtual conference on Library and Information Services in 1999 as part of the 1st Pan-Commonwealth Forum held at Brunei, Darussalam.

In order to make literature on library services to distance learners visible and accessible to interested Librarians and other scholars, three annotated bibliographies (Latham et al, 1991; Slade and Kascus, 1996, 2000) have been published. The fourth edition of this bibliography is available online at http:/uviclib.uvic.ca/dls/bibliography4.html

There were in all 24 papers presented at the Pre-Conference Seminar on "Outreach Library Services for Distance Learners". Of these, this book includes 17 papers that have been revised by the original authors before being edited. The editors have categorized these papers into four parts, viz. Part I: Outreach Library Services to Distance Learners, including three Keynote addresses in the seminar; Part II: Library Services to Distance Learners in India; Part III: Library Services to Distance Learners in other Asian Countries; and Part IV: Library Services to Distance Learners in UK and USA.

In Part I, Andrew McDonald discuss the nature of distance learninga and the need for library services to distance learners in his paper on "Supporting Distance Learners". Defining the distance learners as "those who are separated by distance or by available time from the institution at which they are registered for a course of study", McDonald provides a case of successful deployment of library services for distance learners at the University of Sunderland. Harvey R. Gover in the next chapter uses the phrase "To Still Live Our Ideals" as the title to describe the necessity of providing quality library services in transnational distance learning. He provides an overview of transnational distance learning practice in the Europe and elsewhere. He outlines 10 philosophical percepts from the *ACRL Guidelines for Distance learning Library Services* as key to the rights of distance learners, teachers, and librarians. Olugbemiro Jegede in the Chapter 3 discusses the changing environments of Open and Distance Learning (ODL) and also the library services due to the impacts of modern information and communications technologies (ICTs). Describing the librarians as the new age 'Knowledge Managers' in the context of Knowledge Management in ODL, Jegede outlines the challenges before library professionals to meet the needs of distance learners by adopting new technology. Having discussed various electronic and digital library initiatives, he points us towards greater need of training library professionals on appropriate technologies to develop "Virtual Librarians".

Part II consists of 4 papers from India. Neela Jagannathan and Uma Kanjilal report the "Outreach Library and Information Services for Distance Learners of IGNOU" in Chapter 4. The IGNOU provides a comprehensive package of library services to distance learners by: providing access to the libraries at Regional Centres and Study Centres; establishing learning resource centres in collaboration with local institutions and libraries; putting previous year question papers in digitized form on the Web and CDs. The Central Library caters to the needs of the faculty providing additional services like access to electronic journal and CD-ROM databases, helping teachers to develop up to date quality course materials. In Chapter 5, Madhukar Shewale describes the activities of Library and Resource Centre (LARC) of the Yashwantrao Chavan Maharastra Open University, while in the next chapter B. K. Singh reports the initiatives of Kota Open University (*now renamed* as Vardhaman Mahavir Open University). In Chapter six, V. K. Jeevan discusses the threats and opportunities of IT-enabled library services for distance learning.

Part III has seven papers with case studies from Hong Kong, China, Philippines, Thailand, Indonesia, Sri Lanka, and Bangladesh. Annie Chan in Chapter seven describes the e-library initiatives of Open University of Hong Kong. It also provides special services to people with disabilities, which include text to speech technologies, printed scripts for videos, Braille books, online magnifies, etc. There are initiatives on the way to implement the 'web content accessibility guidelines' of the World Wide Web Consortium (W3C). Findings of his research on the Library resources and services of Chinese Television University have been discussed in Chapter eight by Anthony W. Ferguson. In Chapter nine, Andrey G. Andey reports the efforts of UP Open University Library towards increasing access to learning resources. Apart from the traditional services, they use the web extensively to provide online reference materials to distance learners. Boonta Wissawapaisal in Chapter ten provides an overview of Sukhothai Thammathirat Open University's (STOU) library and information services. STOU library services are organized in three levels: central, regional and provincial. Library cooperation and networking have been highlighted as important means to provide efficient library services to distance learners. In Chapter eleven, Effendi Wahyono discusses the Universitas Terbuka's efforts in making library services more accessible by transforming it into an e-library. K.H. Sellathurai in Chapter twelve describes the library system and services of Open University of Sri Lanka (OUSL). The needs of the students are taken care of by the fully automated central library, with the support of study centres. However, the demands of the learners for library services are reported to be high, and the usage of books increased after lending facilities were offered to students. There are also plans to provide more user education to develop independent and creative library users. In the last chapter of this Part, Muhammad Saadat Ali describes the role of information resource centre of Bangladesh Open University in providing quality education and lifelong learning.

Part IV has 3 papers discussing three case studies in outreach library services in the UK and USA. In Chapter fifteen, Mou Chakraborty and Johanna Tunon discuss the issue of how to provide international overseas students with quality library services. With a case of Nova Southeastern University, USA, the authors suggest that technology can play a major role in document delivery. Also arrangements with local libraries could prove to be very useful. They also indicate that cultural and political sensibilities are important issues that should be considered while developing collaborative library services. In Chapter sixteen, Nazira Ismail-Kaye describes the initiatives of International Centre for Distance Learning (ICDL) to provide services to distance learners. Though primarily a web-based service, open to all, the ICDL is used to provide document delivery services to the students of the Institute of Educational Technology (IET) of UKOU. In the last chapter of this book, Gill Needham provides us a vivid account of how the Open University (UK) supports its students through the library. UKOU uses the power of network technologies to metamorphose from a 'teacher only' library access to 'student too' library services. Using the need-based research approach, the services are designed within five strategic objectives, with focus on developing information literacy skills amongst learners.

The present collections of seventeen papers illustrate the range of library services possible and available to distance learners. In order to provide equitable library access to distance learners as that of their counterparts in the face-to-face institutions, the case studies in the book utilized some of the following approaches and services depending on the need, suitability and context:

- Document delivery
- Collaboration with local universities and libraries
- Joining networks of libraries
- Web access to library catalogue and services
- Lending facilities of books

- Access to e-journals
- Online CD-ROM databases
- Access to previous year question papers
- Bibliographic instructions or developing information literacy skills
- Facilities for information access to people with disabilities

The above analysis also reflects that the nature of outreach library services to distance learners is not uniform though the experiences of learners are similar around the world. It also shows the growing concerns of educators and library professionals to provide better services to the increasing population of distance learners. This book is a testimony to this effect and adds substantially to the body of literature on this topic. There are national standards and guidelines for library services to distance learners in the UK, USA, Canada, Australia and India. It is high time that professional bodies like the AAOU and ICDE take up this important task to develop consensus in the Asian region and all over the world to provide improved quality library services to distance learners. Collaboration with international library professional association like the International Federation of Library Associations and Institutions (IFLA) and several Library Associations of the developed and developing countries should be undertaken to frame suitable guidelines and standards.

The main objective of this book is to share experiences of the librarians of the ODL institutions of developed and developing countries — IT rich and IT poor countries. This book will be useful for all those who are interested in the library support to distance learners, including administrators and planners, librarians and library and information science teachers, researchers and technologists, students of Library and Information Science and Distance Education programmes as well as Directors and Coordinators of the Regional and Study Centres of Open and Distance Teaching Institutions who are directly responsible in serving the counselors and students.

References

Latham, Shiela; Slade, Alexander L. and Budnick, Carol (1991) *Library Services for off-campus and distance education: An annotated bibliography*, Ottawa, Ontario: Canadian Library Association, Library Association Publishing Limited and American Library Association, [contains 535 items ranging from 1930 to 1990].

Prytherch, Ray (1995) *Harrod's librarians' glossary*, ed.8. Aldershot, England: Gower. [contains 9000 terms used in Information Management, Library Science, Publishing, the Book Trades and Archive Mangement]

Slade, Alexander L. and Kascus, Marie A. (1996) *Library Services for off-campus and distance education: An annotated bibliography*, Englewood, Colorado: Libraries Unlimited, [recorded 518 items from 1990 to 1995. Out of these 108 records were dated prior to 1990 but were missed in the first edition].

Slade, Alexander L. and Kascus, Marie A. (2000) *Library Services for off-campus and distance education: An annotated bibliography*, Englewood, Colorado: Libraries Unlimited, [recorded 764 items ranging from 1994 to mid 1999. A few items from the early 1990s missed in the second bibliography are covered in this volume].

Watson, Elizabeth (1992) *Library Services to distance learners: a report to the Commonwealth of Learning*. Barbados: Learning Resource Centre, University of the West Indies.

SECTION 1

OUTREACH LIBRARY SERVICES TO DISTANCE LEARNERS

1

Supporting Distance Learners

Andrew McDonald

Introduction

In the United Kingdom, there is significant trend towards a 50 per cent participation rate of young people in higher education, and many universities are now offering programmes for distance learners whether in the United Kingdom or overseas. The University of Sunderland, is committed to widening participation and to enhancing access to learning. Indeed, the University is recognised as one of the most successful in the United Kingdom in terms of attracting learners from a range of socio-economic backgrounds. In addition to this commitment to widening participation, the University has developed its distance learning provision as an important part of its Learning, Teaching and Assessment Strategy. At the moment there are about a thousand distance learners, mainly in the areas of computing and business, but also in engineering, and this represents about 10 per cent of total student numbers. These distance learners are spread all over the world: Bahrain, Greece, Hong Kong, Ireland, Jordan, Kenya, Macau, Malaysia, Netherlands, Pakistan, Saudi Arabia, Singapore, Syria, Tanzania and United Arab Emirates. Ironically, the United Kingdom is a growing market for our distance learning courses.

The City of Sunderland sits proudly on the banks of the River Wear in the North East of England. Once famous for its shipbuilding, mining, glass and brewing industries, the City is undergoing a major regeneration with successful new automotive and telematics industries, a new National Glass Centre and an impressive Stadium of Light housing the City's football club. The new award-winning riverside campus is an important symbol of the City's regeneration, not only of the physical regeneration of an area formerly occupied by shipyards, but also of the skills regeneration within the region's population. It houses the centres of learning and research in the key areas of business and computing, and shortly of digital media, and it boasts cutting edge facilities including a stunning terrace of some 500 PCs and a splendid new library. These are wonderful, state-of-the-art facilities for the campus learners, but how to create a similar experience for the growing number of distance learners, is now the latest concern.

This paper discusses this question and three particular themes: the nature of distance learning, the services provided by the Library at the University of Sunderland for its distance learners, and the range of issues and challenges involved in developing library support for distance learners.

What is distance learning?

In the United Kingdom, The Society of College, National and University Libraries (SCONUL, 2001a) has recently produced an excellent Briefing Paper on *Access for Distance Learners* in which it very simply defines distance learners as "those who are separated by distance or by available time from the institution at which they are registered for a course of study". This means any students who live so far away from the institution at which they are registered as to make it difficult or impossible for them to derive the same benefit from existing library services as campus-based students. It also means students whose personal or work circumstances may prevent them from attending at times, which make it possible to benefit from those services. Some students, of course, fall into both categories.

The Quality Assurance Agency for Higher Education in the United Kingdom (QAA, 1999) defines distance learning a little more broadly as "a way of providing higher education that involves the transfer to the students location of the materials that form the main basis of study, rather than the student moving to the location of the resource provider". It goes on to identify four broad types of distance learning:

- materials based learning,
- courses where parts are delivered by travelling teachers,
- learning that is supported locally, and
- learning that is supported by a remote provider.

Distance learning offers the exciting potential for the local delivery of learning within what is a fast growing global market. It is crucial for widening access to education and for providing opportunities for an increasing diversity of learners. These new learners may be geographically remote, or may have a disability or learning difficulty, or may be disadvantaged in some other way (reference is made to women, migrating populations and mobile groups, for instance). They may be what might be called 'lifestyle' learners who are learning at work, at home or at a centre. They may be undergraduates or postgraduates, or they may simply be enjoying small byte-sized pieces of learning for pleasure as much as qualifications. Increasing participation in learning in general, and in higher education in particular, is an important part of the UK Government's policy for social inclusion. It is evident that if people are denied access to learning throughout their lives, then ultimately a social underclass of people is created who are effectively excluded from the economic, cultural, democratic and intellectual benefits of information, knowledge and learning.

A significant challenge for universities is to provide a similar quality of learning experience for their distance learners as their campus-based students, and a key question for librarians is how to offer equality of access for distance learners to library and information services. However, people's lives and their learning is not tidy and defined and must not fall in to the trap of thinking of distance learners as a discrete or homogeneous group. The boundaries between what may have come to regard as various types of learner are increasingly becoming blurred. Courses are now being delivered in a mixed way with both on- and off-campus components, and students are often choosing a mixed mode of study, perhaps attending less than they used to and engaging with remote provision rather more. Some students effectively become distance learners when they go on work or study placements away from campus. A further trend in the United Kingdom, rather like the United States, is for students to work through college and require support out of traditional hours or even at their work. In a way 'everyone is a distance learner'.

Why library services for distance learners?

The university library may wish to develop services to support its distance learners for a number of reasons. The university, and therefore the library, may have a strategic commitment to distance provision with a view to achieving success in this new global market. Effective library provision will underpin the marketing, recruitment and retention of distance learners, and funding and quality agencies will expect to see suitable learning support services in place. The library itself may have a policy of equality of access for all its users who may themselves begin to exert pressure for more support. It is certainly true to say that providing effective services for distance learners reinforces the value of the library within the institution.

Services for distance learners at the University of Sunderland

Information Services at the University of Sunderland was one of a small group of university libraries in the United Kingdom who first developed services for their distance learners. As part of the Services Strategic Plan, a Distance Learning Services Coordinator was appointed to spearhead development and develop a portfolio of services, working closely with the academic community.

She exploited a variety of routes for communicating with the off-campus learners: phone, fax, e-mail, the Web and even in person (some distance students visit our campus and occasionally we visit them).

The service is mainly offered through the special distance learners Web page. Beyond the welcome page there are six main service options. Distance learners can register, they can use a number of databases most of which are full text, they can make enquiries, they can request books to be delivered (in the UK only at the moment), they can request documents, and they can request literature searches.

There are two further important features. "Information gateways" or Internet subject links that have been created by academics and information professionals to facilitate navigation of the Web in particular subject areas are provided. On a further Web page, information skills support through Internet tutorials and through guides to literature searching, project work, electronic resources and citing references are offered. Information skills training is perhaps even more important for distance learners who have to rely on remote support services and cannot attend the training sessions available to campus-based students.

Distance learners are assisted in gaining access to their local university or public library either directly or through schemes such as UK Libraries Plus and The British Council Distance Learning Zones project.

These then are the generally available services to distance learners. In addition, services in relation to the particular needs of specific courses by working in close cooperation with academic colleagues and local tutors are targeted. For example, the information needs of some Masters in Management students are largely met through local provision and study packs, but we offer a bespoke support service for their project work. The students are required to undertake a literature search, retrieve half a dozen relevant references and write a thesis, all in a short period of time. This project work would simply not be feasible without the support and delivery service and the skills training provided by the Distance Services Coordinator who has even travelled to help the students in their country.

As is the case with all the services, keen to monitoring of usage and feedback are obtained from distance users. Currently about 2,000 requests a year are received, over half of which are e-mail enquiries mostly about Athens registration and access to databases. About 300 documents and 70 postal book loans a year are given. A dozen or so training sessions a year and about 100 telephone enquiries are received. Ironically, the campus-based students are increasingly taking advantage of these services aimed at distance learners, a further example of the blurring of boundaries between traditional categories of student.

Distance learners were surveyed way back in 1998 and this revealed some interesting information about their use of the services and some good suggestions for improving provision. Both have helped in formulating a forward plan for developing relevant distance learning services that are responsive to the needs of users.

It was reassuring that 85 percent of the distance learners said they needed library support. But it was disappointing that 70 percent were unaware of the services provided and that only 37 percent had actually used them. Greatest use (21percent) was made of the electronic database that was provided, 13 percent used the enquiry services, 6 percent used the document delivery service and 4 percent made use of postal loans. The survey showed that students who do make use of the services are very satisfied if not astonished with the level of support provided.

The distance learners made several suggestions for improving services. Most wanted more assistance in using the services, particularly in using electronic databases. There was also demand for more electronic databases, an overseas textbook loans service, greater technical support on site and better local library support.

Clearly, publicity and marketing are important for making distance learners more aware of these important services. There were several other priorities in the development plan for distance services. Library worked more closely with academic staff and the local providers responsible for delivering courses. Access to electronic sources, wherever possible was simplified particularly through authentication and single passwords. Information skills training through the University Web site was provided and this is now made available through WebCT, the new virtual learning environment chosen by the University.

It is planned to continue to monitor demand and usage as part of the strategy for achieving high quality services for the distance learners and it is confidently expected that the next user survey to indicate higher levels of usage and satisfaction.

Several other university libraries in the United Kingdom developed services for distance learners in the mid 1990s, including Leicester, Surrey and Sheffield Hallam. The Open University has an impressive Web-based service with an interactive information skills training module. Many other university libraries now offer services for their distance learners and their Web sites are referred to in the SCONUL Briefing Paper on *Access for Distance* Learners (2001a).

Developing successful services

Library managers should consider a variety of factors when developing successful distance learner services. These relate to providers, users, library staff, legal issues and partnership working. The USA and India have commendably taken a lead in developing national guidelines, but there are no national standards for Library Services to distance learner in many other countries, and this may be an issue for the International Federation of Library Associations and Institutions itself to consider.

It may be necessary to influence university managers and remind them about the importance of developing distance learner services and about the costs involved. In the United Kingdom, SCONUL (2001b) has produced a useful Briefing Paper on the resource issues involved and this is very much aimed at policy makers.

Librarians need to work closely with the academic colleagues who provide the courses and understand the pedagogy involved. Library services must facilitate the learning outcomes for the course and have relevance to the subject concerned. Ideally they should be embedded in the course itself. The development of virtual learning environments provides a good opportunity for librarians to work with academic staff to deliver and support distance learning.

It is important to understand the needs of the distance learners themselves and the learning process they are going through, since these may be quite different from those of campus-based learners. It is useful to know something about the profile of users, their countries, situations, pressures and expectations. Many of the services so far described are delivered over the Web, but in some countries users have limited access to information technology and they may have poor IT and information skills. Indeed, free access to the Internet is denied in some countries. In one way one should encourage distance learners to make full use of our services, but in another, one has to manage their expectations. However, as it has been noted, there are dangers in trying to define distance learners too closely as a group because they are as diverse as the campus learners. Students in general are choosing modes of study and support that suit their particular circumstances.

Services, whether traditional or electronic, must be appropriate, sustainable and affordable. Managers may choose to develop special new services for distance learners or they may simply extend existing ones. They may create a special unit for distance support, particularly in the first instance, or they may seek to integrate these services with general provision. Publicity, marketing and arrangements for authentication require special attention. Provision should be made for information skills training and for arranging access to users' local libraries and learning centres. The quality of services can be assured through service standards and suitable arrangements for monitoring and feedback. Some libraries choose to simplify and customise their computer interfaces to assist distance learners.

Some library directors have found it necessary to change the culture of the library and the attitudes of staff in order to encourage library staff to embrace distance learners as well as campus learners. Demanding remote learners may not always seem to be a priority when staff is faced with equally demanding queues of students at the counter! This culture change may flow from an explicit strategic commitment within the university but will almost certainly require strong managerial direction and support and may need additional staff and resources.

Even when the librarian has identified suitable electronic databases and services, delivery can be constrained by copyright, licensing and authentication issues and this can be complicated by international boundaries. It used to be the case that suppliers could be restrictive about permitting access to their products in different sites in the United Kingdom, let alone overseas. However, it was found that a growing understanding on their part of the importance of distance learning and of the needs of the remote learners (who can be authenticated as studying on the university courses) for access to electronic databases.

Few libraries can support their distance learners by themselves and services can usefully be enhanced by collaborating with local, national and global partners. As well as working with providers and users, managers should cooperate with information and communications technology experts, content providers, local tutors and other libraries and organisations. Indeed, as library professionals, one need to work in collaboration and not in competition with each other in order to respond to the needs of distributed and remote users. Developments in reciprocal access schemes in libraries have greatly benefited distance learners. Under a recent scheme called UK Libraries Plus, distance learners in the United Kingdom now have access and borrowing rights in their local university library or at least in the 100 or so libraries that have joined the scheme. Would it not be wonderful if university libraries around the world could be similarly hospitable to distance learners on an international scale?

Conclusion

Providing services to meet the needs of distance learners is a considerable and complex challenge for library managers. An increasing number of university libraries in the United Kingdom and indeed all over the world are now providing services for their distance learners. May I say I am hugely impressed by the leadership shown by the profession in the US and India in developing useful guidelines for provision. The world of e-commerce is developing at a staggering rate and has developed a great deal of experience of providing e-services. The world of universities and their libraries should embrace this expertise in moving forward with their ambitions for providing high quality distance learning.

Achieving equality of access and support with campus learners is an even more challenging task. It is arguably more important to make suitable, realistic provision for your distance learners than to try to emulate the campus experience completely. That having been said, it is ironic that some remote services are becoming popular even with campus students. Could it indeed be true that everyone is really a distance learner?

Unless librarians successfully respond to the challenge of distance learning and 'think out of the box' and develop the necessary services, other organisations will step in and provide support for distance learners. Indeed, even the private sector itself may become interested in what is an expanding and potentially lucrative global market.

References

Quality Assurance Agency for Higher Education (QAA). (1999). *Guidelines on the quality assurance of distance learning*. QAA, Gloucester.

The Society of College, National and University Libraries (SCONUL). (2001a). *Access for distance learners:* report of the SCONUL Task Force. Briefing Paper prepared by Elizabeth Heaps. SCONUL, London. (http://www.sconul.ac.uk/publications/publications.htm#2)

The Society of College, National and University Libraries (SCONUL). (2001b). *Distance learners: information resource issues for policymakers*. Briefing paper prepared by Elizabeth Heaps on behalf of SCONUL's Task Force on Access for Distance Learners. SCONUL, London. (http://www.sconul.ac.uk/publications/publications.htm#2)

2

To Still Live Our Ideals: International or Transnational Distance Learning and Distance Learning Library Services

Harvey R. Gover

Where are we right now in the development of international or transnational distance learning and distance learning library services? The word I would use to most closely characterize our present state is "thresholding". That is, of course, to convert threshold from a noun to a verb. To threshold, then, is to step out or forward onto a threshold. In the process of thresholding, every step we take puts us onto a new threshold, as we constantly evolve and adapt and undertake to move with a sense of some meaningful direction. Although always being on a new threshold can be exciting, even exhilarating, it does not tend to engender much in the way of individual security. One is literally always "on the edge," and at times the edge can take on the proportions of a cliff.

We are all asking questions these days, and that is nowhere truer than in the arena of our professional lives. In announcing its April, 2002 conference, the Illinois chapter of the U.S. based Association of College and Research Libraries, the IACRL, opens with a metaphor for rapid change and a series of follow-up questions as given below. One is reminded, in reading these IACRL questions that one should seek not for answers only, but should strive first to pose the strongest, most effective questions. Thanks to IACRL, we begin our study with a series of strong questions:

We feel the tides of rapid change carrying us to new, uncharted destinations.

- How can we meet challenges as we progress along our odyssey?
- How can we
  - continue to serve our users?
  - meet information needs across the board?
  - be viable contributors to the educational process?
  - and still live our ideals?
- How can we share those ideals with new generations?
- And how will we build partnerships for the 21st century? (*IACRL*, 2001)

As one can readily discern, because of the breadth of these questions, there are potentially scores of valid responses to each. The fact that there is no single "best" answer for each question greatly magnifies the challenge, as well as the potential for achieving a wide range of solutions. The methods which one may employ in devising answers are likewise limitless. With no little irony, the process of developing strategies through posing and responding to questions perpetuates the thresholding effect.

The IACRL opening metaphor of "the tides of rapid change carrying us to new, uncharted destinations" is perhaps no more true for any other area of librarianship than for distance learning library services. Although otherwise true across the entire scope of the library field, to some extent the metaphor of change is true for other areas of library service because of the sudden growth of distance learning and the necessity for serving distance learning students in or away from many different library settings. The IACRL statement is another metaphor for the "thresholding" effect. What we want to avoid, of course, is simply being tossed about randomly in choppy waters. Not only do we want a sense of direction, but we also want to continue to "live our ideals...and share those ideals with new generations" (IACRL, 2001).

In terms of library services for distance learning programs, the *ACRL Guidelines for Distance Learning Library Services* (*Guidelines*) can provide a Rock of Gibraltar to which we can anchor ourselves in these stormy seas of change; even though, reflective of the seas of change, the *Guidelines* themselves are in a state of frequent, near ongoing revision. However, the elements of the *Guidelines* which do not change and to which we can turn for stabilization, are the ideals embodied within them. That guidelines and standards of any kind exist is in itself an affirmation of the significance attached to the processes they are intended to govern. Many of the ideals by which we wish to live in distance learning librarianship are eloquently expressed in the philosophical precepts of the *Guidelines* and provide an excellent vehicle for sharing these ideals with new generations. The *Guidelines* will be covered in more detail in Part II.

Using the same approach as the *Guidelines*, P. Tapio Varis, in his essay, "The Goals of Global Learning," applied principles to transnational institutions that have long been used for traditional ones. In doing so, Varis begins for us a list of elements essential for the successful establishment and sustenance of transnational education. Varis uses the term "dimensions" for these essential elements:

> ...The quality of higher education is a multidimensional concept, which should embrace all its functions, and activities: teaching and academic programmes, research and scholarship, staffing, students, buildings, facilities, equipment, services to the community and the academic environment. Internal self-evaluation and external review, conducted openly by independent specialists, if possible with international expertise, are vital for enhancing quality. Independent national bodies should be established and comparative standards of quality, recognized at the international level, should be defined. Due attention should be paid to specific institutional, national and regional contexts in order to take into account diversity and to avoid uniformity. Stakeholders should be an integral part of the institutional evaluation process.
>
> Quality also requires that higher education should be characterized by its international dimension: exchange of knowledge, interactive networking, mobility of teachers and students, and international research projects, while taking into account the national cultural values and circumstances.
>
> Marco Antonio Dias, the former Director of UNESCO, has noted that globalization is consolidated by the extraordinary invasion of higher education by new technologies, especially the Internet. The development of communication and information technologies

> makes it possible for distance teaching institutions to strengthen their position in the educational landscape. They also pave the way for lifelong education for all and at the same time are spreading the traditional universities, more and more of which use distance teaching methods in their activities, thereby making the distinction between the two types of institutions virtually meaningless.
>
> There are an increasing number of university networks of this kind all over the world, and the use of computers in the learning process, access to the Internet by students as a vehicle for self-directed learning, educational broadcasting and videoconferencing are all being stepped by.
>
> Higher education cannot, however, be visualized any longer in purely national or regional terms. Future graduates have to be in a position to take up the complex challenges of globalization and rise to the opportunities of the international labour market. The equitable transfer of knowledge and the mobility of students, teachers and researchers, and also the mobility of learning environments using eLearning applications, are crucial to the future of peace in the world.
>
> We realize that after so much talk of technology and eLearning we are now talking of peace, cultures and human development. It is not too late to think of the goals of global learning (Varis, 2001 a).

Peace, prosperity, understanding, successful communication and cooperation among peoples and nations are the fundamentally essential requirements for the establishment and conduct of effective transnational education. These, then, are the foundation blocks upon which can be placed the desired pedagogical elements. Together these two layers of requirements form the lower, basic tiers of a three-dimensional model for transnational education.

Successful partnerships make up another essential foundation element. Partnerships between public and private entities, such as governmental agencies and private corporations, and partnerships among institutions and among nations are but two examples.

One of the largest scaled partnerships is the recently undertaken European Higher Education Area. The thirty-one European Ministers of Education who signed the Bologna Declaration on June 18, 1999, proposed a deadline of 2010 for achieving the initial structure of the Area. The number of participating partner nations has grown a bit since the original core signed the initial agreement. Andris Barblan, Secretary General of the European University Association, in his keynote address to the 13th annual conference of the European Association for International Education, Tampere, Finland, December, 2001, comments that the exact size and membership of the Area is not as important as its content, and then proceeds to provide this vision of the Area:

> Educational services will be flowing freely from one side of the continent to the other, like material goods do today; the providers of education will draw resources - people or money - from all parts of the area - like industrial firms do today when assembling cars or telephones - in order to develop and package the most enticing products, be they courses or research projects, data or publications. Providers will be institutions resembling today's universities but also networks involving publishing houses, media companies, and other specialised communicators. Students of all ages will draw on the most convenient services, relevant in terms of their intellectual interests, career development or social commitments. And there will be common measurement to compare the value of the service, a Euro of the intelligence

allowing for the compatibility and cohesion of the promised knowledge society - the same way tomorrow's common currency will bind the production and trade of goods all over Europe.

For learners, teachers and administrators, the freedom of movement in a common European intellectual space should offer:

- equal conditions of access to the many providers and users of higher education,
- equal conditions of support to knowledge development, in people and institutions,
- equal conditions of assessment and recognition of services, of skills and competencies,
- equal conditions of work and employment.

In Bologna, six action lines were proposed:

- the adoption of a system of easily readable and comparable degrees
- the adoption of a system essentially based on two cycles
- the establishment of a system of European credits
- the promotion of mobility
- the promotion of European cooperation in quality assurance
- the promotion of the European dimension in higher education.

Prague...added three items to the menu of activities leading to the Berlin Summit, two years from now:

- lifelong learning,
- the social position of the learner and
- the competitiveness of higher education (Barblan, 2001).

Barblan's remarks from December 2001, were rendered even more timely by the introduction of the Euro in January, 2002. With what facility and with what a sense of excitement and potential accomplishment can we transpose these goals for the European Higher Education Area into goals for global transnational higher education and global transnational distance learning library services!

Like the *ACRL Guidelines* all of these proscriptions provide principles for application to all global learning development. The phrase "lifelong learning" strikes a very definite chord with distance learning librarians, and there is a precept of the *Guidelines*, to be examined later, which specifically notes the importance of information literacy in engendering and sustaining lifelong learning as a desired outcome of all post-secondary education.

Although P. Tapio Varis does not identify the European Higher Education Area in his keynote address, "21st Century Challenges of Higher Education," Varis in effect projects a *virtual* European Higher Education Area. Like Barblan, Varis was a keynote speaker at the 13th Annual Conference of the European Association for International Education in Tampere, Finland, in December, 2001. Varis was speaking from his home base, for he is Professor and Chair of Media Culture and Communication Education Hypermedia Laboratory, University of Tampere, Finland, and Acting President of Global University System (GUS). The GUS project was initiated at an August 1999, workshop/conference on the "Emerging Global Electronic Distance Learning" held at the University of Tampere. Professor Varis is also Chairman, GLOSAS/Finland. GLOSAS is the GLObal Systems Analysis and Simulation Association.

At the 2001 conference Varis expressed the need for a unified European virtual education which would seem to coexist with that described by Barblan. Quality issues began in Varis's opening statement. Later Varis pointed out that with virtual as with traditional education, the guarantee of quality resides with the faculty. Beyond that, Varis identified "the experience and critical function of the traditional universities" as being "central in the efforts to create new eLearning environments."

> There is now a need for common European virtual education and common European degree system. The content of a European virtual university gateway service would be a portal to net-based or net-supported courses and programmes, information search, collaboration and exchange, common denominators, ownership and endorsement label. The quality issues include transparency, benchmarking, meta-data structure, user and peer reviews, sharing of models and best practice, sharing system and tool description, and user experiences.
>
> Virtual education in Europe has mainly taking (sic) place within national level so far and there is not much transnational collaboration yet. National consortia with centre of expertise have (sic) been formed in many countries (France, the Netherlands, Finland, etc) while some single e-universities and project-based national initiatives also exist. Public-private partnerships are also developing and there are new providers of content from corporate and media linked sources. The issues of quality assurance and accreditation as well as international strategic alliances are widely discussed.
>
> The introduction of eLearning also requires new competencies. A competency is an area of knowledge or skill that is critical for producing key outputs. The competencies can be grouped into generic categories such as general, management, distribution method, and presentation method which help illustrate the relationship among certain competencies.
>
> Transnational education is not necessarily international in the sense that this term has been used before in the context of international education. Courses and learning materials and environment are simply offered beyond national borders. However, a university is more than a library of courses. It is still the college and the professional faculty who can give the quality guarantee to credits and credentials, degrees and diplomas. Governments will have their responsibility in quality assurance especially in courses delivered from non-accredited institutions from abroad.
>
> The quality assurance for virtual education can follow external and internal models. The external models include multi-lateral agreements, accreditation, licensing, kite-marks, and consortia arrangements. The internal models include codes of practice and quality, and management systems. The assessment of on-line universities is often accompanied by three principles. First, the institution must demonstrate how it will achieve its goals, particularly student learning goals, and maintain high standard of quality in doing so. Goals must be stated which are specific and assessable. Second, the assessment should provide assurance that standards of quality are successfully maintained at an appropriate level regardless of the medium of the course or the methods of instruction adopted. This is a concern that students have a reasonable assurance that the course offerings they believe they are taking, based on public descriptions, are accurate regardless of where or under

what format the course is offered. Third, the responsibility for the conduct of assessment should be appropriately delegated and shared.

The philosophy of eLearning focuses on the individual learner although it recognizes that most learning is social. In the past training has organized itself much for the convenience and needs of instructors, institutions, and bureaucracies. Now eLearning is the convergence learning and networks, the Internet. New university systems are being developed to new global needs.... The experience and critical function of the traditional universities is central in the efforts to create new eLearning environments.

The European eLearning summit emphasized the importance of assuring quality and certification in eLearning. Co-operation in the production and selection of best practices is needed between the private sector and teachers, instructors, ministries and pedagogical experts. Forums for peer reviews could create a useful, informal way of evaluating eContent. Existing eLearning portals could also be enlisted to function as quality filters.

The practical solutions are being made now and many standards do not go through an official and formal standardisation procedure. When everybody starts (sic) using a given standard it becomes de facto the standard without having a prior rule on it. Cooperation between traditional institutions of higher education, the private sector and governments is continuously needed (Varis, 2001b).

One of the greatest ironies concerning the elements essential to the effective *establishment* of transnational distance learning is that these very same elements are also among the most important desired *outcomes* of transnational education. As listed earlier, peace, prosperity, understanding, successful communication, cooperation among peoples and nations, and successful partnerships are *sine qua non* for establishment and sustenance of transnational education programs, and yet at the same time, are among the elements which we hope to foster in the cultures we serve.

Does this not then provide us an immovable paradox, a *Catch 22*, to draw upon a phrase that has become a cliché of our era, that the very desired outcomes of our enterprise must already be present for us to be successful? Professor Brenda Gourley, (then) Vice-Chancellor (Designate) of the U.K. Open University, discussed in detail the current, near overwhelming ramifications of this paradox in an Open University Council Lecture delivered September 21, 2001. Using the term "covenants," Gourley, also identified partnerships as "necessary to our survival." Professor Gourley subsequently took her post as Vice-Chancellor the first week in January, 2002. However, the September 21 date on which Professor Gourley delivered this address should be recalled, when she refers below to "...this week and this month and this very year...."

Not the politics of the nation state, not the politics of the city, not even the grand unifying ideal of democracy itself have so far managed to halt the growing divide of rich and poor. Technology gives every indication of increasing this divide. In the global context we know that in India, for example, only 1% of households have Internet access while in Singapore access is close to 50%. In a country as large as the United States, access is somewhat over 45% and in Britain somewhat less than 30%.... What these figures do not tell you are the disparities they hide.... In the United Kingdom a Family Expenditure Survey released in July last year shows not only the vast differences in access but that those differences relate to income and that they are growing. Single-parent families and pensioners living alone have least access of all and they will be even more marginalised in a Western society than they would be in an African or more Eastern society, where community and family structures are still stronger.

Scenarios, stories and conferences such as these lead us to the ineluctable conclusion that we are, this week and this month and this very year, at an important turning point. One author calls it a "hinge of history", a time when one ill-considered decision by the powerful could swing the balance and make all the difference. If we keep our heads through this crucial time we are still in a very precarious state and it will take all of our collective and individual wills to do whatever it is that we are required to do to make a better world, a more peaceful and equitable world.

All universities have a social responsibility in this matter.... Some may imagine that this task is not ours, but rather that of the nation state. Yet we have seen globalization demonstrate just how helpless the nation state can be. It is one of the great ironies of our time that thanks to the spread of democracy, more people than ever before in human history have a chance to influence their governments while at the same time globalization is eroding government's ability to act on their behalf.... Some people may imagine that the task is that of large economic blocs. Yet we have seen in Europe the helplessness of a large bloc to deal with tides of refugees, for example, and ethnic war. The reality is that none of us, on our own, can undertake all that is necessary to the task.... Covenants are necessary to our survival. Corporations – especially those with global reach – governments, international development agencies, institutions such as the United Nations, the fast growing organs of civil society: all these must be involved. Universities must involve themselves in this endeavour or forever abandon any pretense they may have to educating.

Reflection in this case...should include consideration of the main drivers for change in Higher Education: the pressure for equity and access, for social inclusion, on the one hand and on the other the forces of globalization which have made lifelong learning an economic necessity and put education on the map as one of the biggest businesses in the world, an intensely competitive arena where only the strong and the focused will survive. The Internet alone makes literally thousands of degrees available, some of them with brands that our consumerism culture recognizes and, indeed, to which it responds. Microsoft is a good example. The Open Source ware movement adds impetus to the competitive dimensions which our institutions have to accommodate. The recent decision of MIT to put all its material on the Web is the first indication of what this might mean.

...One of the blessings in South Africa during a time of change was great leadership.... But we have learnt in South Africa, and there are many examples all over the world, that leadership does not reside in one person. Indeed it is dangerous if it does. Leadership can and should be shared. It needs to be cultivated and nurtured and developed wherever it is found. Building a culture of leadership, encouraging enterprise and being tolerant of mistakes are all necessary to a change process, where people need to be given room to grow, accommodate to new realities.

A special kind of leadership seems to be a necessary condition as well. I have been privileged to live in a country, South Africa, where all these elements were at work and where deep and profound change and learning has taken place. The question that needs to be answered is whether or not the South African transition was anything more than an interesting episode in history and whether or not it can be transported as a learning experience to any other place in any other time. I believe it can.

> ...We stand at the dawn of a new tomorrow. We can either embrace the rich mosaic of our human cultures, races, religions, gender, to name but some of what could reaffirm our faith in the triumph of the human spirit, or we could seek refuge within the familiar. The natural reaction is not always the smartest. In a global age it is even dangerous. This is not a time for competition, for winners and losers, but rather a time for collaboration and reconciliation. This is not a time for the faint-hearted but for the courageous. It is a time for strong intellectual leadership – leadership which affirms the ties that bind us as citizens of the same planet, and which affirms the ethics of a common humanity (*Gourley, 2001*).

Thus, Gourley adds a culture of shared leadership to our list of elements essential for the effective establishment and sustenance of transnational distance learning. To synthesize Gourley on leadership: a special kind of great leadership is required, a leadership capable of effecting deep and profound change and learning; a leadership that can be shared, cultivated, nurtured, and developed, building a culture of leadership, encouraging enterprise and being tolerant of mistakes; a leadership which affirms the ties that bind us as citizens of the same planet, and which affirms the ethics of a common humanity.

December, 2001 also saw the publication of a report on how satellite technology can be used to improve education in Africa. The report, a product of significant trans-national partnerships of government and private business, was commissioned by Imfundo: Partnership in IT and Education, which is a development initiative for African education of the U.K. Department for International Development (DFID), http://www.imfundo.org.

The report, entitled "Improving Access to Education via Satellites in Africa: A Primer" was written by Mathy Vanbuel of ATiT, Belgium, and is published online to provide an overview of the opportunities afforded by recent developments in satellite technology in meeting educational and development needs, especially in Sub-Saharan Africa. While the contents are available publicly on the Imfundo web site, the ownership of the contents remains with Imfundo and ATiT. Only Imfundo and ATiT have the rights to publish this document or to allow its use by a third party. The report may be found at: http://www.imfundo.org/satprimer/contents.htm (Utsumi, 2001)

> The profile of ATiT may be found at its Web pages as given below:
>
> ATiT is an audio-visual and information technologies company based in Belgium since January 99 specialising in the field of Education and Culture. The principles, Sally Reynolds and Mathy Vanbuel, have extensive experience in managing leading edge telematics-based projects in the educational and training sector. This includes training programmes whereby potential users of technology for pedagogical purposes have successfully made the transition to a technology supported environment.
>
> ATiT provides audio-visual production, project management, training and consultancy services to clients all over Europe, which includes large organisations like the European Commission, European Space Agency and the UNESCO as well as corporate and smaller agencies and university clients.
>
> Activities also include specific specialised event organisation such as conference broadcasts and two way video links as well as consultancy and support services for conferences like agenda design, content development and speaker identification and orientation. The ATiT team are multilingual and creative and work in a flexible and goal-driven manner (ATiT, 2002).

Imfundo, a veritable prototype of trans-national distance learning partnerships, is defined and its mission is likewise described at its Web pages:

> Imfundo (im~fun~doe) n. The acquisition of knowledge; the process of becoming educated.
>
> The name Imfundo is from the Nguni languages [of] Southern Africa.
>
> We chose the name because it reflects the aims and objectives of the project and describes our values and what we are trying to achieve (DFID, 2002).
>
> Imfundo is a unique initiative, providing partners with a rare opportunity to help transform the education sector in Africa.... The provision of quality education for young people in Africa is one of the most important tasks for all of us in the international community. Working together with African governments and teachers, we can help to provide relevant and high quality training and knowledge for future generations. But this requires considerable investment and commitment. Imfundo is specifically designed to help make available such resources to African countries (Unwin, 2002).
>
> Imfundo will work with other Department for International Development (DFID) programmes to direct the resources, energy, expertise and ideas of business, educational institutes, NGOs, multilateral organisations and donors into more strategic and sustainable outputs which bring about real change in education. We are asking for contributions to a "Resource Bank". The Resource Bank is a unique way for business, academic institutions, NGOs and multilateral organisations to support education in developing countries.
>
> Organisations willing to give resources to education sector reform sign an MOU with the Imfundo initiative pledging their support, and indicating what type of resources they are able to give.
>
> Activities which use ICT to improve education are developed by governments and donors. Organisations which have pledged support are then asked for specific resources which are needed to implement the activities.
>
> Pledges might include staff time and consultancy time, e.g. to design computer networks, or provide training; equipment such as computers, routers, and printers; intellectual property, e.g. software licences; access to infrastructure in developing countries, such as telecommunications and satellite, buildings and distribution networks.
>
> For Imfundo partners, the initiative offers them a chance to show their commitment to corporate social responsibility, gives their employees new and challenging staff development experiences, and includes them in a network of organisations involved at the interface between education, ICT and development.
>
> Last year the Imfundo team held two private sector seminars at No 10 Downing Street. The aim was to test our proposal for a Resource Bank, to identify potential risks and to explore how the Resource Bank could be improved. We also looked for advice and comment on our draft prospectus which will be sent to potential private sector partners (Resource Bank, 2002).

In still another address of major import from still another December 2001 international conference, Professor Sheung-Wai Tam, President of the Open University of Hong Kong presented his lecture on the occasion of his being awarded the 2001 Prize of Excellence for Individuals from the

International Council for Open and Distance Education. Professor Tam shared his insights on current issues in global distance learning, described the development and current status of his institution, and provided his vision of the future for worldwide open and distance education. Tam identifies the factors that have made open and distance education a global mainstream activity:

> Due to a number of factors which have emerged in recent years, open and distance education has become a mainstream activity engaged in by all countries and virtually all institutions, educational companies and institutional consortia. Some of the reasons are:
>
> - the need for enhanced access to the provision of equitable and quality education;
> - the demand for higher education at an unprecedented pace and with numbers which traditional forms of teaching could no longer cope with;
> - the need for institutions to seek alternative sources of income in the face of dwindling national and institutional budgetary allocations;
> - the effects of globalization on higher education world-wide; and
> - the substantial changes which the advent of ICT unleashed on the world's education scene (Tam, 2001).

Based upon the developmental leadership his Open University has provided, Tam projects that new ideas will emerge on open and distance education from all developing countries, making them future resources for guidance and leadership. Tam begins this segment with a global perspective, then focuses on Asia, then the city, and then the Open University:

> Given the phenomenal increase in the world's population, it is virtually impossible for any country, especially in the developing world, to provide educational facilities for all its citizens within specified physical locations. The latest projection of the world's population is that the current 6 billion will rise to 9 billion in the next 25 years, with developing countries constituting over 60 per cent of this figure. It has been estimated that over 900 million of the world's poor live in the Asia-Pacific region. The region has the world's highest rate of illiteracy and, by implication, the largest number of those needing access to education. There can be no doubt that they need to rely much more on education, especially in non-traditional forms, for the development of their human resources. Economic and other opportunities in the next 50 years will depend very heavily on a new generation which thrives on knowledge. This might be the reason why in Asian countries the use of distance education as a vehicle for human and other resource development is fast becoming the 'traditional' form of education. To date, seven out of the ten mega universities identified in the world are located in Asia. Open and distance education is growing by leaps and bound (sic) in the Asian region as it has become accepted as a viable and cost-effective means of providing affordable, convenient and efficient quality education. One implication of this for the future is that significant developments and new ideas about open and distance education will begin to emerge from developing countries, and the rest of the world will shift its focus to these areas for guidance and leadership (Tam, 2001).

In the following passages, Tam uses the term "tertiary" to refer to institutions of higher learning. The term "post-secondary" is often used in the United States. Later, Tam uses the term "off-shore" to refer to those distance learning instructional programs offered in Hong Kong which originate from other nations. Still further down, Tam uses simply "ODL" to designate open and distance learning.

Hong Kong, with a population of over 6.5 million people living within a relatively small area, is one of the most densely-populated cities in the world. There are ten tertiary institutions: eight universities (one of which is self-financing and non-traditional); the Hong Kong Institute of Education which is responsible mainly for teacher training; and the publicly-funded Hong Kong Academy for Performing Arts. About 60,000 full-time and 20,000 part-time students pursue sub-degree, undergraduate and postgraduate courses in the seven traditional universities while over 26,000 pursue their education through the distance learning mode at the Open University - the only single-mode distance learning institution in the Hong Kong SAR. While the Education Department makes provision for adult education at secondary levels, almost all institutions of higher learning provide continuing education opportunities to the public. Also, the Vocational Training Council caters for about 21,000 full-time and 42,000 part-time students who need technical education.

Hong Kong has one of the largest concentrations of off-shore distance education provision in the world. As at (sic) June 2001, there were 570 non-local programmes in Hong Kong, offering more than 60,000 places. Of this total, the British programmes make up the largest share of (57%), followed by Australia with (31%), the USA (7%) and Mainland China (4%) while Canada, Macau and Ireland jointly make up the remainder.

Such a large-scale off-shore contribution to meeting the upsurge in demand for education in Hong Kong derives largely from universities in the developed world seeking to augment their progressively diminishing government funding from other sources. Marketing education overseas is an attractive option as it gives relatively huge returns for comparatively less work when compared with what they offer to their home-based students.

There are at least eight distinctive features of the model of open and distance education practiced at the OUHK which have contributed to its becoming an institution of excellence within the Asian region. These include (1) its open access policy; (2) the range of its academic programmes; (3) its course development, programme planning and quality assurance procedures; (4) its credit transfer and advanced standing systems; (5) its provisions for student support; (6) its research activities; (7) its self-financing status; and (8) its international outreach and collaboration. While some of these were part of the original design of the University, others were introduced during the process of development.

Open and distance learning, unlike the traditional face-to-face teaching and learning environment, is characterised by distinctive course development and delivery features. First, a team must design the courses with members bringing their expertise to the instructional design process. Second, the courses must be presented in a way which facilitates study by students who are separated from their lecturers, study independently and have limited time each day to devote to self-study. Third, several means, including appropriate multi-media, must be used to deliver the courses to wherever the students are located. In the unique case of Hong Kong, 'distance' is not a geographical concept as most of the students are located within a radius of 25 km from the University. In this case, 'distance' relates more to limitations on access due to, for example, work demands and family commitments.

A comprehensive student support system is the hallmark of a quality distance education institution. The OUHK's courses and programmes are offered through study materials in various combinations of print, audio, video, CD-ROMs and online (electronic courses). The University now has over 150 courses running online, and by the year 2010, the Information Technology Plan makes provision for almost all of the OUHK courses to run online. Particularly when faced with such an array of learning materials, distance students clearly need guidance and support in their studies. The University, therefore, provides extensive support through tutorials, day schools, telephone tuition and, increasingly, online communication with tutors and fellow students - as well as self-study centres and both a physical and an electronic library (Tam, 2001).

A unique strength of Tam's institution is its emphasis on research in distance learning, an outcome of his leadership:

The OUHK gives serious consideration to the impact of research on distance and adult learning

on its daily operations as a distance teaching institution, which sets it apart from similar institutions in Asia. I personally championed the need for the University to embark on research activities as a way of supporting, through empirical results and information, how it performs all its functions, including teaching and learning, the development of courses, the use of technology and student support. As a first step, in 1995, the institution set aside HK$7.5 million for its Research & Development Fund in readiness for the setting up of a Centre for Research in Distance and Adult Learning (CRIDAL) to, for example:

- enhance the quality of scholarship and research activities;
- provide leadership through an approach to open and distance learning research that is responsive to the needs of the community; and
- foster a collaborative research culture within the University and, eventually, with our counterparts around the world.

Since its inception in May 1997, CRIDAL has made significant contributions to the development of open and distance learning research at the OUHK, within the Asian region and, indeed, within the global ODL environment. Within the University it conducts frequent training and surgeries in research methodology, colloquia, seminars and workshops to assist staff to acquire or renew their skills and knowledge about ODL research. The Centre undertakes three kinds of projects: (i) locally, within the University, involving staff from the various units of the University for hands-on skill acquisition and development; (ii) CRIDAL staff conducting research as part of their normal employment; and (iii) consultancy and externally funded research. In its relatively short period of existence, CRIDAL has enhanced the research culture at the OUHK, embarked on capacity-building activities with staff and undertaken research projects. CRIDAL has become the East Asia regional site for the World Bank Global Distance Education Network, has established and is serving the AAOU Net, and has recently co-ordinated the ICDE Task Force on Research. Recently the Centre won three external research grants (totalling HK$1.6 million) from the Research Grants Council of Hong Kong.

...The OUHK generates almost all of its revenue from the fees which students pay for their courses. For capital projects such as buildings, laboratories and the electronic library, government makes one-off subventions. The OUHK also benefits from the generally favourable atmosphere of endowment and charity from sources such as the Jockey Club, the Croucher Foundation and many other charitable and business and commercial organisations in Hong Kong. Self-financing status has helped the University to focus on a market-oriented strategy of providing courses for which there is high and sustained demand, applying differential fee-charging criteria, and conducting regular market surveys to determine the needs and relevance of courses directed at the Hong Kong public.

Having reflected upon ODL and what it has meant to the world, and Hong Kong in particular, it now remains...to look ahead and contemplate what the future scenarios might be. There are three major areas on which I would like to place emphasis.

The first is global demographics, ageing and lifelong education, especially in Asia. As mentioned earlier, it has been forecast that the world population will grow to about 9 billion within the next 25 years. This will have a significant impact on education and the quality of life. Many people will live much longer, but will retire early, and literacy and continual updating of one's knowledge will be of critical importance. Only a small fraction of those needing education will receive it in classrooms. Hence open and distance learning will become even be more popular in the future than it is now. If the current pace of knowledge generation continues, it is likely that the half-life of the knowledge we hold will be reduced from 5 years to about 2 years. This means that there will not only be a need for continual updating and renewal of knowledge, but also that many new areas of knowledge and new careers will emerge and will need be serviced. Lifelong learning will become even more mainstream than it is today and will play its part in educating people about how to handle the key challenges which will face humanity in the near future: how to keep the spiralling population down, or at least constant, and how to manage ageing with the increased number of older adults in society.

Second, global development, especially in relation to the Internet, will see online education become pervasive. By the year 2025, the Internet will have penetrated every corner of the world as satellite communication makes it easy to reach anyone, no matter how remote. Almost every institution will invest in e-education, and the skills of designing online education will become commonplace even at the primary school level. This implies that there will be more intense competition to market online courses around the world. Scandinavia has been in the forefront in the development of mobile phones, which has led to the emergence of wireless application protocols which will have a significant impact on the delivery of instruction to learners at a distance. With hand-held devices which will have considerable memory and processing capabilities, students will be able to access their lecture notes or other resource materials without any restrictions of time and space. It may well mean also that the desktop computer as we know it today will become obsolete. For most learning activities, it will neither be necessary for teaching to occur in a designated area nor for the printing and distribution of hard copies because everyone will carry with him or her some form of viewing device to enable the accessing of information online anywhere. The world will draw closer to the so-called 'paperless society'.

A third major future development will be the changes that will take place in Web-based instruction due to the emergence of new and more robust technologies. While it is difficult to conceptualise the new technologies which might emerge, it is possible to hazard a guess that the language of the Web will change remarkably and be much easier for all to learn and use. For the delivery of instruction, everyone will need to master the new technologies, and the choice of which technology is to be used for learning and teaching will no longer be determined mainly by the teachers but by students.

For distance education institutions or open universities, the implications of all these future scenarios are of major significance and all their ramifications must be closely analysed to make them responsive to the needs of society. Education reform will be more regular as

> nations struggle to keep pace with rapid developments. Globalisation and ICT will become a dominant feature of the learning landscape of individuals and communities. The emergence of learning communities will overshadow the development of specific study or resource centres. Institutions like mine will have to respond much more quickly than we do today to the needs of society, otherwise they are in danger of going out of fashion (Tam, 2001).

What a brave new world Professor Tam envisions for global distance learning. All the factors Tam covers should contribute to the growth, complexity, significance, and effectiveness of distance learning programs throughout the world. For many students, perhaps even for the majority, some form or forms of distance learning will simply be the way to learn. For those of us who are purveyors of distance learning in all its manifestations and applications, an expanding and exhilarating market is burgeoning before our eyes.

As one can see from the Hong Kong population and enrollment figures which Professor Tam supplied above, the OUHK with its 26,000 students from a city population of 6.5 million is a microcosm compared with, for instance, the Indira Gandhi National Open University IGNOU. IGNOU boasts a student enrollment of about 800,000 students scattered throughout the nation and serves them through forty-six Regional Centres and above 1000 Study Centres across all of India. As is so often the case with distance learning institutions, IGNOU has "crossed national boundaries providing higher education as well as assisting other developing countries in this regard (IGNOU, 2000).

The following passage, also from December, 2001, concerns the growth of corporate distance learning adaptations in response to the post September 11 business environment in the United States. The passage is included because of its possible implications for the future of global academic distance learning. The socio-cultural elements identified earlier in this study as necessary to the establishment and sustenance of global distance learning programs is obviously not universally available throughout the world. In fact, some individual elements are frequently missing in any given geographical setting, while the availability of each element often varies from place to place. Nevertheless, global distance learning programs are being established anyway, in spite of adverse local conditions and even, to some extent, expressly to overcome these conditions. The following passage provides some insight into the enabling adaptive processes involved:

> Demand for video conferencing has rocketed.... Even when business travelers return to the skies, video conferencing is likely to remain as a mainstream corporate technology. While video conferencing technology has been around for years, until the onset of a crisis mentality most companies had considered using it for exotic rather than everyday purposes.
>
> Similarly, distance learning and presentation systems, such as Net Meeting, Place Ware, and Ten TV, are getting more attention. While companies curtail their travel for reasons of cost, safety and inconvenience, they still must keep their employees, distributors, dealers, and customers trained. Such concerns may finally cause technology to substitute for many types of in-person meetings.
>
> Telecommuting is also likely to become more widespread. Even companies that do not encourage employees to work from home on a routine basis will incorporate telecommuting technology as part of their disaster recovery plans (Greenhouse, 2001).

The following checklist represents a synthesis of the factors which have been identified throughout this study as essential to the establishment and sustenance of international distance learning programs:

Essential Elements for Institutions of Global or Transnational Education:

Socio-Cultural Base:

- International Peace
- International Prosperity
- International Understanding
- Successful Communication among Peoples and Nations
- Successful Cooperation among Peoples and Nations
- International Strategic Alliances
- Successful Transnational Partnerships of Institutions, Governmental Agencies, and Private Businesses
- Culture of Shared Leadership

Quality Assurance Through:

- Internal Evaluation
- External Evaluation
- International Expertise in Evaluation
- Established and Equitable Standards of Quality in Evaluation
- Professional Faculty Standards and Practices
- Equitable Assessment of Student Skills and Competencies
- Demonstration of how Institutional Goals are to be achieved
- Maintaining Quality across Variations in Course Media and Methods
- Maintaining Accuracy of Course Descriptions across Variations in Course Format
- Drawing upon the Experience and Critical Function of Traditional Universities
- Establishment and Selection of Best Practices through Partnerships
- International Exchange of Knowledge
- International Interactive Networking
- International Mobility of Teachers and Students
- International Research Projects
- Comparable Degrees
- Comparable Credits
- Account for National Cultural Values and Circumstances
- Internet Access
- Internet Based Courses and Programs
- Internet Supported Courses or Programs
- Internet Based Information Searching
- Internet Based Collaboration and Exchange

- Institutional and Inter-Institutional Networks
- Interactive Compatibility of Institutional Systems
- Equitable Transfer of Knowledge
- Teaching Electronic Learning Competencies or Information Literacy
- Teaching of Lifelong Learning Skills
- Preparation for Complex Globalization Challenges
- Preparation for the International Labor Market
- International Free Flow of Educational Services
- Equality of Access
- Equal Conditions of Support to Knowledge Development

Is our list complete? No list ever is! But this one is inclusive enough that it will carry us very far, indeed, and prepare us to recognize the elements omitted and the new elements we will encounter that will have come into being well after we have first made the list. One of the most significant challenges generated by the list itself at the moment of its completion is to start brainstorming for the missing elements. Posing new questions, as in the process with which this study opened, can lead to new items for the list. One of the most valuable characteristics of the list is that it has both direct applications, as for program development and assessment, and theoretical applications, as a springboard for research.

The ACRL guidelines for distance learning library services: beacon lights for ensuring provision of global distance learning library services

The ACRL Guidelines for Distance Learning Library Services (ACRL Guidelines or Guidelines) are a product of the work of the Guidelines committee of the Distance Learning Section of the Association of College and Research Libraries, which is a division of the American Library Association, U.S.A. (Guidelines, 2000). Although comprising a forward looking and progressive document, the Guidelines trace their origins back to the original 1967 Guidelines for Library Services to Extension Students (Guidelines, 1967). The present document is the product of four subsequent revisions.

The current *Guidelines* are very broadly based, having been expanded in scope with each one of the four revisions, making the *Guidelines* very widely applicable to all types of distance learning programs throughout the world. Further, because of their breadth of scope, the 2000 *Guidelines* provide an excellent prototype for those wanting to devise their own locally applicable guidelines for distance learning library services.

In India, the Sectional Committee on Distance Education of the Indian Library Association (ILA) has prepared *Guidelines for Library Services for Distance Learners*. The ILA *Guidelines* are keyed to the unique circumstances and institutional structures of the nation which they are intended to serve (ILA, 2001). These ILA *Guidelines* are no doubt harbingers of those national guidelines to be produced by other nations over the coming decades, each addressing the needs unique to its circumstances.

One of the most significant qualities of the ACRL Guidelines is that they carry, by their very nature, a certain sort of moral force. This phenomenon of the ACRL Guidelines extends well beyond their nation of origin. Throughout the world, the ACRL Guidelines are cited again and again by those who wish to ensure that library services are provided in newly developing distance learning programs. So also are the Guidelines cited by those who want to ensure that library services of academic superiority are provided to existing distance learning programs.

Another way in which the *Guidelines* are frequently cited is by institutions under accreditation review, which want to assure accrediting agencies that standards of high academic quality are being maintained in their distance learning library services programs. The *ACRL Guidelines* are cited to accreditation agencies even when the agencies themselves have provided their own skeletal "guidelines" for distance learning programs specifying that library services must be included.

The *Guidelines* are further used internally within the institutions themselves by academic librarians who are involved in distance learning library services and who want to promote the use of the *Guidelines* by their upper-level institutional administrators. These administrators include academic vice presidents, and/or provosts, and especially college or university presidents, and members of boards of regents. The intent of these librarians is to engender a broader-based institutional awareness and commitment to distance learning library services among these upper-level institutional administrators, who are responsible for setting levels of support for academic units, including the library and its programs.

The 2000 *ACRL Guidelines* themselves are available at the ACRL Web pages at the following URL: http://www.ala.org/acrl/guides/distlrng.html. In addition to a brief, general introduction and definitions, the *Guidelines* consist of two major components. First is a set of philosophical precepts or principles. The second, following the precepts, is a series of categorized lists of recommendations for achieving or ensuring adherence to the opening philosophical principles. The lists of recommendations are provided in the following categories: management, finances, personnel, facilities, resources, services, documentation, and library education.

The moral force of the *Guidelines* is found in the philosophical precepts and is derived from their being intended to secure and protect the rights of those for whom they were written: the rights of distance learning students, faculty, and related personnel to library services *equivalent* to those available to students in traditional campus settings. What follows is an examination of those philosophical precepts themselves.

The Guidelines assume the following precepts

Precept one: superior academic skills.
Access to adequate library services and resources is essential for the attainment of superior academic skills in post-secondary education, regardless of where students, faculty, and programs are located. Members of the distance learning community are entitled to library services and resources equivalent to those provided for students and faculty in traditional campus settings. (Guidelines, 2000)

Precept two: lifelong learning skills.

The instilling of lifelong learning skills through general bibliographic and information literacy instruction in academic libraries is a primary outcome of higher education. Such preparation and measurement of its outcomes are of equal necessity for the distance learning community as for those on the traditional campus. (Guidelines, 2000)

Precept three: equivalent teaching and learning results through equivalent library services.

Traditional on-campus library services themselves cannot be stretched to meet the library needs of distance learning students and faculty who face distinct and different challenges involving library access and information delivery. Special funding arrangements, proactive planning, and promotion are necessary to deliver equivalent library services and to achieve equivalent results in teaching and learning, and generally to maintain quality in distance learning programs. Because students and faculty in distance learning programs frequently do not have direct access to a full range of library services and materials, equitable distance learning library services are more personalized than might be expected on campus. (Guidelines, 2000)

Precept four: responsible institutional support through separate funding.

The originating institution is responsible, through its chief administrative officers and governance organizations, for funding and appropriately meeting the information needs of its distance learning programs in support of their teaching, learning, and research. This support should provide ready and equivalent library service and learning resources to all its students, regardless of location. This support should be funded separately rather than drawn from the regular funding of the library. In growing and developing institutions, funding should expand as programs and enrollments grow. (Guidelines, 2000)

Precept five: technical linkages.

The originating institution recognizes the need for service, management, and technical linkages between the library and other complementary resource bases such as computing facilities, instructional media, and telecommunication centers. (Guidelines, 2000).

Precept six: compliance with national, regional, and professional accreditation of programs.

The originating institution is responsible for assuring that its distance learning library programs meet or exceed national and regional accreditation standards and professional association standards and guidelines. (Guidelines, 2000)

Precept seven: library involvement in program development.

The originating institution is responsible for involving the library administration and other personnel in the detailed analysis of planning, developing, evaluating, and adding or changing of the distance learning program from the earliest stages onward. (Guidelines, 2000)

Precept eight: program accountability through outcomes assessment.

The library has primary responsibility for identifying, developing, coordinating, providing, and assessing the value and effectiveness of resources and services, designed to meet both the standard and the unique informational and skills development needs of the distance learning community. The librarian-administrator either centrally located or at an appropriate site, should be responsible for ensuring and demonstrating that all requirements are met through needs and outcomes assessments, and other measures of library performance, as appropriate, and as an ongoing process in conjunction with the originating institution. (Guidelines, 2000)

Precept nine: equivalent services through innovative approaches.

Effective and appropriate services for distance learning communities may differ from, but must be equivalent to, those services offered on a traditional campus. The requirements and desired outcomes of academic programs should guide the library's responses to defined needs. Innovative approaches to the design and evaluation of special procedures or systems to meet these needs is encouraged (Guidelines, 2000).

Precept ten: resources and services consistent with broader institutional mission.

When resources and services of unaffiliated local libraries are to be used to support information needs of the distance learning community, the originating institution is responsible, through the library, for the development and periodic review of formal, documented, written agreements with those local libraries. Such resources and services are not to be used simply as substitutes for supplying adequate materials and services by the originating institution. The distance learning library program shall have goals and objectives that support the provision of resources and services consistent with the broader institutional mission (Guidelines, 2000).

In using the on-campus provisions of traditional colleges and universities as benchmarks, the Guidelines follow a principle expressed by P. Tapio Varis in Part I: "The experience and critical function of the traditional universities is central in the efforts to create new eLearning environments." (Varis, 2001 b). The Guidelines, of course, apply the principle far more broadly to library services for all aspects of distance learning. The Guidelines are very much like the checklist at the end of Part I. In fact, there may very well be some items in the Part I checklist that will be incorporated into the next revision of the Guidelines. The list building processes are organic. The processes never end, and the checklists are never complete. The power of the checklists, or with the Guidelines as a check list, is their stabilizing effect, identified as anchoring in Part I and as beacon lights in Part II. Beyond stabilization, the checklists ensure that program developments are as complete as possible and that their users are as adequately served as possible.

References

Association of College and Research Libraries. (2000). *ACRL Guidelines for Distance Learning Library Services.* http://www.ala.org/acrl/guides/distlrng.html ATiT. 2002. http://www.atit.be/

Barblan, Andris. (2001). "When European relations become local agreements ....2010." Keynote Address, *International Education: Realising Human Potential*, 13th Annual Conference, European Association for International Education, Tampere, Finland, 5 to 8 December. http://www.eaie.nl/conf2001/barblan.asp

"Why are we called Imfundo?" DFID, (2002). DFID, U.K. Department for International Development Imfundo Web pages. http://www.imfundo.org/imfundo/imfundoword.htm

Gourley, Brenda M. (2001). "Diversity and Change in a Global Context." The Council Lecture, The Open University, 21 September. http://www.open.ac.uk/vcs-speeches/BGourley/VCs_council_lecture.doc

Greenhouse Associates, Inc. (2001). "...How Trauma Accelerates Technology Change." *Greenhouse Effects*, December. http://www.greenhousegrows.com/id47.htm

Guidelines for library services to extension students. (1967). *ALA Bulletin*, 61 (1), 50-53.

IACRL Publications Committee. 2001. IACRL 2002 Spring Conference: Pioneering a New Librarianship: Illinois Academic Libraries and the 21st Century Odyssey, April 3-5, 2002. http://servercc.oakton.edu/~iacrl/conference.html

IGNOU. (2000). "A Brief Profile." Indira Gandhi National Open University Web Pages. http://www.ignou.org

Indian Library Association (2001). *Guidelines for Library Services for Distance Learners.* New Delhi: Distance Education Council (IGNOU)

"ResourceBank." (2002). From the DFID, U.K. Department for International Development Imfundo Web pages. http://www.imfundo.org/resource/resourcebank.htm

Tam, Sheung-Wai. (2001). "Reflections on Open and Distance Learning." Public Lecture on the occasion of his receiving the International Council for Open and Distance Education: Prize of Excellence for Individuals, 2001. Oslo, Norway. December.

Unwin, Tim. (2002). "A message from the team leader - Professor Tim Unwin." From the DFID, U.K. Department for International Development Imfundo Web pages. http://www.imfundo.org/imfundoname.htm

Utsumi, Tak. (2001). "Improving Access to Education via Satellites in Africa" by Mathy Vanbuel. E-mail message, December 30, 2001. http://www.friends-partners.org/pipermail/gu-l/2001q4/date.html

Varis, P. Tapio. (2001). "The Goals of Global Learning." From Utsumi, Tak, "The Goals of Global Learning by Tapio Varis." E-mail message, December 15, 2001. http://www.friends-partners.org/pipermail/gu-l/2001q4/date.html

Varis, P. Tapio. (2001). "21st Century Challenges of Higher Education." Keynote Address, *International Education: Realising Human Potential*, 13th Annual Conference, European Association for International Education, Tampere, Finland, 5 to 8 December. http://www.eaie.nl/conf2001/varis.asp

3

Management, Processing and Distribution of Knowledge in the Emerging Open and Distance Learning Environment

Olugbemiro Jegede

Introduction

The Open and Distance Learning (ODL) environment requires the librarians of the open universities to apply their drive and vigour in their day-to-day life. They have challenged the administrators, planners, teachers, professionals and other staff to continue to put the distance learner uppermost in all they do. Besides, no infrastructure no matter how extensive; no technology no matter how modern; no curriculum, programme and course no matter how up-to-date can replace the provision of adequate, timely and appropriate library services to students. This is even more important in the case of distance learners who are remotely located from the providing institution. The task of a librarian at any ODL institution has become an enormous one as we march into the modern age of information and communications technologies (ICTs). The challenges are formidable and yet the librarians in many institutions especially of the developing world are continually faced with lack of resources, dwindling volumes of books and printed materials and shrinking space as the student number grows. With the emergence of knowledge management, librarians are now being called to do what they either never learnt during their professional training or forced to add on to their normal schedule. Librarians are no more seen in the restricted sense of taking care of a physically located building for the provision of reading materials to students. They are now becoming knowledge managers undertaking versatile responsibilities. They are, in addition, expected to 'encourage the development and sharing of open learning/ distance education materials, expertise, technologies, and other resources'. It is in this regard that I propose to share my thoughts on what I see as the challenges which face librarians in the management, processing and distribution of knowledge in the today's world of education and especially in the emerging open and distance learning environment.

The changing world of education

Education is going through a period of turbulence unprecedented in history. Institutions of higher learning are increasingly being called to justify their existence, be more responsive to their students and the larger society, continually cut cost in the face of dwindling financial allocation from proprietors, and transmit relevant knowledge to students in a world characterised by a movement towards global economy. Added to this, is the explosion and coming unto the mainstream of open and distance learning for a variety of reasons which include being responsive to the need for mass higher education, access and equity, cost-effectiveness using efficient system of delivery, being flexible, fast and yet fluid with the provision of education, and the elimination of distance and isolation of the learner from the institution, teacher and peer. Thesc contemporary changes in education and the dclivery of instruction are significantly affecting and being affected by a paradigm shift with regard to how information and knowledge is transmitted, distributed, accessed and processed. This shift has been propelled by several developments, which interact and integrate to impact on how teaching and learning occur. One of these is the exponential growth in knowledge with which the world is finding difficult to keep pace. According to Marshall, the half-life of the knowledge we currently hold is limited to just three years. This means that in three years' time all the knowledge we currently hold in our long-term memory and guard so jealously will become irrelevant, redundant or dated forcing us to continually 'go back to school' again. Another reason is the emerging postmodernist view of knowledge generation that is responsible for a move from looking at knowledge generation as hierarchical and restrictive to being regarded as non-linear, socially negotiated and should be accessible to anyone and everyone through a variety of ways. This has led to the need to look at the various ways in which knowledge, its generation and transmission can be effectively managed to aid in personal and societal development and global economy.

How knowledge results and grows

Flemming (1996) argues that a collection of data is not information and a collection of pieces of information is not knowledge unless they have some patterns and relations and are contextual. Bellinger (1999) represents this diagrammatically as follows:

Learning takes place when we connect new information to patterns we already hold in our long-

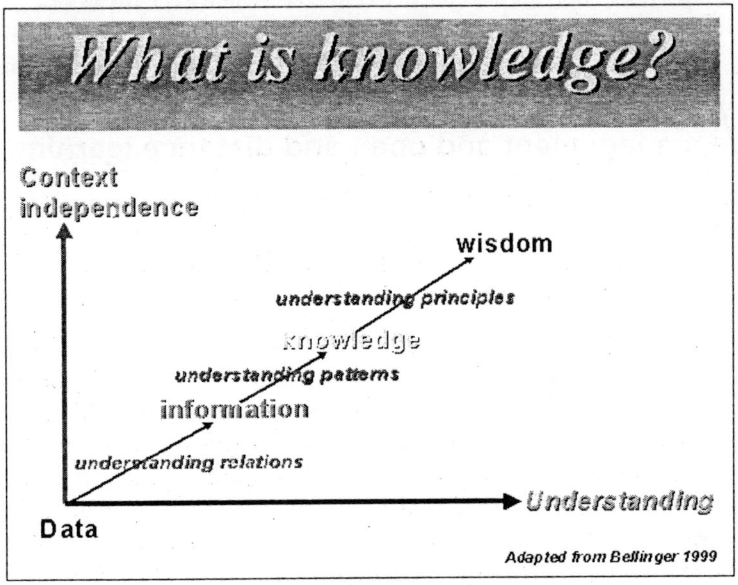

Figure 3.1

term memory. This becomes knowledge. Knowledge therefore becomes ideas and understandings, which can be used to take some action in order to achieve some goals. Knowledge is stored in many ways and places. For example, it may be stored in a person's brain, stored in an organisation, or held in a repository such as a library, or organised in a database. Human beings engage in finding, selecting, distilling, organising, and presenting information in a way that within contexts can be used for several things once patterns and association can be discerned from them. Given the rate at which knowledge is generated today, individuals, organizations, and educational institutions must manage information and knowledge effectively and efficiently. One of the roles of librarians is to assist the distance learner to effectively process knowledge and information available in their libraries to gain wisdom.

Knowledge management

Knowledge management is the capturing, processing, storing and sharing of data, information and knowledge through reliable, fast and rapid access. Knowledge management is increasingly being utilised in many areas of individual, organisational and national operations including strategic planning, decision-making, training, control and effectiveness. Knowledge management is exerting significant impact on the need for mass education, access and equity, cost-effectiveness and efficient system of delivery of instruction.

The concept of knowledge management is a recent one emanating from commerce and industry where there is increasing need to utilize knowledge for many areas of their operations such as strategic planning, corporate decision making, workplace training, control and effectiveness and competitive edge. According to Davidson (1996) knowledge management in an organisation must align with its mission (i.e. what are we trying to accomplish?), respond to competition (i.e. how do we gain a competitive edge?), should focus on performance (i.e. how do we deliver the results?), and anticipate and address change (i.e. how do we cope with change?). Many organizations have now corporatised knowledge management as a way of continuous development and improvement of their operations and marketing. Hewlett Packard is one example of an organisation which has developed a knowledge management system called 'Knowledge Links' for identifying, codifying and storing company knowledge and accessible to all of its employees.

Knowledge management and open and distance learning

Open and distance learning is changing within a larger global environment that is also changing in a number of ways. First, the world has moved from an industrial-based economy to an information-based one in which knowledge is seen as more profitable than capital services. Indeed there are many organisations existing today just to sell information, and they are doing so with high profits.

Second, the need to transmit the high volume of information and knowledge being generated in an emerging information-based economy has led to the phenomenal development we are witnessing in the area of communication. This development in information and communication technologies has transformed how, where and what is communicated at a speed far greater than what was imagined a few months ago. As a result, the variety of technologies available for transmitting information has changed the world's view of what information and communications are. It has globalised information and has brought world economies to the doorsteps of even the remotest farmer.

These recent developments in technology as mentioned above have two facets, which are now transforming teaching and learning. A few years ago we saw the emergence of affordable, portable, personal computers laden with multimedia capabilities. Next was the availability of networking, which allows global contact asynchronously or synchronously. These have unleashed a tidal wave of unlimited growth of the Internet, which has made the use of the Web in open and distance learning and teaching possible. The indications are that we have not even scratched the surface of the tremendous potential of its use in instruction.

It now means that individuals, institutions and organisations must device means of managing knowledge in a ways that would be efficient in meeting the needs of their customers. We need to give to the customer or learner the right information and knowledge they require at the point and time needed. For want of time I shall restrict to the role of libraries and librarians in the knowledge management.

Libraries

Before the advent of non-contiguous education which was variously known and labelled as 'correspondence', 'off-campus', 'extension', 'part-time', 'continuing' and 'distance' education, libraries have serviced learners through the professional delivery of information and knowledge. The collection, storage, and distribution of knowledge and information followed as a set pattern of management and served mainly on-campus learners and staff. Their system was closed and not often accessible to the public. The realisation of the need to provide the community with some limited form of information and knowledge led to the establishment in many parts of the world of community libraries. These are open to the public and all the information and knowledge contained in them is accessible to all. What needs to be mentioned is that the 'knowledge' within libraries is not strictly speaking managed as such. They are, from our definition of knowledge above, pieces of information and data which the learner or reader would need to acquire and attach some patterns and understanding to in order to become knowledgeable. However, libraries have always engaged in and perfected their knowledge management system, which focuses on the acquisition, storage, and distribution of knowledge to their customers. There has been a shift in non-contiguous education both in practice and in nomenclature as outlined above. Now variously known as 'open', 'distributed', 'flexible', 'synchronous', asynchronous', and 'virtual', the offering of education at a distance has now taken a new dimension in which technology plays an increasingly dominant roll in the delivery of instruction and therefore of information and knowledge.

Furthermore, the emerging focus or refocus on life-long and life-wide learning will mean that libraries need to manage literacy instruction to the public in greater dimension than currently occurs. The library is therefore facing the challenge of providing information and knowledge to customers through reliable, rapid and secure access. Several libraries are therefore turning to the Internet as a solution and they are going electronic or virtual.

Virtual library and virtual librarianship

Virtual libraries started as a small experiment in the USA less than ten years ago are having an effect all over the world. Many developing countries and institutions are establishing electronic or virtual libraries. Nigeria has recently launched its nation-wide virtual library project and it is the most extensive national virtual libraries so far.

Scanning through the literature, it is noticed that the main reasons for establishing electronic library resources include

- to provide easy, fast, round-the-clock and flexible access to the retrireview and processing of information to support learning,
- to eliminate unnecessary duplication and thereby maximise the cost-effective use of material resources,
- to provide a friendly learner-driven library support services to all learners, especially those remotely located from institutions and necessary facilities,
- to harness current development and global effort in information and communications technology for the provision of education for all, and
- to provide greater opportunity as well as reliable platform for research, ease of collection and monitoring of user statistics of library resources.

The justification for Virtual Libraries is not far fetched. Any educational system or institution worth its salt must provide information and material resources centre to support teaching, learning and research. Library resources centres provide access to literature and space for private study and referencing. Traditionally, library resources are housed in physical space locations, often hold multiple copies of materials, require extensive human and financial resources, and demand constant updating, replacement, and refurbishment of the resources. Apart from the fact that this situation exerts extensive strain on the system, it depletes resources, and increases wastage. In addition, as has occurred in recent times, it has been difficult if not impossible to keep up with the library resources needs of the ever-growing population of students and staff in developing countries. As a result it is possible to proffer as many reasons as one may think of but just a handful of the more listed here for an electronic library system.

First, it is the issue of the sheer size and scope of library resources provisions for education today. With the constant explosion of knowledge each institution will continue to require both qualitative and quantitative expansions to cope up with the resources required for teaching and learning. As a result an alternative system which is cost-effective, relatively cheap to maintain, and provides access to current and latest materials needs to be found. Electronic library resources can be shared by all students within an institution or all institutions within a country at a fraction of the total cost required to support as all the physical libraries within the higher education system in the country. Furthermore, it is projected that 1,000 electronic databases/resources are equivalent to 300,000 volumes of printed materials. These will require 2,650 square metres of shelving space alone, which is saved if the library is electronic.

Second, the use of distance education methods to educate people in massive scales has become quite pervasive all over the world due to its obvious advantages in providing education services without compromising quality. The progression is that for the immediate future distance education mode would be the default mode rather the alternative mode. Therefore, the availability of a library resources centre, no matter how remotely located, that is accessible via electronic means at the convenience of students and staff, is of utmost importance. All students can share this sort of electronic provision in the system with little or no difficulty at all.

Third, the phenomenal development in telecommunications, computing and information and knowledge management has led to the advent and use of virtual education. The trend now is for institutions to go virtual in thc delivery of instruction. A virtual education institution, as defined by the Commonwealth of Learning (COL), is an organisation that directly, or indirectly, uses information and communications technology (ICT) to provide educational services; this includes traditional agencies such as universities or non-educational organisations that distribute virtual educational services. Virtual education is profoundly affecting access to educational services; online distance learning is less onerous than a correspondence course. Furthermore, virtual learning has affected the ways and means with which people learn, the role of community tele-learning centers that provide access to ICTs has assumed greater significance.

Fourth, in recent times post-secondary educational institutions have been under tremendous pressure for change as a response to diminishing budget, need to reach students other than their traditional clientele, and adapt current development in information technology for the delivery of instruction. As a result, many institutions of higher learning worldwide have turned towards electronic networking in academic services. In summary, some of the advantages of an electronic library resources system are mentioned in Table 1.

Challenges of modern-day librarianship

The challenges, which face librarians in the management, processing and distribution of knowledge in the today's world of education and especially the emerging open and distance learning environment are multi-faceted and compelling.

As you may well imagine, the emergence of virtual libraries has thrown up several challenges to nations, institutions and librarians. The training of library professions will now have to change. Librarians must first and foremost be proficient in the use of ICTs and especially web-based environment and become conversant with the daily changes in and on the Internet. It also means that for librarians in open and distance learning, understanding all of the issues, which surround the provision of knowledge and information resources to remotely located learners must be central to their training. Above all, improvisation especially in rural areas where the infrastructural provisions are either inadequate or non-existent becomes a challenge.

However, there is another challenge which we must not lose sight of. In spite of all the noise being made about the ubiquity of emerging information and communications technologies, thousands of learners in rural and remote locations or even in urban areas but cannot access the Internet due to financial means; and this still needs to be catered for. At the moment, from my subjective observation, about 90 per cent of those who live in developing countries are yet to have any contact in one form or the other to the Internet due to illiteracy, poverty, physical distance or bureaucratic obstacles. Even for those who have access to the Internet, the issue of free access to all libraries or to all the information in libraries, which may not be those they are directly registered with, needs to be sorted out.

For librarians and administrators, providing electronic libraries is one thing but proving distance learners with library skills is another. It might not just be taking what is available for on-campus on-site users and dumping it on the Internet. Using the Internet requires completely different protocols and orientation, and one would hope that libraries would not fall into the same mistakes that web-based instructional developers are making. A secondary consideration is that in the old system, knowledge management was undertaken in the libraries by a few senior staff, especially the librarian and senior administrators. The concept of knowledge management makes available all in-house information and knowledge including decision making to all staff in the organisation.

My limited experience with the electronic library of the Open University of Hong Kong and the Virtual Library project for Nigeria brings me to the next challenge. One great challenge that has

Table 3.1: Comparison of library services

No	Library Services	Traditional Library	Electronic Library
1	Opening hours	Limited	Round-the-clock, all- the-year round
2	Student remote access	Not possible	Possible
3	Services to non-traditional students	Grossly limited	Online delivery
4	Access to resources	Limited to shelf search in physical locations	Instant and electronic
5	Search engines	Manual and tedious	Electronic, easy and extensive
6	Time factor	Does not save time, in fact wastes time	Significant saving, no travel time required
7	Seating space and Shelf space	No saving	No seating space required
8	Manpower requirements	High	Low
9	Multiple access	Not flexible	Easy and cheap
10	Resource sharing	Inconvenient, slow turn-around time	Convenient, fast turn-around
11	Migration	Limited	Use the Internet to access other libraries and materials

arisen today is how do we train a Virtual or an Electronic Librarian? What should constitute the curriculum of a degree in Virtual Librarianship considering that the various areas of knowledge and information that a librarian must learn continue to increase by the day? Who should do the training of Virtual Librarians when our current crop of librarians were not trained as Virtual Librarians and have not the opportunity of becoming familiar or proficient in virtual librarianship? For a start, we may have to look for support and assistance in the direction of current databases in the world such as the International Centre for Distance Learning (ICDL) in the UK, the CRIDAL of The Open University of Hong Kong, The World Bank Global Distance Education Network, and the recently established Commonwealth Open and Distance Learning Knowledge Network (CODLINK).

Another area of formidable challenge is how librarians can help distance learners to learn more efficiently. Distance learners are used to self-paced individualised learning supplemented or complemented by some tutorials and some form of conferencing with peers and tutors. Modern distance learners cannot avoid the explosion of knowledge or the necessity for using ICT in their studies, especially for retrieving information. Therefore, in addition to providing information and knowledge, libraries and organisations should provide them with guidelines for managing the knowledge they are bombarded with in libraries, databases and other sources. How for example should a learner browse through hundreds of materials and web sites systematically to eliminate what is not significant or relevant to the information and knowledge essential for the course? How can learners keep their mind focused on accessing relevant information while ploughing through hundreds of web sites capable of sidetracking them? We need, as facilitators of learning, to guide learners towards efficient management of knowledge.

Conclusion

As professionals interested in being at the forefront of development in our respective areas of specialization as well as in ODL in general, we need to consider many of the issues I have raised above. I intentionally decided to bring them up again with a view to reiterating some of the salient features of the changing needs of the emerging Virtual Librarian. We also need to deliberate further on issues such as how to train a Virtual Librarian, how to create an effective working environment for a Virtual Librarian, and how the librarian can meaningfully contribute to the quality of learning by a distance learner will engage our discussions.

References

Bellinger, G. (1999). Knowledge management – emerging perspectives. http://www.outsights.com/systems/kmgmt/kmgmt.htm

Davidson, M. (1996). *The transformation of management.* New York: Butterworth-Heinemann.

Flemming, N. (1996). *Coping with a revolution: Will the Internet change learning?* Canterbury, New Zealand: Lincoln University.

SECTION 2

OUTREACH LIBRARY SERVICES IN INDIA

4

Outreach Library and Information Services for Distance Learners of Indira Gandhi National Open University

Neela Jagannathan and Uma Kanjilal

Backdrop

Distance education has grown tremendously all over the world during the last three decades. The growth in number of distance teaching institutions, increase in number of programmes/ courses, exponential growth in literature on open and distance education (ODE), increasing number of conferences/workshops and the growth in number of distance learners – all these have contributed immensely towards the development and maturation of a strong and sustainable system of education.

Genesis and development of distance education in India

There had been a rapid and remarkable proliferation of educational institutions and universities after independence. But, they were not adequate to meet the ever-growing demand for higher education. To reduce the pressure on existing formal universities and colleges, the Union Ministry of Education constituted a committee under the Chairmanship of Dr. D.S Kothari to examine the possibility of commencing correspondence courses in India. Based on the recommendation of the Committee, the University of Delhi started correspondence education as a pilot project in 1962. The Andhra Pradesh Open University, renamed as Dr. B. R. Ambedkar Open University (BRAOU), was established by an Act of State Legislature in August 1982 at Hyderabad, as the correspondence courses did not prove effective due to several limitations already inherent in the conventional education system.

Imbued by the success of Dr. BRAOU the Indira Gandhi National Open University (IGNOU) was established at the national level in Delhi on September 20, 1985 by the Act of Parliament. Eight more state open universities are established: in Rajasthan in 1987, Bihar in 1987, Maharashtra in 1989, Madhya Pradesh in 1991, Gujarat in 1994, Karnataka in 1996, West Bengal in 1997 and Uttar Pradesh in 1998.

Indira Gandhi National Open University (IGNOU)

IGNOU has attained popularity as a premier distance teaching institution not only in India but also across the world. IGNOU has at present over 800,000 students on rolls. The University follows a multi-media approach in producing learning packages and imparts instruction through self-instructional materials, face-to-face contact sessions, audio-video programmes, broadcasting, telecasting and teleconferencing. In the last one and a half decade, IGNOU has produced 74 programmes consisting of 850 courses, from certificate to post graduate / Ph.D. levels; published 3342 blocks of self-instructional materials, produced 1051 audio and 1102 video programmes.

Unique features of IGNOU

- National jurisdiction
- Flexible admission rules
- Individualized study: flexible in terms of place, pace and duration of study
- Use of latest information and communication technologies
- Student support services network
- Cost-effective programmes
- Modular programmes
- Resource sharing, collaboration and networking with other Open Universities
- Relevant programmes
- Comprehensive evaluation scheme.

Organizational structure

The organizational structure of the University has been designed to reflect each major functional area of operation. At present, there are nine schools of studies and sixteen divisions. IGNOU has established a network of 44 Regional Centres and over 1000 Study Centres spread all over the country to provide support services to distance learners. The student support services include counseling sessions for providing guidance, peer group interaction, laboratory practical, access to audio-video programmes and library services.

Library system

The Library network of IGNOU operates through a hierarchical system having Central Library at the zenith and the branch libraries located at the Regional and Study Centres. The Library and Documentation Division (L&DD) at the headquarters caters to the needs of academic, administrative and support staff. On the other hand, while the Regional Centre Libraries cater to the library requirements of their staff and those at the Study Centres are meant exclusively to meet the needs of the students and counselors.

Objectives of the university

In order to fulfil the vision of democratizing higher education and providing access to all citizens of India, the University Act (1985) states that the University shall:

- impart education and knowledge through various means suited to the open and distance education system;
- provide higher education not only to large sections of the population but particularly to disadvantaged segments of society;
- encourage, coordinate and assist open universities and distance education systems to uphold standards in such systems in India; and
- provide national integration and strengthen the natural and human resources of India through the medium of education

Objectives of IGNOU library

The Library and Documentation Division was established in 1986 to fulfil its objectives in tune with those of IGNOU. The objectives of the Library and Documentation Division are to:

- develop appropriate collections in various disciplines for satisfying the needs of the diverse clientele of the libraries of the University, Regional and Study Centres;
- provide reading, lending, reference, information and documentation facilities to all categories of staff and students, especially the disadvantaged segments of society through multi-media collections;
- develop a special collection of distance education books and journals at the libraries at the headquarters as well as Regional Centres; and
- render comprehensive reference, information and documentation services in areas related to distance education to other Open Universities of the world in general and of India in particular.

Trends

During last fifteen years, the Library and Documentation Division of the IGNOU has been striving hard to provide the books to the libraries of the Regional and Study Centres for reference and consultation for the students who visit the Centre's library. There are constant demands from the students and counselors at the Study Centres to send all the recommended books in the study materials and also issue the same for the home study. But the financial support received for the purpose does not commensurate with the requirements fo the students to satisfy their demands. The trends in development are -

- Increase in number of academic programmes and courses leads to increase in enrollment of students.
- Increase in number of students necessitates establishment of more Regional and Study Centres. The growth of regional and study centers is shown in Table 4.1 below.
- Increase in number of academic programmes/courses as well as Regional and Study Centres requires acquisition of more number and copies of books and hence need for increase in funds for acquisition of books.

Table 4.1: Year-wise growth in academic programmes/courses, regional/study centres, number of books and expenditure

S. No.	Academic Year	No. of Acad.Prog./ Courses	Regional Centres	Study Centres
1.	1986-87	2/13	4	18
2.	1987-88	5/43	8	95
3.	1988-89	7/89	12	120
4.	1989-90	8/128	13	133
5.	1990-91	13/205	16	170
6.	1991-92	26/256	16	202
7.	1992-93	28/296	16	219
8.	1993-94	28/368	16	229
9.	1994-95	34/372	16	247
10.	1995-96	36/435	16	254
11.	1996-97	39/482	17	268
12.	1997-98	39/486	19	315
13.	1998-99	47/553	21	376
14.	1999-2000	50/604	26	504
15.	2000-2001	62/673	44	626
16.	2001-2002	72/854	46	765

Chart 4.1: Growth of study and regional centres

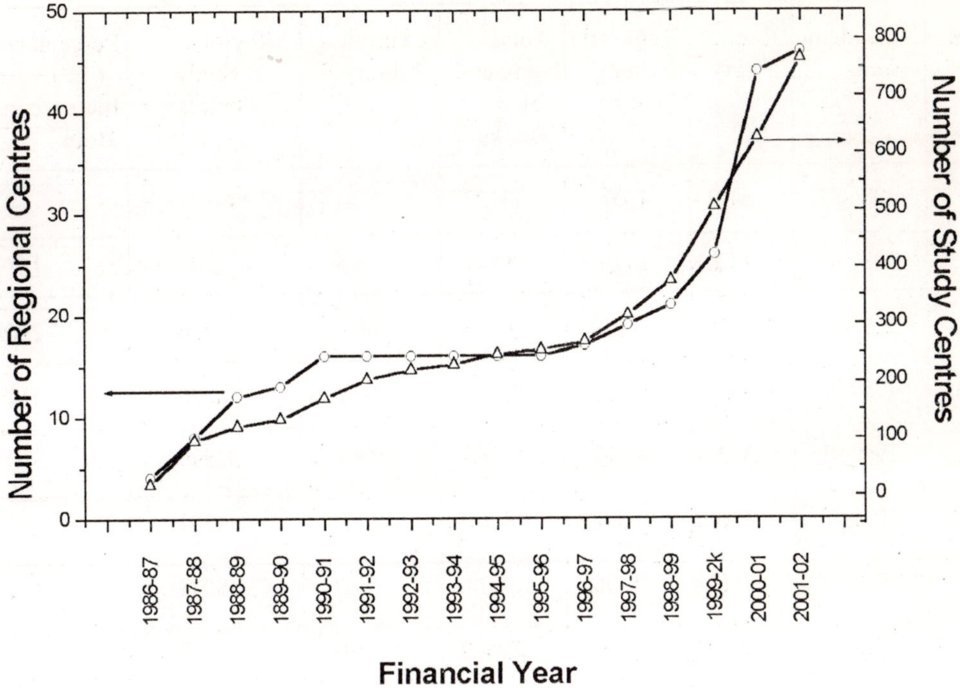

Over a span of sixteen academic years, the total number of books held increased by 2243% from 13,122 books in 1987 to 3,03,433 in 2001-2002, (Table 4.2). This high rate of increase in the collection is in conformity with the popularity of IGNOU programmes and the corresponding increase of 6825% in the enrollment of students (Table 4.3).

Table 4.2: Year-wise increase in number of books at regional and study centres

		Number of Books in			Number of Books Added in		
Sl No.	Academic Year	Central Library	Regional & Study Centres	Total Number of Books	Central Library	Regional & Study Centres	Percentage (%) Increase in Books
1.	1986-87	8422	4700	13122	-----	-----	----
2.	1987-88	16261	13986	30247	7889	9286	131%
3.	1988-89	21254	29242	50496	4993	15256	286%
4.	1989-90	26269	53778	80047	5015	24536	512%
5.	1990-91	31093	96713	127806	4824	42896	878%
6.	1991-92	36162	135917	172079	5069	39204	1216%
7.	1992-93	41183	154965	196148	5021	19048	1400%
8.	1993-94	46332	170304	216636	5398	15339	1584%
9.	1994-95	19661	174419	224080	3080	4115	1639%
10.	1995-96	52219	176869	229088	2558	2450	1677%
11.	1996-97	57561	177282	234843	5342	413	1721%
12.	1997-98	62720	177354	240074	5159	72	1761%
13.	1998-99	67004	187769	254773	4284	10415	1873%
14.	1999-2000	71041	191525	262566	4037	3756	1932%
15.	2000-2001	74546	207085	281631	3505	15560	2077%
16.	2001-2002	77978	225455	303433	3431	18370	2243%

Table 4.3: Year-wise trend in student enrollment, academic programs and increase in books

S.No	Academic Year	No. of Acad. Prog. Courses	No. of Students	No. of Books in Regional & Study centres	% Increase in No. of Students	Ration of Books: Students
1.	1986-87	2/13	4,381	4700	--------	1.1
2.	1987-88	5/43	16,811	13986	384	1.8
3.	1988-89	7/89	42,324	29242	966	1.2
4.	1989-90	8/128	48,281	53778	1102	1.7
5.	1990-91	13/205	52,376	96713	1196	2.4
6.	1991-92	26/256	62,375	135917	1424	2.8
7.	1992-93	28/296	75,666	154965	1727	2.6
8.	1993-94	28/368	84,175	170304	1921	2.6
9.	1994-95	34/372	91,398	174419	2086	2.5
10.	1995-96	36/435	1,30,354	176869	2975	1.8
11.	1996-97	39/482	1,62,540	177282	3710	1.4
12.	1997-98	39/486	1,63,394	177354	3730	1.5
13.	1998-99	47/553	1,72,548	187769	3030	1.5
14.	1999-2000	50/604	1,96,650	191525	4489	1.3
15.	2000-2001	62/673	2,91,360	207085	6651	1
16.	2001-2002	72/854	2,98,987	225455	6825	1

The total number of books in the central library was more than that at the regional/study centres until 1988. By 2001-02 the number of books in R/S centres has grown at a rate more than 5 times that of the central library as indicated in Chart 4.2. A fast increase in the number of books at the R/S Centres compared to the central library fits well with the fact that the increase in the number of students in very high.

Chart 4.2: Growth of books in central library and regional/study centre library

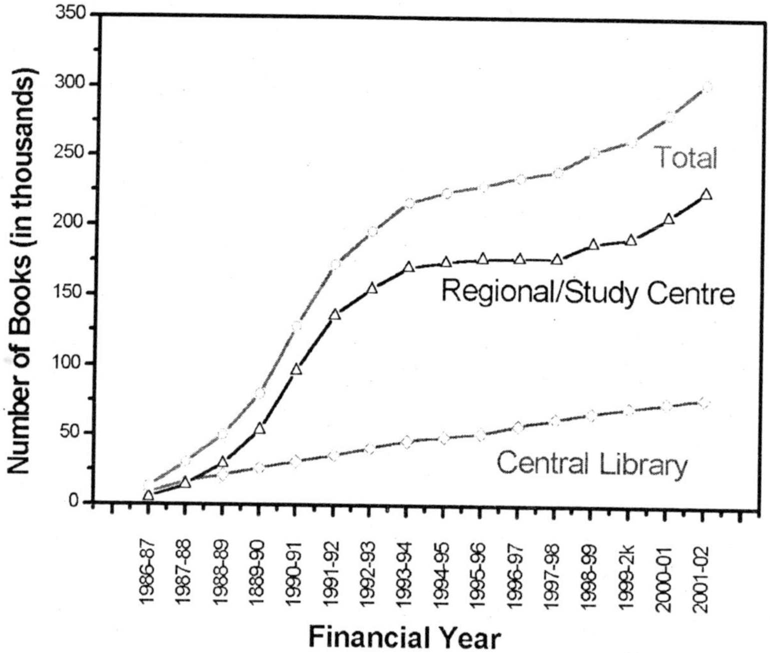

Although the percentage increase in the number of books is impressive, the books to student ratio has fallen to 1. (Table 4.3, Chart 4.3).

Chart 4.3: Comparative diagram showing increase in total number of books and number of students

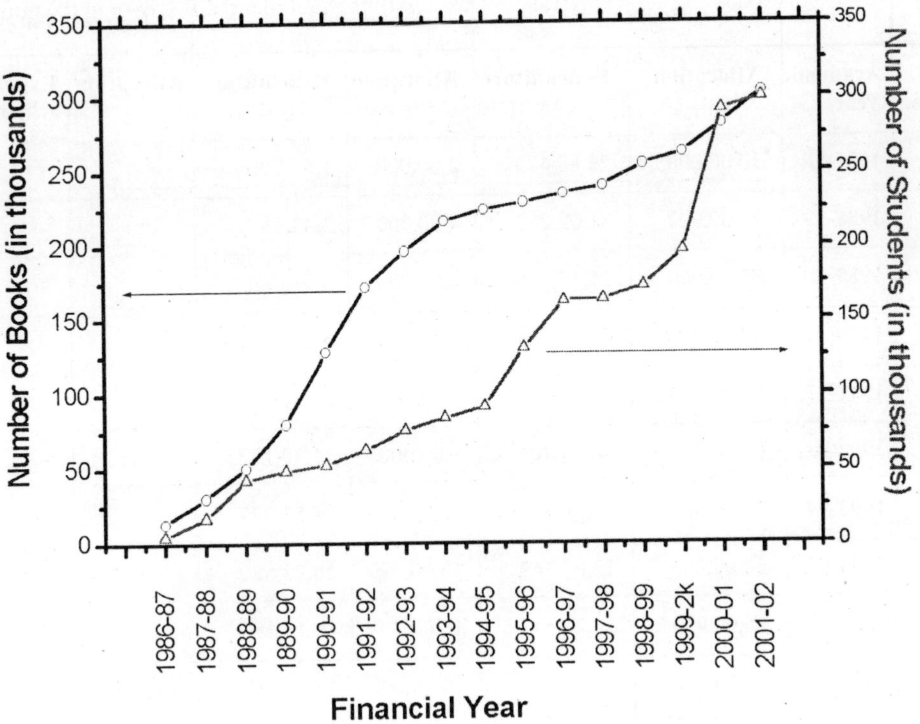

Ever rising enrollment number require, corresponding increase in the budget for books. Although the budget allocation for library has risen from 32, lakhs to 122.5 lakhs, there is marginal change in the book budget (Table 4.4). The trend is now towards procurement of journals and electronic publications (Chart 4.4). With rising cost of books on one hand and marginal increase in the book budget it is becoming difficult to cater to the needs of the learners.

Table 4.4: Year-wise allocation and expenditure for books, periodicals & electronic publishings

		Books		Periodicals		Electronic Publications	
Sl. No.	Academic Year	Allocation	Expenditure	Allocation	Expenditure	Allocation	Expenditure
1.	1987-88	30,00,000	22,88,479	2,00,000	1,67,200	-	-
2.	1988-89	30,00,000	31,02,282	4,00,000	3,42,587	-	-
3.	1989-90	35,00,000	31,17,118	4,00,000	3,91,680	-	-
4.	1990-91	60,00,000	57,62,239	8,00,000	6,28,557	-	-
5.	1991-92	50,00,000	48,44,289	8,00,000	8,25,961	-	-
6.	1992-93	60,00,000	36,89,406	8,00,000	11,19,172	-	-
7.	1993-94	50,00,000	32,98,930	13,00,000	11,53,977	-	-
8.	1994-95	50,00,000	12,07,762	16,00,000	16,73,520	-	-
9.	1995-96	35,00,000	24,22,493	16,00,000	16,13,387	-	-
10.	1996-97	27,50,000	29,54,698	20,00,000	18,90,895	10,00,000	7,83,388
11.	1997-98	45,00,000	45,46,717	20,00,000	20,55,015	35,00,000	36,40,587
12.	1998-99	50,00,000	55,60,861	27,00,000	27,20,281	35,00,000	32,85,293
13.	1999-2000	40,00,000	38,64,793	25,00,000	31,04,360	35,00,000	24,23,254
14	2000-2001	62,00,000	62,35,684	35,00,000	33,03,723	33,00,000	32,69,995
15.	2001-2002	50,00,000	57,03,829	37,50,000	37,17,193	35,00,000	27,87,085

Chart 4.4: Expenditure on Books, Periodicals and Electronic Publications

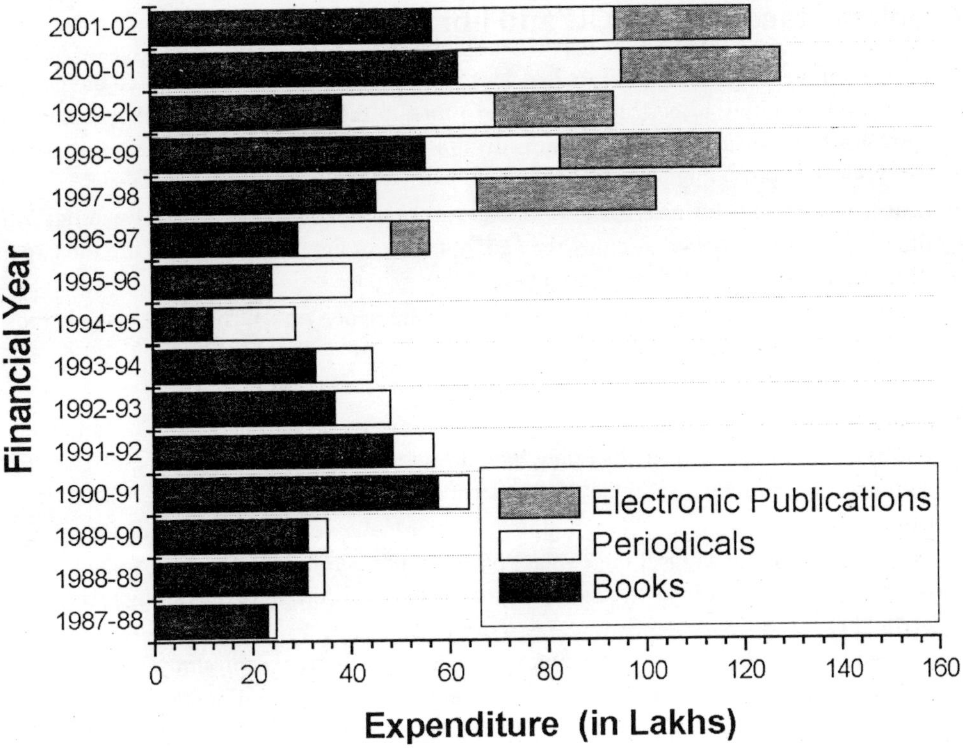

Problems faced by students

- Learners require library services like reading reference and lending similar to their counterparts in conventional universities, but lending service is not provided to students at IGNOU.
- India being a vast country and having huge population scattered all over the country, learners have to travel long distances to reach study centers.
- Learners have to incur expenditure every time they visit their study centre to avail library services.
- As IGNOU students are part-time learners, they cannot get concessions for travelling by train or bus.
- Employers do not permit/grant leave on Saturdays and Sundays if the weekly off is on any week day.
- They have to arrange for lodging/boarding facilities to visit study centre on Saturdays and Sundays.
- Economic background and social commitments on holidays to their families and relatives cause difficulty in visiting study centre.
- Disadvantaged students such as women, physically challenged, residing in rural, remote hilly and backward areas as well as spouses and children of migrating population face problems in availing support services at the study centres.

- They do not get up-to-date information unless they visit the study centres.

Problems faced by IGNOU and library

- Lack of infra-structural facilities such as space, furniture, adequate staff, limited funds, literature explosion, spiraling prices, devaluation of rupee in the international market, complexity of demands from diverse learners of multi-disciplinary choice of programmes, shrinking budget etc hinders in providing support services to learners.
- Learner's demands for providing all books recommended as "Suggested Readings" in their blocks cannot be satisfied as either they are out of print/out of stock or they are too expensive/ difficult to procure from foreign countries.
- Regional and study centres do not have adequate space and furniture for stack room and reading room.
- They also do not have professionally qualified and committed staff.
- Books are issued for consultation only at the premises for reading/reference but students do not have time to sit and read as they have to attend counseling sessions and view/listen to audio-video programmes. So they are underutilized.
- Circulation of books, viz. issuing, adjustments of loans, reservation of books is not possible as attendance at the counselling/contact programmes is optional. Books if issued may not be returned on time and thereby reducing significantly the availability of reading facility to others on the premises.
- Postgraduate students expect the library to subscribe journals for study centers but due to lack of permanent staff to undertake serial control activities, it is not feasible.
- Demand to get books on inter-library loan also cannot be fulfilled as study centres cannot spare books for sharing resources.
- Demand for books in regional languages cannot be satisfied as standard text books in professional subjects such as science and technology, management, computer science, engineering, etc are not available.
- Electronic gadgets like TV, VCR, tape recorder, radio, computer are not equally and adequately accessible to all learners.
- Budgetary constraints are graver and so multiple copies of books cannot be sent to each study centre for providing lending facilities.
- Library has no alternative but to play a significant role by undertaking measures to bridge the gap by outreaching library services to distance learners.

Measures taken to provide outreach library services for distance learners

Establishment of Learning Resource Centre

Library and Documentation Division has established IGNOU Learning Resource Centre on April 23, 2000 to provide reading, lending, reference and information services to students of management, computer science and library information science at – Leela Devi Public Library, A-82, Mohan Gardens, D.K. Post Office Building, Uttam Nagar, New Delhi 110 059.

Membership of DELNET for regional centres

IGNOU's Central Library has been the institutional member of DELNET – Developing Libraries Network since 1991. The annual membership has been provided to 22 Regional Centres to enable the postgraduate and research students visiting the Library of the Regional Centres to access the collection of 233 participating libraries.

Digitization of question papers

In order to satisfy the demands of learners for the question papers of the examinations of previous years, the Library has digitized all the question papers from 1987 to 2000 and has prepared year-wise, level wise and school-wise CDs of papers. They are being provided to all schools of studies, regional centres and regular study centres to facilitate them in providing question papers to students.

Installation of CD-Net workstation

The Library has acquired TNT Server 2000 CD-Net Workstation having capacity of stacking 28 CD-ROMs at a time. Software for accessing CD-Net facilities has been installed on the computers of academic staff networked with the University LAN. It facilitates teachers to browse, scan and download information for themselves as well as for their research and postgraduate students/ without visiting the Library.

Subscription of CD-ROM full-text and bibliographic databases

Bibliographic and multi-user full-text CD-ROM databases have been subscribed for installing on CD-Net workstation for providing easy and quick access to information on their own computers.

Access to electronic journals through J-Gate

The Library has subscribed sixty journals in print format with which on-line access is available free. By entering the on-line gateway called J-Gate, the Library users can have access to 1400 gratis on-line journals linked through this gateway after obtaining a password from the library.

Future plans

Electronic reference library

University is introducing Ph.D. programmes in a few disciplines. Library proposes to install electronic reference library for management, computer science, humanities and social sciences to provide access to exponential literature to the postgraduate and research students.

Packages of reference materials

In order to provide reference materials prescribed for further reading as supplement to self instructional materials provided by the University, the Library will prepare packages of relevant chapters of books and articles of journals for professional postgraduate courses in consultation with faculty members. The same documents will also be posted on the University website after taking necessary copyright permission from authors. Distance learners having access to Internet will download from the website whereas those who do not have access to Internet can request for the packages in the print format. They will be charged minimum photo copying and postal charges.

Mobile libraries

Outreach library services will be provided to learners residing in rural, remote, hilly and backward areas through mobile libraries.

Learning resource centres at public libraries

The Library and Documentation Division is exploring feasibility of establishing IGNOU Learning Resource Centres at various public libraries having adequate infrastructural facilities to provide reading, lending and reference services.

National policy for library services to distance learners

The Sectional Committee on Distance Education constituted by the Indian Library Association (ILA) has formulated Guidelines for Library Services for Distance Learners. The ILA can enter into Memorandum of Understanding with the Distance Education Council at IGNOU - the national body for co-ordination and monitoring of distance education in India - to implement these guidelines at the national level.

Web-based information

The Library also has a plan to provide web based information regarding :

- complete catalogue of IGNOU's print, audio and video programmes
- question papers of the examination of the previous years from 1987 to 2000
- catalogue of the Central Library
- holding of journals received at the L&DD
- catalogues of theses, IGNOU course materials microfiches and microfilms, holding of CD-ROMs and other databases.

Library and information services

After shifting to the permanent central building on the campus, the library will provide library and information services through telephone, e-mail, fax and postal service. Books will be lent through DELNET to regional centres for Ph. D students all over the country. The additional services include the following :

- reading, reference and lending services from the existing library block
- viewing and listening to audio-video programme
- reprographic services on subsidized charges
- information services from multi-media collections at the Central Library.

Library support to physically challenged learners

The Library support will be provided to physically challenged / blind students at the new building campus by procuring necessary hardware, software and braille collections.

Conclusion

With ever increasing students enrollment and escalation of cost of books and journals it is becoming difficult for the IGNOU library system to cater to the basic needs of reading material for the learners. Added to that, the scattering of the learners throughout the country, requires library services to be taken to the learners at their end. Alternate methods of delivery of materials and services are being planned to reach out to the learners. It is hoped that in future with setting up of digital library system it will be possible to provide effective services to the learners.

References

Indira Gandhi National Open University. (1999-2002) *Annual Reports, (1992-2002)*. New Delhi: IGNOU.

Indira Gandhi National Open University. (1989-2002). Statistics compiled from Library records (Unpublished).

Jagannathan, Neela (1997) Rendering Equitable Library Services to Distance Learners in India:Problems and Prospects. In *Library Services to Distance Learners in the Commonwealth: A Reader.* Ed. By Elizabeth F. Watson and Neela Jagannathan. Vancouver, Canada: The Commonwealth of Learning, 1997. p. 135-153.

Jagannathan, Neela (1998) Libraries in Distance Teaching Universities. In *50 years Library and Information Services in India*. Ed. by M. K. Jain et al. Delhi: Shipra, p. 65-76.

Kanjilal, Uma and Jagannathan Neela (2001) Bridging the gap: Experience of the Indira Gandhi National Open University in providing library services to distance learners. *Poster Presentation Sixty Seventh Annual Conference of IFLA,* Boston from August 16-25, 2001.

Kanjilal, Uma and Tripathi S. M. (1995) Collection Development: Planning for IGNOU library system. In *Library Acquisitions: Practice and Theory,* 19(1), 83-95.

5

Status of Library and Resource Centre (LARC) and its Activities Yashwantrao Chavan Maharashtra Open University

Madhukar Shewale

Introduction

The Yashwantrao Chavan Maharashtra Open University (YCMOU) came into existence in July 1989 through Act XX (1989) of the Maharashtra State Legislature. Established to provide quality education through distance mode it is trying to create a distinct identity in the Indian Open education scenario. With its goal of becoming a 'Mass varsity', its emphasis has been on Vocational, Technical, Professional as well as general education programmes.

Objectives of the university

The major objectives of the University are:

- To make higher, vocational and technical education available to the large section of the population.
- To give special attention to the needs of disadvantaged groups, in particular people in the rural areas and women.
- To relate all courses to the developmental needs of individuals, institutions and the State
- To provide innovative, flexible and open systems of education by using distance teaching methodology and by applying modern communication technologies to education
- To provide continuing adult and extension education. Special attention is to be given to retraining adults in new skills to enable them to adjust to a changing technological environment.
- To provide post-graduate studies and research opportunities in all fields of knowledge, especially in Educational Technology, Distance education, and Development Communication.

YCMOU is responsible to provide educational opportunities at State level through Open and Distance mode. The University is committed to becoming self-sufficient in operational costs, which today seems rather difficult. It develops linkages so as to become instrumental in developmental and transformational process of the society around.

Academic programmes

Academic programmes of YCMOU are broadly classified as general programmes, technical programmes, professional/vocational programmes and research programmes. These programmes are not only knowledge oriented but also skill-oriented. The University has 60 academic programmes and more than 250 courses. YCMOU has introduced some of the programmes in the field of Agriculture Science like Floriculture, Horticulture, Fruit Production, Gardening, Vegetable Production, etc. It is the only Open University offering programmes in Agriculture and Agriculture extension.

Organizational structure

The organizational structure of YCMOU is divided into two important areas viz. Development and Operation. The schools of studies have major role of designing curriculum and developing learning material. The Divisions and other Centres facilitate in distribution of the learning materials and management of Students Services. These services include Admission, Evaluation, Academic Counselling and Library Services.

Regional and study centres

YCMOU has developed a three-tier system having Headquarter, Regional Centres and Study Centres for the delivery of different programmes in the State of Maharashtra. It has a network of 8 Regional Centres and 1451 Study Centres. The Study Centres have not only been a medium of transmission of information and instructional materials to the students, but, have also been an effective means of offering academic counselling to distance learners through the planned contact sessions. These sessions are conducted on Saturday, Sunday or on holidays as per the convenience of students and counsellors. The counsellors are experienced teachers at these institutions or are retired teachers living in and around the town. They provide instructional support, guidance and counselling. There are 4521 counsellors offering their services for about 60 programmes throughout the State of Maharashtra. Apart from this, each Study Centre has a coordinator and administrative staff working on honorarium basis.

Library and Resource Centre (LARC)

The Library and Resource Centre (LARC) is playing an important role in fulfilling the objectives of YCMOU. The functions of LARC are to:

- support academic activities of in-house academics and outside experts by providing information sources for the development of learning material;
- support reference and information needs of post-graduate, Research students and students of job–oriented and Agriculture programmes of YCMOU by creating appropriate facilities at the Headquarters as well as post-graduate and research study centres.
- provide documents and comprehensive reference and information services in the area of Open and Distance Education for other Distance Education Institutes in the State.
- provide assistance to Co-ordinators of Library and Information Science Programmes (B.Lib. and M.Lib.) of the University.

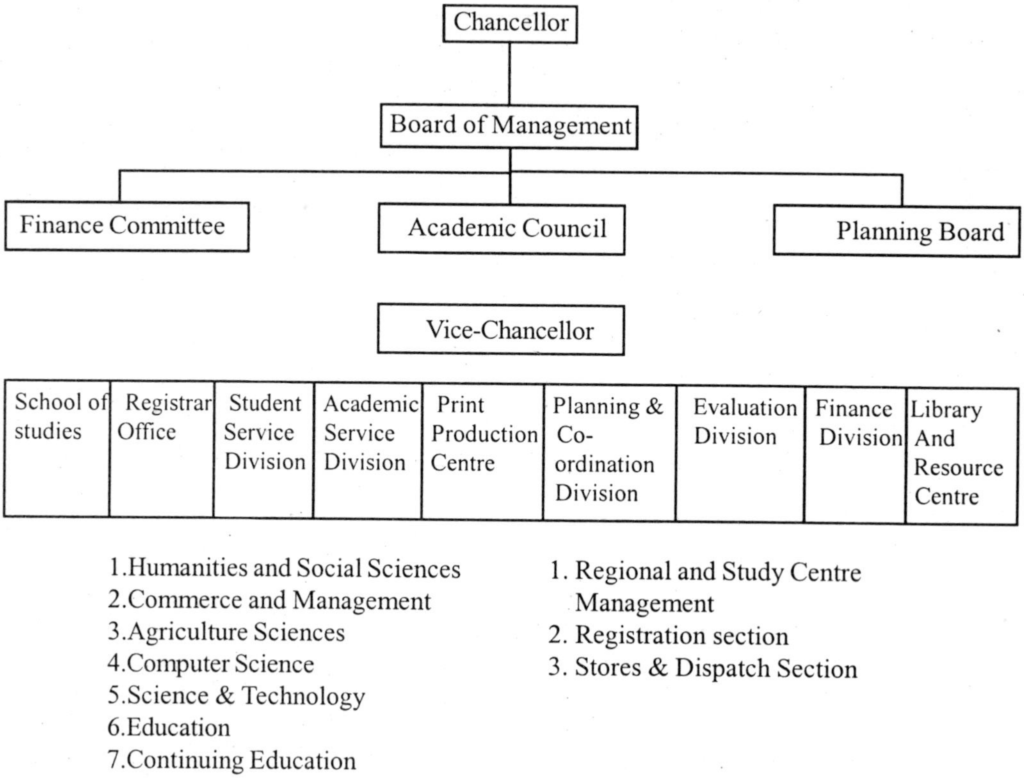

Figure 5.1: The flow chart of organizational structure of the university

LARC resources

In order to fulfil these objectives, the University has developed a collection of printed and non-conventional materials like, Audio, Video, CBTs, CD-ROMs and specially prepared course materials for distance learners (See Table 5.1)

Collection development procedure

The collection development policy for LARC has been introduced in view of programmes offered by the University. The titles required for course development, suggested titles for reading and Distance Education material are the main criteria for collection development.

Academics and the Library personnel share the responsibility for selection of reading material. Many times the titles suggested by outside experts, course writers, scriptwriters and counsellors are taken into consideration. For the purpose of selection, Librarian and the Academics visit bookshops, exhibitions on regular basis. Many times the vendors are asked to hold exhibitions of books in various disciplines at the site. The reading materials are also selected with the help of various bibliographical tools, publishers catalogues, publishers' new arrival announcements, pre-publication jackets, select bibliographies and Book reviews and so on.

Table 5.1: Stock of library materials

Sr. No.	Resource	Number
1.	Printed Books	21,000
2.	Periodicals	250
3.	Audio Cassettes	534
4.	Video Cassettes	537
5.	CBT Packages & CD-ROM	700
6.	Slides	300
7.	Thesis & Project Reports	6000
8.	Photographs	10000
9.	Reports	300
10.	Archival Material	2000

Services offered

At present the Library and Resource Centre of YCMOU offers following services to its users

- Lending services
- Reading services
- User services
- Inter-Library Loan Services
- Reprographic services
- Bibliographic services
- Documentation services
- Current Awareness services
- Selective Dissemination of Information
- Facilities for viewing and listening audio/video and other learning materials

Out of above-mentioned services, the post-graduate and research programmes Study Centres of YCMOU offer Lending and Reading services at their respective places. Post-graduate and research students regularly visit the central library to refer Thesis and Project Reports for their research work. LARC has maintained Newspaper clippings in the area of Education and Distance Education. Also one of the major things added in the syllabus of B.Lib programme of YCMOU is the collection of Newspaper clippings by students. LARC offers their services to student community.

The schools of respective disciplines, Divisions and Centres are connected with LAN. The Current Awareness Service and Selective Dissemination of Information Service offered through LAN by scanning the content page of journals, and putting new arrival list and jacket are provided to the users. Bibliographies are also prepared on various subjects, which are available to the users in the print format. Recently University has started On-line counselling for few programmes and library is participating in these discussion forums for the related queries. LARC is having section of multi-media resources, which include Audios / Videos, CBTs, CD-ROMs, Slides etc. It has an agreement for viewing such material. The students and staff (users) need professional assistance and support in terms of using equipments and facilities in the library. The students also need guidance regarding suitability of material to support their study, assistance in planning their learning and developing study skills for independent learning. The LARC has institutional membership like Asiatic Society Library, Mumbai, British Council Library, Pune, to cater to the needs of users. It has taken institutional membership of **INFLIBNET** and **DELNET** to offer their services to the staff and Distance Learners.

The University publishes the quarterly journal 'Dnyangangotri' to make aware of the current developments in the field of 'Library and Information Science', which includes articles in various disciplines, abstracts from the leading journals, information about useful websites, book-reviews etc. This is another type of library service being provided to the Distance Learners.

Problems faced

Recently library has shifted to the new premises having ample space to store print as well as non-print materials. The work of interior fittings is in progress and will include Circulation Counter, Periodical display, Special corner of Distance Education publications, and Yashwantrao Chavan Special collection, Librarian's office, Technical section, Multi-media learning center, Reading room and so on. Most of the research and post-graduate students visit the library for research work, for their urgent requirements. Due to lack of appropriate furniture, it becomes difficult to provide effective services to the users.

Library services provided by LARC of YCMOU are certainly very cost effective for providing information resources to student in ODL, but they often lack proper funding. It is felt that while planning resources, Library services may be given a priority.

Another important factor is inadequate staff. While providing effective library services, there is an urgent need of professionally qualified and service minded staff to satisfy the users' demand.

Library automation

LARC started its automation programme in 1992. In order to computerise the functions of library the DOS based in-house software was developed to maintain its database. It was somewhat operational for acquisitions, cataloguing, circulation, serials control and housekeeping and not useful for supported network.

Recently 'SOUL' software developed by INFLIBNET Centre of University Grants Commission (UGC) has been installed and data stored in old software has been transported to it. The SOUL software is very user friendly and it satisfies the need of both the staff and users. The 'SOUL' software is also provided free of cost to all the MLIS Study Centres as a part of syllabus for IT component.

Future plans

Taking into consideration requirements of the programmes developed by the YCMOU and the network of study Centre, following are the future plans.

- Development of YCMOU Library website.
- Participation in various discussion forums as some of the schools already started on-line counselling for their programmes.
- Providing students an access to textbooks developed in electronic format by YCMOU.
- Providing access to the Abstracts of Thesis/Dissertations in electronic format to students.
- Participation in various networks and make available its services to distance learners.
- Development of multi-media learning Centre with well equipped resources and instruments.
- Rendering Reference and Information Services through various communication mediums.
- Development and maintenance of libraries at the Regional Centres of YCMOU.
- Establishment of YCMOU corner in all public and college libraries in the State of Maharashtra.
- Making agreement with the institutions in which the YCMOU Study Centres are operational, regarding provision of lending and other library service with some financial assistance and provision of books from the Central library.
- Developing of 'Information Package' for Study Centre counsellors, which is supportive and useful for their contact session.
- Creating 'Information Packages' for job-oriented programmes like Agriculture and technical programmes of the Continuing Education School.

Conclusion

The Open University Central Library has a big responsibility of providing academic support to academics of the Open University as well as to Study Centres also. It has to act as a Resource Centre having important functions of receiving literature, storing and supplying to the needy persons. Many times it happens that the Study Centre Counsellors do not get relevant literature for upgrading their information level. In that case the LARC can play an important role of supplying such literature to Study Centres. It may be done through postal services, Internet or through agencies as and when needed. For this purpose, the YCMOU has to take necessary steps for managing finance and manpower, skilled enough for accepting this big responsibility.

Acknowledgement

I am extremely grateful to Professor Ashok Pradhan, Vice Chancellor, YCMOU for encouraging and allowing me to present this paper for the AAOU Pre-Conference Seminar. I also thank Prof. Manoj Killedar and Dr. Satish Rastogi who have given valuable inputs to this paper.

References

Jolliffee, Alan.,Ritter, Jonathan, and Stevens, David. (2001). *The On-Line learning Handbook; Developing and using web-Based Learning.* London: Kogan Page.

Peter Brophy, Shelagh Fisher and Zoe Clarke (eds.) (2000) Libraries without walls 3: The delivery of library services to distant users. London: Library Association Publishing.

Elizabeth F. Watson and Neela Jagannathan, (eds) (1996) *Library services to distance learners in the commonwealth: A reader*. Vancouver: The Commonwealth of Learning.

G. Ram Reddy, (ed) (1998) *Open universities: The ivory towers thrown open*. Bangalore. Sterling Publishers Private Limited.Perry, Walter.(1976). *Open University: a personal account by the First Vice-Chancellor.* Milton Keynes: Open University Press.

Simpson, Ormond.(2000). *Supporting students in Open and Distance Learning*. London: Kogan Page.

Keegan, D.(ed) (1993).*Theoretical principles of distance education*, London, Routledge.

YCMOU (1998), *Study Centre Management Booklet*. Nashik: YCMOU

YCMOU (1999), *Annual Report*. Nashik: YCMOU.

YCMOU (1999), *About YCMOU*. Nashik: YCMOU.

YCMOU (1999), *Yashwantrao Chavan Maharashtra Open University: Handbook* 1998-99. Nashik: YCMOU.

6

Library Services to Distance Learners: A Study of Kota Open University

B. K. Singh

Introduction

The idea of establishing an Open University in the state of Rajasthan goes back to the UGC Committee set up to study the working of the erstwhile Institute of Correspondence Studies and Continuing Education, University of Rajasthan Jaipur 1985. Also known as Prof. G. Ram Reddy committee, it noted with satisfaction the existing state of the affairs and opined that this could eventually grow into an open university. Thereafter, the state officials and educational experts held a series of preparatory meeting in Rajasthan with the Indira Gandhi National Open University (IGNOU). The ordinance was subsequently enacted by the state legislature as the Kota Open University Act, 1987. The Kota Open University was established on July 23, 1987 as part of the Open University network in the country (art, 4(iv) of the Kota Open University Act (KOU, 1990:1).

In order to strengthen and achieve better co-ordination of the vast scattered resources of distance education in the sate, the Government of Rajasthan decided to merge the assets of the erstwhile Institute of Correspondence Studies and Continuing Education, Jaipur and the College of Correspondence Studies, Udaipur.

The UGC accorded recognition to the University under 12(b) in 1989 and found the University as fit to receive all kinds of assistance / grant including central assistance for instructional development.

Objectives

The objectives of the University are much similar to the objectives of all other major open universities of the world. This University mainly draws its inspirations from Indira Gandhi National Open University (IGNOU) and the United Kingdom Open University (UKOU).

The broad spectrum of objectives set forth for itself by the University are most aptly summed up by Article 4 of the Act. Article 4, while articulating mechanisms for dissemination of education and knowledge in the state, seeks to emphasise the following functions:

- to provide for instructions and research in such branches of knowledge, technology, vocational and profession as the University may deem necessary or proper;
- to prescribe courses of study for degrees, diplomas, certificates or any other purpose;
- to hold examinations and confer degrees, diplomas, certificates and other academic programmes;
- to determine the manner of distance education system so as to organise academic programmes;
- to associate with other universities and institutions of learning especially with the IGNOU in order to have there with inter-locking system in the field of distance education;
- to institute and award fellowships and prizes;
- to establish and maintain Regional Centres and Study Centres;
- to give recognition to examinations, studies and activities conducted by other universities, institutions, academic bodies and organisations; and
- to perform all such functions which are necessary for and incidental to achieving the aims and objects of the University.

Organizational structure

The Governor of Rajasthan is the Chancellor of the University. The Board of Management, Academic Council, Planning Board and Finance Committee are the important University bodies.

The Vice-Chancellor, Directors, Registrar and Finance Officer are the main officers of the University. Competent academics selected from all over the country provide academic services related to programme design, development and implementation. The structure aspires to provide a working arrangement that seeks to establish firm central control of a fully integrated operation.

Programmes offered

Certificate programmes

1. Certificate Course in Food and Nutrition (CFN)

2. Computer Awareness and Training Programme for Beginners (CATPB)

Diploma programmes

3. Diploma in Computer in Office Management (DCO)

4. Diploma in Library and Information Science (DLS)

5. Diploma Course in Culture and Tourism (DCCT)

6. Diploma in Nutrition and Health Education (DNHE)

7. Diploma in Tourism and Hotel Management (DTHM)

P.G. diploma programmes

8. P.G.Diploma in Human Resource Management (PGDHRM)

9. P.G. Diploma in Marketing Management (PGDMM)

10. P.G. Diploma in Financial Management (PGDFM)

11. P.G. Diploma in Labour Laws Industrial Relations and Personnel Management (PGDLL)

Undergraduate degree programmes

12. Bachelor of Arts (B.A.)

13. Bachelor of Commerce (B.Com)

14. Bachelor Degree in Journalism and Mass Communication (BJMC)

15. Bachelor of Education (B.Ed.)

Postgraduate degree programmes

16. Master of Business Administration (MBA)

17. Master Degree in journalism and Mass Communication (MJMC)

18. M.A. Economics

19. M.A. History

20. M.A. Political Science

Research programme

21. Ph.D.: This facility is available in the disciplines/faculties of Humanities and Social Sciences; Commerce and Management, Science and Technology and Education.

The library system

The University started its Central Library during the year 1987-88, but its actual functioning started in July 1988. The library system of Kota Open University comprises the Central Library at the headquarters; six regional centre libraries and 43 study centre libraries. The library system of KOU is being studied in two parts (a) headquarters' Central Library and (b) libraries at the Regional Centres and the Study Centres. The Central Library caters to the needs of the University's teaching and non-teaching staff, councellors/tutors, research scholars, etc.; whereas libraries at RCs and SCs are to fulfil the needs of distance learners and resident counsellors/tutors.

The central library

Management: The library is managed / administrated by the Officer In-charge with the assistance of Assistant Librarian and other supporting staff.

As per the statute of the Kota Open University (1987) (15) (I), there is a Library Committee which advises the librarian for smooth functioning and development of the library services. The constitution of the library committee is as under:

1. One Director/Professor to be nominated by the Vice-Chancellor;
2. One Director to be nominated by the Vice-Chancellor;
3. One Director of the Regional Centre to be nominated by the Vice-Chancellor by seniority;
4. One Professor of the University to be nominated by the Vice-Chancellor by seniority;
5. One Associate Professor to be nominated by the Vice-Chancellor by seniority;
6. One Assistant Professor to be nominated by the Vice-Chancellor;
7. One nominee of the Academic Council;
8. Finance Officer (ex-officio);
9. Registrar or his nominee not below the rank of Assistant Registrar; and
10. Librarian - Secretary.

The terms of reference of committee are as under:

- to consider the appropriate nature of the services the library should provide;
- to advise the librarian of user needs and proposed library developments;
- to advise the librarian on the estimates and the allocation of library funds; and
- to approve the librarian's Annual Report to the Vice-Chancellor.

The modes of operation of the committee are as follows:

- the committee shall meet as and when required but not less than two times in a year;
- the senior most member will be nominated as the chairman by the Vice-Chancellor; and
- the term of the nominated members shall be two years.

Library sub-committee

The library committee adopted a procedure of appointing two Sub-Committees, namely (a) Library Sub-Committee for Central Library and (b) Library Sub-Committee for Regional Services. The functions of the Library Sub-Committee are not prescribed as such, but from the decisions taken during various meetings of these committees, the following functions can be drawn:

- to allocate/ re-allocate budget for the purchase of books and journals in various subjects;
- to draw a broad purchase policy for the library system;
- to advise the librarian on matters where there is a need; and
- to work and advise on the matters as referred to by the library committee.

The number of members in these committees is 5-6, but sometimes all subject heads are invited as special members to attend the meetings of this committee, particularly when the budget is distributed among various subjects. There is no fixed schedule for conducting the meeting of this committee. The committee meets as and when there is a need.

Collection development

Acquisition policies are determined by the range of programmes being offered, the level of courses being delivered, financial allocation for stock acquisition, enrollment numbers, etc.

Selection of material is a pre-requisite for the acquisition of materials. Book-selection determines the quality of the collection. Selection of information sources is the most important and indispensable function of the library. Financial resources play a vital role in selection procedures in KOU. The subject wise allocation of funds is done in the meeting of the library sub-committee and the faculty members select the information sources i.e. books and journals accordingly.

Selection of information sources is the joint responsibility of the faculty members and the library professionals. Selection of information sources includes: publishers catalogue, pre-publication jackets, visits to major book shops, book fairs and exhibitions, etc.

As the books are selected, library staff follow necessary procedure to procure document in the Central Library. Generally the Central Library purchases only one copy of each selected title within the allotted budget in each subject.

The library in general aspires to procure books on all areas, however emphasis is generally on books relevant to the courses being offered or courses under preparation. In addition, the Central Library has a useful collection of books on distance education as a discipline.

As far as the size of collection is concerned, the central library was fortunate to start with a big collection of more than twenty thousand books received from the Institute of Correspondence Studies, Jaipur and College of Correspondence Studies, Udaipur. The library has more than doubled this number since 1987. At present the Central Library has 52,635 books, 255 thesis and dissertations, 1,200 bound volumes previous years journals, 55 video cassettes, 35 audio cassettes. Library subscribes 158 foreign and national journals and magazines.

The Central Library follows Colon Classification 6th edition and Classified Catalogue Code for the purpose of classifying and cataloguing of documents, respectively.

Human resource

The efficiency, usefulness or popularity of a library is measured neither by the size of the building, nor by the large collection, but by the efficiency of library staff which is really the creator and mentor of an efficient and effective library system. At present Central Library has only three professional staff. viz. one Assistant Librarian, one Senior Technical Assistant and one Junior Technical Assistant. Besides four non-technical staff and three peons are working in the library. The position of University Librarian is still vacant.

The library can be defined as understaffed and there is a pressing need for recruiting more trained staff for providing useful services. In the absence of such staff the library is not able to provide the best services. Even the available resources are not optionally used.

Library services to the users of the central library

The prime objective of collection, storage, and organisation of information in the library is to facilitate the academic community to exploit and harness the resources of the library fully. Effective library services make a library more functional to deliver document or furnish information at the right time and in the right manner to the right user.

Central Library is providing the following routine services to the users.

- reading services;
- lending services;

- reprographic services;
- viewing and listening to audio-visual material; and
- reference and information services.

There is a great demand from users to provide the following services as well:

- newspaper clipping services;
- indexing and abstracting services;
- current awareness services;
- selective dissemination of information; and
- bibliographic and documentation services.

The above mentioned specialised service will be provided when the library is shifted from current residential flats to the new library building which is under construction. The new library building will provide the space to arrange the entire collection in helpful sequence.

Problems faced by the central library

There are some problems to the successful development of library services to users faced by the Central Library; these include (among others):

- The University has no separate library building and the library is presently housed in residential flats of the University which does not fulfill the requirement of a good functional building of the university library. Due to lack of space, the growth, the use as well as the functions of the library are adversely affected.

- The library budget is inadequate compared to the demands for documents by users. In addition, the prices of documents are increasing and therefore the ability of the budget to meet the growing demands is shrinking.

- The professional staff plays a vital role in smooth functioning of library but the university has inadequate level of professional staff. The small team of committed and dedicated staff is hard pressed to satisfy user demands. Workload on staff is increasing day by day. As a result, library staff is unable to function effectively and efficiently.

Libraries at the regional centres (RCs) and study centres (SCs)

Libraries at the RCs and SCs have a major role in student support services. As mentioned above the Kota Open University has three types of libraries, namely, at the headquarters. The Central Library, libraries at the RCs; and libraries at the SCs . Libraries at RCs and SCs are housed in the premises allocated for the Regional/Study Centre purposes.

Organisation and management

The Central Library has the responsibility of providing library and information services to distance learners through its libraries at RCs and SCs. There is a Library Sub-Committee known as Library Sub-Committee for Regional Services for the management of these libraries.

The composition of the Library Sub-Committee for Regional Services is as under:

1. Director (Regional Services) - Convenor
2. Two Regional Directors - Member
3. One Asst. Professor - Member
4. One Coordinator of the study centre - Member
5. Librarian - Member-Secretary

There is no fixed schedule to conduct the meeting of this Sub-Committee. Meeting of the same takes place as and when the need arises.

Collection management

There are two ways through which Regional Centres' libraries acquire documents.

- the Central Library procures the documents and sends to RCs
- and SCs as recommended by the faculty members.

The Regional Directors also procure documents as suggested by the faculty members and the tutors and counsellors.

Technical processing (i.e. accessioning, classification, and cataloguing) is done by the Regional Centres themselves. The library staff of the Regional Centre may seek guidance from the professional staff of the Central Library if considered necessary. The part-time librarian at the Study Centre maintains proper record of the library services.

Library and information services to the users of the RCs and SCs

At present the libraries of RCs and SCs provide the following services to the distance learners:

- reading services;
- reference and information services;
- listening to audio materials; and
- viewing to visual materials .

The Regional Centres are well equipped with modern electronic and communication equipments such as telephone, fax, E-mail, computers, television, photocopiers and so on. With the help of these facilities they provide effective library and information services.

Regional Centres' libraries remain open during the office hours, whereas Study Centres' libraries works on week end and remain open during counselling/tutoring sessions.

The libraries of RCs and SCs are housed mainly with study materials, textbooks, audio visual cassettes etc. Some study centres also have a TV set, a VCP and audio cassette players, etc.

An agenda for action

The role of the library is central in all types of education, conventional mode as well as distance mode. Hence, it is necessary to provide a good deal of planning and organisation of library and information services from the headquarters level at the top to the study centre level at the grass root level in an Open University. It is the responsibility of the LIS professionals to provide right library and information services to right user at the appropriate time. Library system of the Kota Open University should seriously consider the following agenda for action for the development of library and information services.

Information technology

Today we are living in the age of Information Society and the role of IT is pivotal in providing library and information services. But at Kota Open University use of IT in library is at its embryonic state. Recently Distance Education Council (DEC) has provided Rs.5,00,000/- or 5.00 lacs for library computerisation and we are planning to computerise our library services in the newly constructed library building.

The Computerisation and Networking plan of KOU's library system will include the following:

- To enter data of entire library collection in appropriate library software packages.
- To connect Regional Centre's libraries located at Ajmer, Bikaner, Jaipur, Jodhpur, Kota, and Udaipur with the headquarter's Centre Library through networking
- To connect Study Centre's libraries located at different colleges with the headquarters' Central Library and libraries of the Regional Centres.
- To link the library system with the Internet and suitable existing system and Networks in the Country, Such as INFLIBNET, NICNET, DELNET, the proposed OPENET; etc.

Satellite collection

Some of the distance teaching institutions have an arrangement with public libraries for the establishment of Library Corners for Distance Learners (LCDL) in their libraries. These collections are based on the needs of distance students who can go to these public libraries and use their collections. Some time in future KOU Library can also introduce such type of facilities with the collaboration of public libraries located in different parts of Rajasthan.

Multimedia

The KOU's library system mainly consists of printed books and inadequate systematic efforts have been made to develop non-print materials in the collection. The apparatuses like TV, VCP, microfilm reader are available in the library, but due to lack of audio visual cassettes, they are not frequently used. Now we are in the process of procuring a considerable amount of audio visual cassettes from several agencies. We are also planning to develop a well-equipped multimedia collection in various physical formats such as compact discs, video discs. CD-ROMs, computer databases, microforms, films, film strips, slides and so on.

Interlibrary cooperation

The use of the resources of one library to satisfy the information needs of another is the fundamental principle of Inter-library loan. Distance education forces institutions to examine other aspects of inter-library cooperation with a view to satisfying student information needs. This service is possible through the resource sharing arrangements with the other kinds of libraries, namely public libraries, academic libraries, special libraries and information centres. Thc KOU's library system has to consider to provide these facilities to distance learners in future.

Information literacy

Learning depends not only on classroom instruction and dialogue but also on the student's ability to search and analyse information.

During the past few years there has been a strong focus on the need for a flexible learning for students to develop information literacy skills. Information literacy is generally understood to include... the ability to locate, evaluate, manage and use information from a range of sources for problem solving, decision making and research (Bruce and Candy 1995: 245).

The ultimate goal of the KOU's library system is to enhance student's ability to retrieve required information. Knowing this reality we are planning to implement this programme in future through the following ways:

- preparing and disseminating printed guides, help sheets and handbooks;
- introducing a special information literacy unit as an integral part in each and every programme; and
- organising special information literacy workshops.

Finance

Financial resources form an essential input for service planning and execution of any library.

Various committees and commissions have recommended that the library should receive six percent of the University's total budget, which in an Open University is urgently required due to the nature of services needed to be rendered to users at various levels. The KOU library system has not followed the norm for many preceding years. Thus budgetary allocation to the library services should be enhanced to the extent of 6 percent of the total budget of the University and in the same ratio at the SCs and the RCs level.

Training of manpower

Introduction of new technologies in library will demand learning of skills by the staff to handle these gadgets. Besides this our system provides multiple services to different strata of readers viz. core faculty, part-time faculty, distance learners etc. To cater to these diverse clientele our staff needs to be informed about the resources and trained in handling such information. The staff we hire at the study centres are not trained to provide adequate services to different types of users. Keeping this in view a series of training programmers should be organised for the staff of library system by the STRIDE of this University. The content of this training programme may cover use and handling of IT as well as distance librarianship.

Personnel

Implementation of the above change will largely depend upon the professional staff of the library. It is strongly suggested that vacant post of the University librarian should be filled up at the earliest and some new posts viz., Dy. Librarian, Documentation Officer, Information Scientist, Programmer and other supporting technical staff should be created and duly filled up. At least one post of library professional staff may also be created for each RC.

Conclusion

Library support is an integral part of quality education and a vital service that should be available to all distance learners. While many institutions throughout the world which are offering distance education programmes attempt to provide pertinent library services, students in developing countries are often hampered by the unavailability of such basics as electricity in their homes, poor telecommunications and postal services and inadequately funded and limited library services. Nevertheless, it remains the responsibility of the home institution to provide, for the library needs of its students with best of its capabilities.

It is essential for Distance librarians to find new and innovative methods to provide the enumerated services. They need to exhibit more dynamism, be more responsive to their clients, needs and become more involved at many levels for actively pursuing the institutional objectives.

Future developments involve the assessment and implementation of appropriate and widely accepted technologies, the extenuation of remote access to information services and the encouragement of the electronic highway as an essential tool for all students.

The general requirements of library services for distance learners are discussed in guidelines produced by several national library bodies. KOU must adopt the guidelines issued by Indian Library Association for effective library services.

References

Bruce, C.S. and P.C. Candy (1995). " Developing information literature graduates: prompts for good practice" in D. Booker (ed.) *The Learning Link : Information Literacy in Practice*, Adelaide: Aslib Press.

Burge, E.J., J.E. Snow and J.L.Howard (1988). *Developing Partnerships : An Investigation of Library Based Relationships With Students and Educators Participating in Distance Education in Northern Ontario*. Toronto : Ontario Institute for Studies in Education and Contact Nord.

Cavanagh, Anthony (1994). "The role of libraries in off-campus study, " in T.D. Evans and D.Murphy (Eds.) *Research in Distance Education* 3. Geelong, Victoria: Deakin University press.

Jagannathan, Neela (1998). "Libraries in distance teaching University " In M.K. Jain et al. (Eds.) *50 Years Library and Information Services in India*, Delhi: Shipra Publications.

Kascus, M. and Aguilar, W. (1988) Providing library support to off-campus programmes, *College and Research Libraries* 49, (1) 29 - 37.

KOU (1990) *Kota Open University: a system view*, Kota: Kota Open University.

Monroe, Margaret E. (1975). Implications of the Open University for changes in library education, *Drexel*

Library Quarterly 11, (2) 54 - 67.

Watson, E (1993). " library services to distance learners in Third World countries: barriers to services", in C. Jacob (comp.) *6th Off. Compus Library Services Conference Proceedings*, Kansas City, Missouri.

Wooliscroft, Michael (1996). "Introduction", in Waston, E.F. and Jagannathan, Neela (Eds.) *Library Service to Distance Learner in the Commonwealth : a reader*, Vancouver : The Commonwealth of learning.

7

Information Technology enabled Library Services for Distance Learning: Threats and Opportunities

V K J Jeevan

Introduction

The terms "distance education" and "distance learning" are used to 'cover any situation when the student and teacher are not in the same place' (Forbes, 2000). In contrast to the erstwhile correspondence courses where the student and instructor communicated by mail which was a 'pretty paltry imitation of a real college class', the radical improvements in educational technology transformed distance learning to a 'key delivery channel for educational content of all types' (Coffman, 2001). Modern technology notably the Internet provides opportunities for really high-quality distance education (Arms, 2000). Distance Learning has become an important stream for providing educational opportunities to a wide group of the community who would not engage in formal regular education channels. Now distance education is offered using various forms of technology such as interactive tele-classrooms, videotapes and the Web (Casado, 2001). Through distance education, 'adult learners can take control of their education and have the opportunity to learn at their own pace, at times and places compatible with the commitments of family, work and leisure' (Forbes, 2000). These days the term distance learning receives vital and enriched importance as it is being used even to encompass the continuing education activities as professions and disciplines are getting increasingly intertwined in a complex fashion and progressing rapidly due to inter and intra disciplinary research activities. Gone are the good old days where the education of a person stops when s/he receives a degree/job. The knowledge intensive work environment stipulates continuously to keep abreast of fast pacing developments in one's fields of specialization.

IT for library services

The library professionals in India are already exposed to the offshoot of Information Technology (IT) for information services such as library software systems to handle the in-house operations, CD-ROM and electronic databases for bibliographic as well as numeric and full text/image information. The availability of a wide variety of library automation software on different platforms (both hardware and software) to suit the needs of libraries of various sizes itself is a reflection of the progress our libraries have made in this important attempt to fine tune the manual operations of procuring, processing and providing information sources. CD-ROM is common nowadays and libraries hold a good amount of them not only of databases, but also those that comes with books and other reference sources. Managing and servicing these high capacity discs were a problem as they are to be serviced only through stand-alone devices. Now, the onset of networking and hard disk cached solutions provide an effective and functional way to enable access to a considerable set of information in electronic form. With the emergence of Internet and web as the global information superhighway, librarians like other professionals are experiencing the benefits of ever-pervasive electronic information. More libraries have now a website and they use the site to inform others about the strengths of the library and to clients as a one-stop forum to receive certain services such as OPAC, on-line access of electronic information. Though the professionals are concerned with the poor search efficacy of Internet search engines, they know the utility of web as a first stop for answering reference queries, and to use it as a platform to furnish electronic information such as web access of subscribed journals.

Another development that has received much enthusiasm in recent times is that of hosting digital libraries on general and special information resources. Libraries in India are also getting engaged in the development of prototypes of digital information resources. There are certain types of contents which lie inaccessible or less used now, due to its present physical form, may be put into a more visible and enhanced use as a result of digitization. Also heavily used contents in limited physical copies can also be identified for conversion to electronic form. To demonstrate the efficacy of digital libraries and collections, libraries must be able to identify materials in the public domain, sources generated in-house etc., by easily bypassing the constraints of copyright. Thus, IT adaptation for library applications is an ongoing process right from procuring IT enabled information products to their computer aided processing and management to IT enriched services.

Library services for distance education

Real learning requires students to explore materials that they have found for themselves and hence colleges and universities have general-purpose libraries, not canned collections of materials tied to individual courses (Arms, 2000). The distance education students' only necessity provided by the university is information (Hooke, 1999) but how many are able to provide this crucial entity is the big question. At a 'closer look at the services offered to distance learners reveals a simple re-marketing of the services that have existed earlier' (Pace, 2001). The ACRL guidelines for distance learning library services consider philosophy, management, finances, personnel, facilities, resources, services, documentation, and library education (ACRL). The Open University Library's research project, OPAL (Online Personal Academic Librarian) attempts to develop a 24-hour fully automated reference service for distance students (D-Lib Magazine, 2001). The National Science Foundation's (NSF) National Sciences, Mathematics, Engineering, and Technology Education Digital Library (NSDL) program seeks to create, develop, and sustain a national digital library supporting science, mathematics, engineering, and technology (SMET) education (Zia, 2001). The status of library services for distance education (though renamed correspondence courses to this glossy term without redoing much of the erstwhile practices) in the country is not at all a matter of pride. Till the start of the Indira Gandhi National Open University (IGNOU), distance education was provided by supplying materials by post or through contact classes at the University's location or in exceptional cases in major cities. The provision of library services, like those rendered to regular students at the conventional universities, were part of the facilities provided to distance students, if at all present, only during the brief contact classes. The IGNOU enriched this practice by opening regional centres in all states and study centres in major cities. However even today, the libraries attached to all these function as independent entities at least to the point of online information sharing. Ultimately, the issue to be highlighted is students in the country tend to use the library just on-campus, the only difference being the distance education students will get this benefit only during a brief intermittent period of their course.

The importance of library services for distance education can be summed up as "when you study physically and geographically alone, any glitch in the supply of reference materials is doubly frustrating" (Hooke, 1999). Library services for distance learning have to take extra care in information organisation, retrieval and dissemination to supplement the contact classes and self-learning modes to achieve the necessary progress. It is not only the off campus location of distance learners that libraries have to face as a challenge, but also the wide variation in their intellectual level as they come from a more varied spectrum in comparison to campus learners, comparatively lesser time and resources than regular learners etc. Since electronic and IT tools are being applied for information services in the country too, some of these barriers must be broken to some extent.

IT for distance education library service

The distance library services include virtual reference services, simplified remote access to licensed indexes and full text purchases of electronic texts, document delivery, reciprocal borrowing with other libraries, etc. (Pace, 2001). The real question to be asked is: are we any way near these services practiced in the industrially advanced regions of the world? 'Unfortunately, advances in distance librarianship have not always kept pace with the rapid developments in distance education' (Coffman, 2001) though 'tailored electronic-delivery methods could facilitate better usage and remuneration levels for the publisher' (Hooke, 1999). To understand the needs of remote users, focus either on interactions with individuals or inferences drawn from statistics of web site usage by remote users (Guenther, 2000). The fruits of IT enabled library environment could be better applied for distance education as we have to service clients located off-campus and electronic access must be better attuned than print access in this environment. Apart from seamless access of contents, electronic contents can be shared easily over many users as their access will not be restrictive like printed sources. Another advantage with electronic contents is the multi-channel access through internet/intranet/modem/video/broadcast rather than personally visiting a library to issue a printed book. It may be difficult to highlight the IT application for distance library services since library services for distance learning itself may be seen as a luxury than as a necessity. There may be cases where the library attached to the distance learning university or its regional centres may be computerized or offering electronic databases locally. But equitable access to all students when they are stationed in their places of domicile/work is a matter of distant propensity. Libraries and publishers need to work together to make off-site licenses a reality to provide better access to library resources for distance-education students (Hooke, 1999).

Inter-library loan and making readers find their own resources on the Internet are bleak prospects for publishers, too, as library revenues are being spent on administration and postage, and readers tend to use free material rather than pay for it (Hooke, 1999). Patrons of all stripes now want information access that is convenient to their life styles and their working needs and if librarians try to ignore this fact, users will want to replace them with the infamous internet (Dempsey, 2001). If you don't have good access to the web, you can attend class via telephone or packet radio and broadcast television (Coffman, 2001). The same situation must be tried for information access also only when distance learning libraries were in a position to offer their resources and services accessible through these channels. 'The libraries should set a priority on acquiring' (books and) 'journals that have electronic versions, to meet the needs of off-campus distance education students as resources tied to one location will become less useful and therefore less marketable' (Hooke, 1999).

IT enabled library services for distance education

Information sources required

Bibliographic

- Online Public Access Catalogue of the Library and/or Union databases from other similar facilities
- Subject/Discipline specific commercial electronic databases such as EconLit for economics, ERIC for education etc.

Full text

- Lecture notes, research reports and course materials produced by the University.
- Proceedings of conferences held locally.
- Resources from friendly/collaborating Institutions.
- Full Text access of subscribed journals, commercial electronic databases.
- e-journals, e-books etc. both free and paid.

Server infrastructure

- *Database server* to hold library automation system and to conduct house keeping tasks.
- *CD-ROM server* to provide on-campus and off-campus access (after validating user name and password plus other security restrictions if any) to bibliographic and full text databases.
- *Web server* to hold and service locally generated digital collection, e-journals, e-books.
- *Multimedia systems/VCP/VCR* to service sources in VCDs/Video cassettes.

Client infrastructure

Multimedia machines set up within the university through LAN as clients to provide access to regular students may also act as clients for distance education students during contact programmes. However, the prime necessity is to arrange these client resources in the student's place either by providing this infrastructure in regional centres and in other places by making an alliance with private computer centres/internet cafes after incorporating the necessary security mechanisms for such public machines to access protected servers of the University. Students would need access to a computer that can send and receive e-mails, that permits access of university's servers with reliable connections to an Internet Service Provider (ISP). They should also need access to a VCR/VCP to play videotaped instruction.

Services

Apart from any/all services of academic libraries meant for regular education (such as OPAC search services, database search services-current as well as retrospective), the distance learning libraries can think of the following:

- Provision to access the library resources and avail library services through various means of WAN.
- Off-campus access to electronic resources for valid distance education students who wish to access them from their home/place of work.
- Web/remote access of course materials.
- Receipt and answer of queries about information sources, services etc., through email/chat.

Threats

The problems the libraries must address to render effective services to distance learners are unstable budget, lesser amount of copyright free contents, inferior IT infrastructure, meagerly increasing national network bandwidth etc.

Distance education programs suffer from the financial dilemma known as "the tragedy of the commons" and many have a separate budget for each course, with no funds available for general services that benefit all students, and this hinders in providing good library services for distance education (Arms, 2000). Also 'as collections and reference services move online, colleges and universities doubt about maintaining expensive physical facilities and staff' (Coffman, 2001).

Since the copyright holder has 'absolute control over any use of every single bit of content', the course designers paid a fee to get over the problem of copyright infringement mooted by a publisher. As the main resource is the process of knowledge exchange, not the knowledge products, then protection of the latter constraining the former looks very odd (Ishii & Lutterbeck, 2001).

There is no doubt about the resourcefulness of Internet/Web, but the crucial issue is the availability of quality content like refereed journals. While there is currently no lack of "great piles of content" on the Web, there is an urgent need for "piles of great content" (Zia, 2001).

The new web based courseware programs permit interactivity, but they are designed to mimic the classroom environment and not for one-on-one reference use because you could have many people in line (Coffman, 2001). Most courseware programs have a limited ability to share content online and make no provision for knowledge bases, scripted chat messages, book marks or other tools that would help a reference librarian (Coffman, 2001).

Normal reference services provided face to face interaction and enough context to understand the user's needs (Guenther, 2000). However electronic reference services have to profile the user based on online interaction and other use characteristics. Email reference services do not offer the instantaneous response and immediate gratification provided by Web (Coffman, 2001). Interactive chat solves the problems of email; however it is primarily designed for one-on-one conversations and not for high-volume question answering services (Coffman, 2001). Videoconferencing requires bandwidth and the connections are too slow to have normal interaction (Casado, 2001).

Though praised from many corners as an IT giant/superpower, inferior IT infrastructure and meagerly increasing national network bandwidth are to be addressed seriously. This is limiting the significant utilization of IT for various social applications.

Opportunities

But as a country with a large number of research and academic institutions as well as manpower with substantial intellectual activity, it is high time for libraries attached to different institutions in India to gather and conserve the research output lying ill-disseminated outside the formal publishing channel such as research/status reports.

Web based contact centre software based on the call centre model which queues and routes calls to the next available agent, and supports built-in knowledge bases, customer profiling, and usage tracking tools (Coffman, 2001) may be better applied for automating reference services for distance learners.

Voice over Internet Protocol (VoIP) allows the librarian and user to browse the web and talk back and forth at the same time. Coffman (2001) dreams about the arrival of virtual libraries with well selected electronic content coupled with online reference services to help students which schools may be able to subscribe them just like electronic databases. Virtual reference services integrate more easily the wealth of print and online resources that are available rather than current reference services which focus on local collections.

Offering basic materials online gave students to choose what and when to read leaving much more time for classroom discussions (Ishii & Lutterbeck). Massachusetts Institute of Technology Open Course Ware (MIT OCW) attempts to make course materials used for teaching undergraduate and graduate subjects available freely on the Web (MIT). MIT OCW will only provide the content of MIT education as the cornerstone of the learning at MIT is the interaction between faculty and students and amongst students (MIT).

With the Internet, the web and digital libraries, distance education programs can mount sets of materials on web servers to support each course and as the materials are accessible only by specified students, licensing problems are unlikely to be a serious barrier (Arms, 200). It is possible to have richer interaction in the digital environment not only as more content is put within reach of the user, but also as more tools and services are put directly in the hands of the user (Zia, 2001).

Conclusion

It is unclear which kind of rules should govern the potentially extraordinarily valuable education market and what issues of sustainability, democracy and public access have to be taken account of and how as the current answers are largely based on the assumption that knowledge is a commodity and education is a product (Ishii & Lutterbeck, 2001). As distance learning at least in the country is followed by capsules of course materials with little or meager library support, it is unclear what sort of track the distance library services in the country would pursue. However, the expression and intent towards IT enabled library services for regular education support might be applied to distance learning too, provided the distribution of clients beyond the campus is properly placed in information acquisitions, organization and services. Such a set up requires enough monetary support and can only be generated by entering into some sort of a consortia approach among the different distance education entities in the country. Let us hope that distance education may not distance library and its services from learners.

References

ACRL, Guidelines for distance learning library services, http://www.ala.org/acrl/guides/ distlrng.html

Arms, William Y. (2000), Digital Libraries for Distance Education, Editorial, *D-Lib Magazine*, 6 (10).

Casado, Margaret (2001), Delivering library services to remote students, *Computers in Libraries,* 21 (4), pp. 32-38.

Coffman, Steve (2001), Distance education and virtual reference: Where are we headed, *Computers in Libraries,* 21 (4), pp. 20-25.

Dempsey, Kathy (Miller) (2001), Reaching faraway patrons, editor's notes, *Computers in Libraries*, 21 (4).

Forbes, Judith L. (2000), Perspectives on Lifelong Learning: The View from a Distance, *First Monday,* 5 (11), http://firstmonday.org/issues/issue5_11/forbes/ index.html

Guenther Kim (2000), Designing and managing your digital library, *Computers in Libraries*, 29(1), pp. 34-39)

Hooke, Julie (1999), Distance Education: The Perils of the Virtual Student in Cyberspace, *The Journal of Electronic Publishing*, 5 (1), http://www.press.umich.edu/ jep/05-01/hooke.htm

Ishii, Kei & Lutterbeck, Bernd (2001), Unexploited Resources of Online Education for Democracy - Why the Future Should Belong to Open Course Ware, *First Monday*, 6 (11) http://firstmonday.org/issues/ issue6_11/ishii/index.html

MIT (2001), MIT Open Course Ware Factsheet, http://web.mit.edu/newsoffice/nr/2001/ocw-facts.html

Pace, Andrew K. (2001), Distance learning services; It's closer than you think, *Computers in Libraries*, 21 (4), pp. 49-51.

Zia, Lee L. (2001), Growing a National Learning Environments and Resources Network for Science, Mathematics, Engineering, and Technology Education: Current Issues and Opportunities for the NSDL Program, *D-Lib Magazine,* 7 (3).

SECTION 3

OUTREACH LIBRARY SERVICES IN OTHER ASIAN COUNTRIES

8

Providing Library and Information Services for the Visually Impaired: The Experience of the Open University of Hong Kong Library

Annie Chan

Background

The Open University of Hong Kong (OUHK) is the first organization set up by the Hong Kong Special Administrative Region (HKSAR) Government to provide distance education in Hong Kong. As its mission statement proclaims, the OUHK "dedicates itself to providing sub-degree, degree and post-graduate courses leading to awards and qualifications principally through a system of open access and distance education; thereby making higher education available to all those aspiring to it regardless of previous qualification, gender, or race". The goal of the OUHK is to provide distance education and education for all.

As an institution serving basically in a Chinese community, the OUHK also aims at serving as "a model for Chinese-medium distance and open learning, providing resources and expertise to meet the needs of the Chinese distance learning community globally", as stated by Professor S.W. Tam, the President of the OUHK, in the 10th Anniversary publication, Learning for all: the First Ten Years of the Open University of Hong Kong (1999, p.83). The Library, as a supporting unit in the University for distance learning, teaching and research activities, is important in providing quality information services and access to information resources.

With rapid development of the Internet and information technology in recent years, there have been revolutionary changes in the delivery of information and the mode of learning. Information can now be accessed round-the-clock and off-campus, extending to a much wider scope through the intricate connectivity of the web. Learning is made more convenient and flexible where students can access information and resources anywhere, at any time and learn at their own pace.

To people with physical disabilities, distance learning has been a very suitable mode of study. Since the establishment of the OUHK in 1989, over 270 students with impaired mobility, hearing or vision have registered in OUHK courses. In the past 7 years, a total of 39 students with disabilities have graduated. With rapid development of information technologies, there comes the issue of equity in web accessibility for the visually impaired. In this paper, the development of the OUHK Electronic Library with highlights on its contents and services is outlined and the experience of providing information services to the visually impaired is shared, with the last part focused on the issues that have been encountered in web browsing support and future prospects to eliminate obstacles.

The electronic library

The OUHK Library is located at the Homantin campus of the University. It has a total floor area of 2,121 sq.m., a size not comparable to other university libraries funded by the University Grants Commission in Hong Kong. It is currently providing services for a total of 25,000 students and 1,500 staff and tutors. The total collection consists of about 83,000 print and non-print items and about 1,500 printed serials in the physical library.

A survey was carried out by the OUHK in 1996 on students' computer readiness. It was found that around 90 per cent of the students had access to a personal computer either at home or in their workplace. Taking this advantage, the development of the Electronic Library (or E-Library) was started in 1997. Phase I was completed in November 1998 and focus was mainly on the development of hardware and supporting infrastructure for linking up electronic databases, providing remote access via dialup and creating a document management system to host past OUHK exam paper and additional reading.

Phase II developments included the provision of secure access via virtual private network technology for students using their own ISP, capacity enhancement of established infrastructure and expansion of the electronic collections by the setting up of an e-Text Centre. It was completed in December 2000. The OUHK is proud to win the Stockholm Challenge Award conferred by the European Commission and the City of Stockholm in May 2000.

Phase III development has started in 2002 and is on good progress with three major projects nearly completed or underway: the Feasibility Study of Building a Chinese Distance Education Database, an Electronic Thesis and Dissertation Collection, and an OUHK Digital Archive.

Following is an outline of the means of access and the contents and services provided in the E-Library.

Means of access

To provide authorized access to restricted resources for students, the Library has acted as an Internet Service Provider (ISP) by offering 144 direct dial-in lines for remote access. Alternatively, students may join the dial-up service of an appointed ISP, or continue to use their own ISP using secure connection provided by virtual private network technology. With later upgrade of the Virtual Private Network software, Broadband users can now enjoy full E-Library services via broadband at much faster response time.

Contents and services

The E-Library can be accessed at the URL http://www.lib.ouhk.edu.hk. All resources and services in the E-Library are provided on a common user interface for easy access. The user interface is easy to use with options of browse by title, by course code, by format, by subject and by providers etc. Keyword search using relevancy searching logic and advanced search using Boolean logic are also provided for simple and advanced searching of information resources. A universal search was launched in September 2000 for simultaneous search of multiple databases and the Library Catalogue. The common user interface is bilingual. Users can choose between English mode and Chinese mode to navigate within the E-Library.

Electronic databases

There are about 1,000 electronic resources currently made available to staff and students. They are equivalent to 500,000 volumes of printed materials, a size that requires much space in physical libraries. Moreover, when kept in electronic format, information can be updated online. These electronic databases include CD-ROM, electronic newspaper/ journals as well as bibliographic and full-text databases etc, providing good sources for information gathering and research activities.

In addition to this, about 580 more new free electronic resources have been sourced since March this year. They have been passed to the schools for selection. Most of them have been selected and recommended by academics and will be added to the E-Library.

E-text centre

The E-Text Centre is another prominent electronic collection in the E-Library. It currently includes three major electronic book collections: eBooks hosting service provided by net-Library; free eBooks found on the Internet and digitized eBooks hosted in the Library's database server. There are now over 7,000 titles in the E-Text Centre with about 65 per cent in English and 35 per cent in Chinese. Set-books are among the printed books to be digitized by Library if right-to-use can be cleared with publishers. Regarding eBook reading system, it is found that different viewers are required for reading eBooks from different sources. net-Library has developed its own online and offline readers. The Library has also developed its own OU viewer. Another Chinese eBook supplier also requires users to download its viewer. Links to vendors' downloading page are provided in the E-Library for users to download the various eBook readers. Keeping in line with the overall E-Library design, keyword and advanced bibliographic search are provided in the E-Text Centre. With the application of XML tagging in OUHK digitized eBooks; full text searching is made available to users for navigation within the eBooks and search for relevant information.

Electronic reserve collection

Printed copies of OUHK past exam papers and recommended readings have long been kept in the Reserve Collection for loan of two hours and use within the Library. With the creation of the Electronic Reserve Collection, students can now access these materials anywhere at any time via the Internet. Several users may be able to view the same copy of exam paper at the same time, with no restriction on the number of copies available. Access is controlled by account login and password and users can access this collection using any PCs with internet connection. The only problem that has been encountered is the clearing of copyright for recommended readings.

The materials in this Electronic Reserve Collection is stored and viewed in pdf (Portable Document Format). Both bibliographic and full-text searching is available for this collection.

Links to library catalogues

Students can access the Library's online catalogue on the web via telnet. Links are also set up to provide a one-stop search for library catalogues of local and overseas higher education institutions through the web.

Links to distance education institutions

The E-Library also provides links to distance learning institutions around the world for easy access.

Interlibrary loan services

To support teaching and research activities by students and staff, the Library has set up an interlibrary loan system to borrow printed materials from other university libraries. A web-based system has been established to allow full-time staff, postgraduate and project-based undergraduate students to submit their interlibrary loan request and monitor the progress of their requests on the web.

User support services

Videos on demand and user guides are available in the E-Library for users to learn how to use the electronic library services. Orientations and Seminars on Remote Access are held for students at the beginning of each semester in April and October. Both ITU and Library provide hotlines to answer user enquiry on technical issues and E-Library searching and services.

Before sharing the issue encountered in providing access for the visually impaired to the E-Library, the general support services provided by the OUHK for students with disabilities are briefly outlined below.

Support services for the physically disabled

The OUHK has a delegated unit, the Student Affairs Office, to centralize and co-ordinate units for the provision of support services for students with disabilities.

Pre-enrolment course counseling

Before enrolling for OUHK courses, students with disabilities are encouraged to contact the relevant Course Coordinators to see what difficulties may be encountered and explore if special arrangement can be made to support their studies. For blind students, the OUHK has prepared Braille version of study advice letter and pamphlets introducing services for students with disabilities.

Course materials and video programmes

Soft copies of course materials, if available and copyright cleared, will be provided to students with visual impairment. With the soft copy, students may either print it in Braille or read it online in Braille. Magnified copies of course materials can also be provided to students of low vision. Printed scripts of video programmes will be provided for students with hearing impairment.

Campus facilities and special arrangements

Special campus facilities are provided for students with disabilities. If possible, the OUHK will try to provide special arrangements in the allocation of tutorial centres, and assignment of tutors with fax. Special equipment and paper is also provided for examinations.

Special learning equipment in library

Special equipment and software have been donated to the OUHK by charity funds to assist students with disabilities in their study. Some of the equipment is placed in the library for use on campus. Some are loaned for use at home during the semester while some are placed at the Hong Kong Blind Union, a well-known voluntary agency serving the Blind, providing alternative venue for access to the adaptive equipment.

The special learning equipment in Library serves mainly visually impaired students. They include:

(i) A DOS personal computer installed with Vista and Lynx colour interface and connected to Colour CCTV Chroma CCD.

- The CCTV consists of a video camera and a television-type screen for enlarging display of printed text or image for users of low vision. The Vista and Lynx colour interface in the PC allows display of the enlarged image (e.g. of a reference reading) on the computer screen as well while the user is editing documents (e.g. writing an essay) on the computer at the same time. Vista and Lynx work only in DOS or win 3.1 environments.

(ii) A DOS personal computer installed with:

- CREDIT *(Cantonese Reader Electronic Document in Text Format)*, a software that can read Chinese text files in Cantonese for blind users. It can handle text files only in DOS environment.

(iii) An English Windows 98 PC installed with:

- Powerbraille
- Embosser, an equipment for printing out documents in Braille (by punching dots into paper)
- JAWS *(Job Access with Speech for Windows)*, a screen reading software with output in voice or in Braille *(using Powerbraille or embosser)* for blind users. It works only in English windows environment.
- Zoomtext, a screen enlarging software for users of low vision. Zoomtext Level 2 provides also a screen reading functionality for English windows only.
- Scanner and Omnipage

At this station, a printed document can be scanned into the computer and then JAWS can read the scanned document to blind users or display it in Braille. Or users can print out in Braille using the embosser.

(iv) A Chinese Windows 98 PC installed with:

- Powerbraille
- ASAB **(Access with Speech and Braille System)**, a screen reading software with output in voice (Cantonese) or in Braille for blind users. It is developed by the Hong Kong Polytechnic University in collaboration with the Hong Kong Society for the Blind. It has similar functionalities as JAWS supporting Traditional Chinese.
- Zoomtext (It also works in Chinese Windows)

(v) Reading Edge, an equipment that can scan and read book or document contents for blind users in the absence of a computer.

Special learning equipment for loan

They include:

- Cassette tape recorder/ radio/ 4 track cassette tape recorder
- Fax machine
- Notebook computers installed with Zoom-text, a screen enlargement software for users of low vision
- Notebook computers installed with JAWS for blind users
- External modem
- Litetalk (a screen reading equipment for use with a computer)
- Powerbraille
- HP LaserJet printers

Web accessibility for the visually impaired

Feasibility study by the UST

While the trend is to provide web access to or to link up information resources on the web, there comes the issue of providing web accessibility for visually impaired students so that they can enjoy the same kind of accessibility as ordinary OUHK students for various E-Library resources and services. Valenza (2000) commented in her article "Surfing Blind" that the web is primarily a graphic and highly interactive interface. If one can't see the graphics, one can't interact.

To cope with this, the E-Library has offered a text version for users to select at the top of the entry page. Also separate pages have been used for English and Chinese version. To investigate further, the Library has sought the assistance of the E-Library Project Team of the **University of Science and Technology** (UST) to undertake a feasibility study last year on making E-Library access available to the visually impaired. In this study, adaptive technologies for the visually impaired were examined. Visually impaired students were also invited for a user interview session. Recommendations were prepared for making the E-Library accessible to the visually impaired. The findings from this feasibility study are as follow:

- JAWS is one of the most popular accessibility tool used by the visually impaired for web navigation. Training is easy to get locally from the Hong Kong Blind Union (HKBU). However, it is a bit expensive, costing about US$800 for one user license. A trial version can be downloaded at http://www.hj.com. It does not support Chinese.
- ASAB has similar functionalities as JAWS and supports Traditional Chinese. Testing found that its performance is satisfactory in accessing normal OUHK E-Library pages. However, when using the software to access E-Text Centre, a lot of content in E-Text Centre can't be read out because they are encoded in Simplified Chinese.
- The entry page of the E-Library cannot be accessed by normal screen readers due to the use of java-script and "frame"
- The E-Library contains a lot of graphical information at the top pages, creating obstacles to access.
- Tables at the second level of the E-Library can't be transformed gracefully.
- Pop-up windows found on the front page of OUHK web site create another problem.

Issues of web accessibility for the visually impaired

The issues are summarized as follow:

Technical issues

- Adaptive technologies, including hardware and software, are needed for visually impaired users to access the web. At the present stage, screen-reading software seems to be the most common tool being used.
- Chinese is not supported by popular screen reading software like JAWS. Adobe acrobat has provided online conversion tools for converting pdf files into text files for visually impaired users. The conversion tools are found at http://access.adobe.com/onlinetools.html. However, online conversion of Chinese pdf files is not available.
- The problem of Chinese is further complicated by the compatibility of screen reading software with internal encoding of Traditional Chinese, Simplified Chinese and Unicode among the Chinese reading communities.
- Apart from the requirement for accessibility software to be installed in users' computers, the major obstacle for web surfing come from web page design as screen reading software follows a pattern of reading from left to right. The use of frames, complicated tables and graphics will pose difficulties to screen reading.

Financial issues

Adaptive equipment and software are not cheap and some users may not be able to afford to have a copy for their own use.

Administrative issues

- As identified by the UST in the feasibility study, visually impaired users usually need different kind of training and support at different stages and a "Do-It-Yourself scenario" is not suitable for this kind of users.
- Library staff may not be well trained in support services for the visually impaired.
- Visually impaired students may not have a clear picture of the contents and services provided in the E-Library.

Recommendations and future prospects

Despite the difficulties posed in web surfing by the visually impaired, the Internet remains a rich source of information readily available for remote access at any time and any place. Given below are some recommendations and suggestions to overcome the difficulties:

Web page design

To create web pages friendly to the visually impaired, the 14 W3C guidelines listed in "Web Content Accessibility Guidelines 1.0" (dated May 5, 1999) should be followed. The guidelines can be found at http://www.w3c.org/WAI as follow:

- Provide equivalent alternatives to auditory and visual content
- Don't rely on colour alone
- Use markup and style sheets and do so properly
- Clarify natural language usage
- Create tables that transform gracefully
- Ensure that pages featuring new technologies transform gracefully
- Ensure user control of time-sensitive content changes
- Ensure direct accessibility of embedded user interfaces
- Design for device-independence
- Use interim solutions
- Use W3C technologies and guidelines
- Provide context and orientation information
- Provide clear navigation mechanisms
- Ensure that documents are clear and simple
- The Hong Kong Blind Union has also consolidated users' experience and worked out some concise guidelines at: http://www.hkbu.org.hk/english/web_assessment/guidelines.asp such as:
- Using Alt-text for hyperlinks accessible through image map.
- Providing a brief descriptive text for significant diagrams and pictures such as when the whole screen is occupied by a picture.
- Avoiding complicated frames.

- Avoiding animation effects, such as flash, animated GIF, marquee effect etc.
- Providing navigation anchors for hot links.
- Keeping good color contrast and selecting colors that will make the pages easy to read by people with color blindness. One good test is to see if the pages are readable in black and white.
- Using separate pages for Chinese and English versions.
- Providing file attachments in text format.
- For complex tables, e.g. those that require several row / column headings to describe a single data cell, a text equivalent of the table should be provided.

A free web-based tool, Bobby is provided by the Centre for Applied Special Technology at http://www.cast.org/bobby. It can be used to test the accessibility of a web page to the visually impaired. One can type in the URL of a web page and the problems that would present to visually impaired users will be displayed.

Enhancement of adaptive equipment & software

- The feasibility study by the UST suggests that further collaboration with the Hong Kong Polytechnic University to develop ASAB may help to make the software more suitable for E-Library access.
- The development of server software for supporting voice and Braille output for Chinese web pages in Hong Kong is in and may be launched at the end of this year. If it can be successfully applied to web servers, visually impaired users may not have to install screen reader in their own computers. Output in voice or Braille becomes an alternative mode of reading offered at a web site.

User support and training

- Provision of training and support to visually impaired students at different stages e.g. dialup kit installation, using screen reader, web navigation technique etc.
- Training for Library staff themselves may also be needed for better and quality user service to the visually impaired
- Promotion of the E-Library is also good to highlight useful contents and services to visually impaired users.

Joint collaboration

In the course of providing support services for the visually impaired, it may involve the input of financial, technical, administrative and professional resources at different stages. Joint collaboration by the Government, educational institutions, social welfare agencies, software development vendors and information technology professionals can surely bring about significant improvement in web accessibility for the visually impaired.

Loan of equipment at the OUHK has proved to be a good arrangement for students with disabilities. The Hong Kong SAR Government announced in June this year that a 3-year programme would be launched to promote access to information technologies among people with disabilities. A total sum of HK$30 million will be spent on installation of computer facilities with internet connection at rehabilitation service units at different localities, construction of a portal web site and implementation of IT awareness and training programmes for people with disabilities. This kind of programme will surely help to alleviate the physical, technological and financial obstacles to the visually impaired in accessing information technologies or the web.

Lastly, local needs and requirements should be catered for as development in one community or region may not apply to another. Chinese is one good example. It may not be an important issue in western countries, but different Chinese coding may be used even in Mainland China, Taiwan and other Chinese communities, thus imposing problems of access. As a conclusion, there are surely obstacles for the visually impaired in web accessibility. The problems may be more effectively tackled by joint collaboration of different parties. Future prospects are positive but require more attention and further investigation.

References

Valenza, Joyce Kasman (2000). "Surfing Blind", Library *Journal Netconnect Fall*, 34-36

The Open University of Hong Kong (1999) *Learning for All: the First Ten Years of the Open University of Hong Kong.* Hong Kong.

The University of Science & Technology (2000) *Feasibility Study of Access to OUHK E-Lib by Visually Impaired Students.*

9

Chinese Television University Library Resources and Services

Anthony W. Ferguson

Introduction

Chinese Television University libraries (TVU libraries)[1] are appendages to study centers where students come to watch taped lectures and to receive supplementary instruction provided by local instructors or tutors. Television Universities in China provide part-time and full-time learning opportunities. Many are beginning to look and feel like traditional Chinese universities with dormitories, halls, fields, and lovely campus gardens. Many others, however, look like office building and factories.

After collecting data during a four-week period in summer 2000, a dissertation by the author was completed at Columbia University Teachers College in April 2001, and the present chapter is based on those findings. As part of the research exercise, the author visited 21 different TVUs in five provinces i.e. Shandong, Anhui, Jiangsu, Jiangxi, and Yunnan and TVUs in Shanghai and Nanjing. These findings were also supplemented with interviews and surveys during short visits in 1998 and 1999 to Tianjin. Data was collected by personally meeting individuals and small groups of students, teachers, librarians and university administrators by tape recording their Interviews and administering written surveys. Only selected important parts of the results are presented here. The reader is invited to examine the entire dissertation to obtain the complete findings[2].

This chapter describes what TVU libraries are like, why students value them, what limits their effectiveness, and how important the participants in this study felt it was to build stronger libraries.

Television University library characteristics

Physically, the most basic TVU library was usually composed of two reading rooms and several book storage rooms. The reading rooms would usually include one for reference books and another for periodicals and newspapers. The storage rooms would be composed of row after row of double-faced book shelving units. Additionally, there would be what librarians would consider a "reserve library" collection; that is, a collection of books reserved by the faculty to support the immediate curricular needs of each class and placed in a separate area where access can be closely monitored. Many of these collections, contained most of the newer books owned by a library and not just those recommended.

Large TVU libraries had more than the two basic reading rooms, with different rooms for the humanities, social sciences, and other subjects, including special rooms for the faculty to use and several floors in a building devoted to open or closed stack book storage. Many libraries also had special computer labs, including a few terminals connected to the Internet. Most computers were for students to learn skills in word processing and spreadsheet use. Small libraries had only one or two floors of book-stacks, a one or two-sided glass lined reserve library materials collection, and no computers at all.

The physical condition of these library buildings differed depending upon the economic conditions and the goals of the university itself. In one major city, for example, while the books were stored in an older building that appeared to have been constructed shortly after World War II, they also had a new library devoted to computers with the required reference and magazine reading rooms. The floors in the latter facility were beautiful terrazzo and the walls were freshly painted white with lovely accents of natural wood. Because many of China's universities are located near the coast and in a sub-tropical part of the world, the moisture that produces mildew was present in the libraries. In general, most of the libraries were simple structures, swept daily, and treated no better or worse than the classroom buildings.

Library resources

All sixteen librarians were requested to complete a survey about the kinds of resources in their libraries. The results of the survey mirrored what I had observed. The table records the types of Material in TVU Libraries. It might seem surprising that fewer than half of the TVU libraries had televisions and just a bit over one-third had video playback machines. This lack of televisions in libraries is possibly because the classrooms are already equipped with television sets. TVU students watch televised lectures as a group in these classrooms which also function as study halls for the students all day long and into the evening hours. A second reason might be that the archived video-tapes are held elsewhere at the TVU. In Nanjing, for example, video resources are apparently kept in an Electronic Teaching Center. Yet, it was not always evident that archived copies of past lectures were held in each classroom or in a resource center. The fact seems to be, that TVU students rely more upon the teachers who are physically in their classrooms than the ones brought to them via the medium of television or some other form of technology. So perhaps the relative lack of these technology-related resources in libraries reflects this reality.

Acquisitions funds

On asking these 16 librarians about the adequacy of their acquisitions funds, it was noticed that only seven chose to answer this question, none chose the "completely adequate option;" three indicated that their funds were about "50 percent adequate;" and two each chose "75 percent adequate" and "completely inadequate" options. The reason for nine librarians declining the opportunity to discuss the adequacy of their budget is not known. It might be because they viewed that their funding as inadequate, but it was embarrassing to talk about this problem with an outsider. Librarians typically are only too willing to complain about their lack of funds.

Jiangsu province, compared to the other provinces, seemed to be especially strong in the area of in-service training. The Nanjing City TVU librarian reported that one of their librarians was a library science graduate, but that the rest had all taken part in library-related workshops (Interview,

Table 9.1: Types of Material Available at TVU Libraries

Type of Material	No. of Librarians Reporting	Percent Librarians Reporting
Magazines, Journals	16	100%
Newspaper	16	100%
Reference Books	15	94%
Teaching Materials	15	94%
Supplementary Teaching Material	14	86%
Computers	9	56%
Audio Tapes / Machines / Tapes	7	44%
Televisions	7	44%
Video Tapes Machines / Tapes	6	38%

Public services

In terms of library public services, each of the TVU libraries seemed to operate like other libraries throughout the world. For example, all sixteen librarians participating in the study indicated that they provided reference services to their library patrons: answering questions of varying length and helping students find the materials they needed. In addition to reference desk help, 10 of the 16 librarians indicated that provisions had been made so that their students could use the resources of other libraries. This sort of cooperative access service is critical for distance students who may live closer to other libraries.

Library staff preparedness

Since the level of training experienced by TVU librarians would affect the kinds of services provided, the educational opportunities available to them were explored. Of the sixteen librarians who completed the survey, 14 indicated that they had some library science training, one had no training, and another did not respond to the question. A common pattern seemed to be that, depending on the size of the overall staff, one librarian might have graduated in library science, or otherwise formally trained, and the rest would have been trained on the job with additional in-service workshops provided by provincial or national authorities.

June 28, 2000). Another Jiangsu librarian indicated that all of their staff had taken part in "short term training" in addition to the one or two who had an associate degree or who had graduated in library science (Zhenjiang interview, June 29, 2000). A county-level TVU librarian in Jiangsu Province indicated that they had all attended training workshops at Nanjing Library, one of the major public libraries in all of China (Wujin interview, June 28, 2000).

The pattern in the other provinces, while not as strong, was similar with librarians in each province indicating that in addition to one or two librarians with a library science related-degree, they had all taken part in workshops provided by the provincial or national authorities. Only two librarians complained about the lack of training opportunities. Another librarian, however, viewed that while library management training opportunities were there, training in the use of computers was insufficient. She perceived librarians were not sufficiently computer-literate. While the lack of computer literacy largely appeared to be the case, in a few locations it was noticed that some recent college graduates with computer expertise were working in the library. It was apparent that each TVU had a core group of computer / systems staff members who took care of all the computers on campus, including those in the library.

Technical services

In addition to public services, most of the librarians indicated that they also carried out a range of technical services duties. For example, all, but one of the 16 librarians interviewed indicated that one of their jobs was to select books. This level of involvement was likewise the case for cataloguing books where most of the librarians seemed to be involved in cataloguing work to one degree or another. It was noted that only one case, at a county level TVU in a poorer province, where books were not catalogued at all. Here the books were sorted much like a bookstore with paper labels pasted on shelves to indicate where various subjects like history and literature books were located. At least half of the libraries had computer catalogs and the rest had traditional card catalogs. The libraries could obtain cataloguing records for books processed by the National Library in Beijing and the basic cataloging elements, including simple call numbers, are found in most contemporary books. Finally, one librarian indicated that their library did not circulate books. His library, however, was for the use of those who developed the courses at the provincial level and these teachers simply used the books at will and did not formally check them out.

Libraries as places: content and contact

Besides wanting to learn about the services and content provided by China's TVU libraries, the degree to which these libraries were used as places for students to contact each other, to come together to study was also examined. It has long been supposed in the United States that students learn not only from their teachers and textbooks but from each other as they live and study together. The study showed that TVU libraries in China were able to play a role in bringing students together. Nine of the 13 librarians (69 percent) who answered, indicated that they viewed that all or at least three-fourths of the students used the library to study with each other. One librarian (8 percent) indicated that only half of the students studied together in the library and three of the nine librarians (23 per cent) believed only a quarter of the students used the library to study together. Consequently, it could be concluded that most of these librarians (77 percent) believe that their libraries do serve as places for student contact as well as places to find content.

The importance of TVU libraries

As many teachers in Beijing and Tianjin during my 1998 and 1999 visits to China mentioned that TVU students did not require library resources and services, more intensive data were collected in 2000 to prove that TVU students did not need libraries. Interestingly, only twenty-one percent (137) of the 654 participants filling out the survey concurred with the statement "Some people feel that TVU students don't need libraries because their success depends solely on their ability to pass tests and because libraries cannot help them better prepare to take tests." Of the 21 percent who agreed that libraries were not required, most indicated that it was because "libraries cannot help students prepare to pass tests."

The next most popular reason was because they felt "success depends solely upon one's ability to pass tests." Both reasons, however, focus on the importance of tests. This "exams are the only important thing" mentality is reflected in many of the comments on the surveys completed by the participants:

- [teacher] The educational system is exam oriented, [students do] perfectly fine without libraries. (Anhui Province, A\nhui Provincial TVU)
- [student] In China, to be employed one has to obtain an advanced degree. Therefore, students should make studying their first priority. If they have time, they can go to the library. Currently, I think reading in the library is a waste of time. (Tianjin TVU)

While still agreeing that libraries were not needed to pass tests, others gave additional reasons for not going to the library. A student from Tianjin stated that -"part-time TVU students just didn't have the time to go to libraries" (Tianjin TVU). Another Tianjin student suggested going was a waste of time because "the library materials are out of date" (Interview October 19, 1999). An Anhui student wrote, "Most references cannot be located in the library because the quantity [of books] is limited so that not all people can borrow [what is needed] (Anhui Province, Maanshan City TVU).

Seventy-four percent of those who responded to the survey, on the other hand, disagreed with the statement that libraries were not needed and felt strongly about the importance of libraries. In most of the world where libraries are synonymous with institutions of higher learning, the idea that libraries are important might not seem like an unusual finding. However, after seeing the very modest libraries that exist at most TVUs, and understanding somewhat the degree to which Chinese possesses an exam-based educational system, it was amazing to note the allegiance paid to libraries by these students.

The survey respondents were asked to explain why they disagreed with the "TVU students don't need libraries" statement. The most frequently given reason was that students simply needed more information to function effectively. A student in Shandong wrote, "TVU students need libraries greatly. Libraries help them understand the teaching materials and enlarge their vision of the things around them" (Shandong Province, Jining City TVU). The idea that library use broadens one's horizons was echoed by a student in Yunnan who wrote, "Even though TVU student success depends upon one's test-taking abilities, students still need the library to learn more and develop their abilities" (Yunnan Province, Kunming City TVU).

Other reasons given were that examinations were not the only measure of success and libraries are important in and of themselves:

- "It is true that one's success is due to passing the exams. However, [getting] good scores does not mean that the student will be an effective member of society". (Yunnan Province, Kunming City TVU)
- Exams are the means, not the end of learning. (Shandong Province, Jining City TVU)

Another theme was the relationship between knowledge acquired in libraries and getting a job, an important measure of success for many students. Many students on their surveys volunteered comments which suggested that they were resigned to the need to read very broadly to help them be more competitive in the future:

- The current society is highly competitive - we would be kicked out of the competition if we do not have abundant knowledge and strong learning abilities [obtained from doing research in libraries]. (Shandong Province, Jining City TVU)
- The library covers extensive knowledge and one can obtain even more knowledge and information. Examinations do not reflect the practical abilities needed in jobs and lives. (Tianjin TVU)

Yet another reason frequently given by participants was libraries provided access to interesting information not covered by lectures and textbooks. These students were not necessarily faulting their exam-based educational system nor were they looking at libraries as a means of helping them get jobs; they just saw libraries as places with information of interest to them. A student in Jiangxi wrote, "The library provides us the needed materials to deepen our understandings about professional knowledge and extracurricular interests" (Jiangxi, Jiujiang City TVU). Another student wrote, "The library helps us to acquire the extracurricular knowledge in areas of interest. It helps us to be self-directed learners" (Shandong Province, Jining City TVU). An administrator in Anhui also saw the lack of extracurricular reading materials as an important reason to have libraries, but expanded upon this theme to include the value of the technology that can be found in libraries: "TVU students need the library to provide extracurricular reading materials, social science and natural science information, and knowledge and technology to develop their overall quality." (Anhui Province, Shou County TVU)

A librarian in Nanjing perhaps best summed it up by observing that students, at different times in their careers, need libraries:

Beginning students use the library to read their personal books. Over time, however, their interests change and their use of libraries depends upon their interests, the degree to which they have mastered their subject matter, and what is expected of them. 70 to 75 percent of the students who visit the library, come to read novels or essays of interest to them. At mid day the periodical and newspaper reading room is full of students. Other students who are having difficulties in school come for additional information. Foreign language students who are having trouble, for example, need the library's reference books. Some students need the library as a place to read, others to find additional information. Others hope to get an additional certificate in English or computers so that they can compete for jobs. (Interview, June 26, 2000)

Factors limiting the use of Television University libraries

The foregoing analysis has established that while TVU students may not require libraries to get the minimum score to pass their exams, they do want and need libraries to accomplish a host of other common goals. However, even if students want to go to a library, several roadblocks limit the effectiveness of their library use. The three major limitations identified during the interviews and surveys are the lack of time to go to a library, the lack of knowledge about what libraries might do for them, and the lack of sufficient library resources.

The no-time problem was suggested to me as early as 1998 when the discussion took place with CCRTVU leaders regarding TVU students and libraries. The curriculum development team members observed that the major problem was TVU students didn't have time to go to libraries. Twenty-six percent of the survey participants during the current study picked the lack of time as a factor that might limit student use of libraries and 27 percent of those interviewed also mentioned the lack of time as a reason for not going to libraries.

The lack of time problem seems to be as serious for younger and older students alike.

- A librarian in Anhui noted, "For adult students, it is not easy to go to libraries after 8 hours of work, classwork, and two hours of homework". (Maanshan interview, June 24, 2000)
- A teacher in Jiangsu echoed the importance of the lack of time problem when he wrote, "Older students have families, [therefore] they prefer to read at home or while they are at work – [they have] no time for libraries". (Jiangsu province, Wujin County TVU)
- Another younger student who had evening classes indicated, "In the afternoon the library is closed [when I have time to go] and in the evening it is open, but we need to go to the classroom to do the required self-learning". (Yunnan Yuxi, interview, July 12, 2000)

The second major limitation to library use mentioned in both the surveys and interviews is students' lack of information about what libraries can do for them and how they can use libraries effectively. While no one mentioned the effect of insufficient information upon library use during my initial visit in 1998, 27 percent of those interviewed in 2000 mentioned student ignorance about libraries as a problem, and 22 percent of the survey participants picked student lack of knowledge about libraries as the reason why students don't use libraries. In addition to those who perceived that students didn't know what libraries had to offer, an additional 14 percent of the survey participants indicated that students didn't know how to use libraries.

The third major limitation mentioned in both the surveys and interviews was the lack of library materials. Thirty percent of those interviewed mentioned the lack of materials as a reason for students not using libraries and 7 percent of the survey participants identified the scarcity of library materials and having too many out of date materials as limiting factors:

- A member of the curriculum development team in Beijing noted, "Libraries have not played a full role in TVU education because they do not have enough books and they do not cover all the fields [studied]. [Libraries] are also not suitable for distance education because there is no money for new books". (Interview, June 15, 2000)
- A teacher in Shandong summed it up as "the collection is so limited that it cannot meet student needs thoroughly". (Jining interview, June 21, 2000)
- A student in Nanjing further noted that "the library's books are out of date and there are few new books or good books". (Interview, June 28)

Virtually every student survey indicating a lack of library resources included such a comment.

In addition to these three major factors, a whole host of other reasons were given for students not using libraries, including not enough space to study, loan periods are too short, limited hours, too few services, books are poorly catalogued and cannot be found, you have to be quiet and limited socialize with friends, and the libraries are too far away from where students like.

Some of these "other" reasons relate to the three major problems discussed above. If students had more time to go to libraries, the problems of the library being too far away or a short check-out period might be eased. Similarly, if students were more sure of what the library had to offer and how to use ineffectively, the problems related to inadequate cataloging and perceptions of poor service might disappear or at least become less significant.

The relative importance of building stronger Television University libraries

Since it was already clear in 1998 and 1999 that at least a portion of China's TVU students, teachers, and librarians felt the need for stronger libraries, it was necessary to understand the relative importance of improving their libraries. During the interviews, they were asked to explain the major problems or challenges facing TVUs and how the need to strengthen libraries compared to solving these other problems. The problems they discussed included the lack of experienced teachers, inadequately prepared students, irrelevant courses, the weaknesses of distance education as a pedagogical concept, and the lack of sufficient access to the Internet.

With so many problems facing China's TVUs, how many of the people/groups actually favored strengthening libraries over working on these other problems? Basically, except librarians, none felt this way. A group of adult students in Nanjing, for example, indicated what they needed were "better teachers with more experience" (Nanjing interview, June 28, 2000). Most indicated that they needed better libraries but these other problems were more pressing.

As indicated, many of the librarians felt just the opposite that their students needed libraries. A librarian in Kunming declared:

If I am an adult student, I need the library and the Internet because I don't have time to wait for the teacher's instructions. If I am a younger student who just graduated from high school, I need libraries and the Internet because I have my own time after class to study independently. (Kunming interview, July 10, 2000)

And a librarian from the Nanjing TVU poetically noted, "The path to becoming educated is long, but the library helps you take your first step." She used a further metaphor to explain that "knowledge is like a vast river. You need a bridge to cross it and the library is just such a bridge". (Interview, June 26, 2000)

Conclusions

TVU libraries are typically fairly minimal physically and terms of their staffing, intellectual resources, technical processing and services. TVU students wish their libraries were larger, had more materials, had longer checkout periods, would allow more socializing, and were closer to where they lived. Yet, the same students and their local teachers seem to treasure them. Still, when asked to decide what was more important, to improve their libraries or solve the non-library problems faced by TV universities, these same library patrons favour solving the latter problems. It is a tribute both to the work of the librarians in most TVUs who do much with little and an indication of the significance of the problems faced by the TVUs themselves.

What needs to be done to improve China's TVU libraries? Two brief suggestions are given, and these are not unique to Chinese distance education. First, distance educators need to recognize the value of libraries to the needs of their students. Students want more information than the learning packages they are given with each course. If there were a greater acceptance of the need for libraries, the second suggestion would not be needed. This suggestion is to simply increase the funds these libraries have to hire and train better library staff members, to increase the hours they are open, to provide more and better space and equipment, to process and shelve their collections, and to buy more content. The content needs to be both digital and print.

Notes

1. The use of the term "Television Universities" refers to the national system of such universities which come under the leadership of the Ministry of Education. The central body of this system is the China Central Radio and Television University. There were 44 provincial Radio and Television universities, 814 company and city branch schools, and 1,742 county level study centers at the time this research was conducted.

2. 'The Library and Information Needs of Chinese Undergraduate Radio and Television University Distance Education Students. Ed. D. Dissertation. New York: Teachers College, Columbia University.

10

The University of Philippines Open University Library: Towards Increasing Access to Learning Resources

Audrey G. Anday

Introduction

Library support is an integral part of quality education and a vital service which should be available to all students whether on-campus or off-campus (Kascus & Aguilar, 1988). Libraries have enjoyed a long and colorful history in their efforts to deliver information services to patrons outside the library. These services have ranged from bookmobiles to remote airdrops. The advent of electronic networks and interlibrary cooperation now permit vast amounts of information to be delivered to patrons without having to set foot in the institution where the information originated or for that matter in the same continent. Faxes, phone lines, computers and satellites all constitute an awesome telecommunications infrastructure that stretches around the globe to link individuals effectively and efficiently (Ferrel, 1983).

Adequate access to good library facilities is a criterion that applies to campus-based and franchised courses, but it does not seem likely to be any less important for distance learners despite the provision of self-study materials. A study by Unwin in 1994 reports that distance learning students wish to see themselves as "real students" and that using the library is regarded as an important component of an authentic learning experience. Students need to go beyond the provided materials in order to develop investigative skills and adequate subject matter expertise (Stephens, Unwin and Bolton, 1997).

To address the unique learning styles of distance learners, a broad range of library resources and services can be offered in different formats. This allows some choice on the part of distance learners, thus contributing to a successful learning experience. Formats may include but are not limited to print, video, audio and electronically delivered text – which may be accessed through the World Wide Web or other appropriate networks or software.

The University of the Philippines Open University

As an educational institution, the University of the Philippines (UP) is mandated to provide quality tertiary education to as many Filipinos as possible. Because of the limited facilities, however, only a small percentage of those who wish to study in UP can be accommodated in the traditional residential setting.

Distance education offers an alternative. This system of self-study allows students to learn at their own time and pace, aided by communication technologies—print, audio, and video. Distance education at UP, however, is not totally devoid of face-to-face interaction between teachers and students as this interaction occurs from time to time through orientation, consultations and examinations. Also a telecommunications network system provides opportunities for teachers and students to interact with one another through electronic means. Students are also provided with a learning support system through the Learning Centers where study sessions are conducted monthly.

The UP System formalized its activities in distance education in 1992 when it implemented the UP Distance Education Programme headed by an executive director. The programme was further strengthened in 1994 when in addition to the Executive Director at the system level, a Director for distance education was appointed in each of the autonomous universities.

On the February 23, 1995, the UP Board of Regents approved the establishment of the UP Open University (UPOU) as the fifth autonomous member of the UP System. Since the establishment of the U. P. Open University on February 23, 1995, distance education in the Philippines has flourished. The UPOU started with one academic programme six years ago. Today, it offers seventeen degree programmes in various disciplines. It continues to develop more programmes that respond to the needs of a wide range of learners within the Philippines as well as those in other countries, particularly the overseas Filipino workers.

The phenomenal growth and development of the U. P. Open University is perhaps exemplified by the designation by the Commission on Higher Education as the National Center of Excellence for Distance Education, which places it at the forefront of educational development in the country. At the same time, it is recognized as one of the growing open universities in Asia having been elected not only as a member of the Asian Association of Open Universities but as host of the Association's Conference in the year 2000. This has widened the horizon of influence of the UPOU beyond national boundaries of the Philippines to include the Asian Region. As it seeks to influence educational thinking, it shall as well be influenced by the developments in the region and the world in the field of open learning and distance education.

The UPOU is exploiting the advantages of technology in the development and delivery of courses to make quality education more accessible to more learners. It shall maintain its leadership role in the study and practice of learning and distance education in the Philippines, and strives to make its presence known and felt among distance education providers in the Asian region.

Objectives

The UPOU seeks to provide wider access to quality higher education. As an autonomous unit (AU) of the UP System, it adheres to the highest standards of academic excellence, guarantees academic freedom, encourages social responsibility and nationalistic commitment among its faculty, staff and students.

Specifically, the UPOU seeks to:

- provide opportunities for alternative access to quality higher education by offering baccalaureate, post baccalaureate degree programs and non-formal courses by distance education;

- develop a system of continuing education for sustaining professional growth and improving technical skills especially for those who cannot leave their jobs or homes for full-time studies; and
- contribute towards upgrading the quality of residential instruction in the university and the educational system of the country by developing, testing and utilizing innovative instructional materials and technology and sharing these with other colleges and universities through cooperative programmes.

The administration

The UP Open University is headed by a Chancellor who is then helped by four Vice Chancellors, namely: Vice Chancellor for Academic Affairs, Vice Chancellor for Student Support Services, Vice Chancellor for Finance and Administration, and Vice Chancellor for Research and Development. UPOU has four different discipline-based faculties, which is equivalent to a College in a residential UP campus. A Dean heads each Faculty office.

Delivery of instruction

Instructional delivery in the distance education mode begins with the planning, designing and preparation of self-learning packages. All learning packages are prepared by course teams, which are also known as quality circles. The quality circle is composed of the writer, instructional designer, reader, language editor, and media specialist. The UPOU believes that to deliver quality distance education, it must be able to provide quality instructional materials. Delivery of instruction is primarily through printed self-learning modules supplemented with other media including video, television, and computer networks.

Upon receiving their learning package, the student assumes autonomy over the learning process. This provides the student a high degree of independence and self-reliance.

Learning support is provided through tele-tutorials and study sessions in the learning centers where students may also access other instructional and supplementary materials. Students may also consult with the tutors and faculty via electronic mail.

To ensure that courses are effectively and efficiently delivered to the students, UPOU conducts tutorials and provides support facilities. Students can avail of tutorials and other support facilities in the Learning Center (LC). The LC is the link between the UPOU and the learner. It is the place where students meet for various reasons, primarily social reasons. A Learning Center Coordinator oversees the Center's operations.

Learning Centers are located in some campuses of the UP System and in cooperating state colleges and universities all over the country. UPOU faculty, senior faculty of cooperating state colleges and universities, or other qualified professionals usually conduct study sessions. Study sessions are held either in the learning centers or through tele-tutorials and electronic correspondence via the Internet. For specific courses that require practical work, summer residential sessions are conducted. At present, there are 22 learning centers located in different provinces all over the country and in Hong Kong.

In the course of their study, students are expected to submit written assignments. At the end of the semester, they must take supervised final examinations in Learning Centers. UPOU faculty marks the examinations and gives the students their final grades.

UPOU uses audiotapes and videotapes for instruction. However March of 2001, UPOU instituted the use of the Internet thus reaching more students.

The UPOU library

The UP Open University Library is envisioned as a service for distance learners, as it is one of the most heavily used units in the university. It is one of the key components of a scholarly communication system. Thus, the following mission and goals of the UPOU Library was conceptualized:

Mission

The mission of the UPOU Library is to provide library resources that meet the information needs of the UPOU faculty, staff and students of the UPOU wherever these individuals are located; and to provide an information service to UPOU constituents that is responsive and innovative.

Vision

It is envisioned that the UPOU Library shall have goals and objectives that are consistent with the broader institutional mission and services that are supportive of the needs of the distance learning community. The UPOU Library shall provide fast access to information resources required by the distance learning community. It will provide services that will enable the onsite and offsite users to retrieve information in various formats and receive information literacy instruction. The UPOU Library will be an electronic library with collections in multimedia formats that are accessible to all the members of the UPOU community and will have pointers to other information sites where information could be downloaded either for free or for a minimal fee. It will eventually become part of library network so that resources could be shared among the members.

Though at present the UPOU Library exists, but it is not yet functioning as a library should. The library of the UPOU is located at the ground floor of the UPOU Headquarters in Los Baños, Laguna. It has an area of 69.15 square meters. Some of the furniture and equipment have already been purchased. The building is connected to the PH-net through the UPLB backbone while those offices in UP Diliman are connected to the UPD backbone, hence there is a connection to the Internet.

The library materials (approximately 250 titles of books and journals) are housed in the shelves in the main building and some are still in Learning Centres. The materials are accessioned depending on the code assigned as to where the books can be found. There are no acquisitions policies yet. Policies regarding collection development are still to be drawn up so that there would be equity in the acquisition of materials among the different courses taught in the UPOU. Copies of publications of the UPOU are deposited in the library for the purposes of access and preservation. Library materials need to be catalogued to provide an access to the collection (David, 1999). It has been agreed that the core collection of the UPOU Library will be more on the fields of distance education, open learning, distance learning, educational technology, information technology and other disciplines that pertain to education, that is of relevance to UPOU. However, some reference materials in support of the programs offered are also being acquired and sent out to learning centers since not all learning centers are within or near locality of a UP campus.

Cataloging of the books have been started. Bibliographic information of the library materials can be retrieved through the mini-card catalog provided or through the use of CDS-ISIS. In addition, the ITS for Windows software has been purchased as a cataloging tool. Also a library web page, connected to the UP Open University main page, is being prepared so that students from all over the Philippines can access the collection, and make arrangements so that these students can utilize the books available in the library and those in the learning centers. For the mean time, the library is still making use of CDS-ISIS and is in the process of upload it to the library web so that students can access the card catalog of the library.

For those books in the library that have already been cataloged using the Library of Congress system, they are arranged according to their call numbers. For those books yet not cataloged, they are arranged alphabetically. To facilitate ease in borrowing, a temporary borrower's card is issued to bona fide faculty, staff and students. Books can be loaned for two weeks only so that all have a fair chance of borrowing the books. For those library materials provided to the learning centers, they are for room use only since only one or two copies of the book is being provided for learning center offering a specific course. The Internet connection is in the process of being completed, and a workstation is being prepared. Due to budgetary constraints however, integrated library system software cannot be purchased yet.

With regards to the modules, an arrangement with the UPOU Printing Unit was facilitated in order for the library to have a complete set of the modules being used. These materials are for room use only for the UPOU faculty and staff have access to these materials. Students who are interested to use the modules are advised to make a request to purchase module/s.

A library homepage is now under construction. It provides information about the UPOU library, its policies, some updates on newly acquired books, with some links to other libraries that would be of interest to students. It is hoped that through the library homepage, UPOU distance learners will gain access to the available resources and services the UP Open University can provide. There are pilot projects to start digitization of materials and searching for online references in preparation for offering online courses. However, only the Faculty of Management Sciences has done work in its Web page. Thus their link is only one operational in the homepage. See Figure 1 for the sample main page. When one clicks on Faculty of Management Sciences, the online reference materials for Diploma/Masters in Environmental Sciences and Management (D/ENRM) will appear on the screen. The online reference materials are results of the pilot project of UPOU regarding the digitization of materials. Figure 2 shows the index of online references for the ENRM program. Continuous updating and searching for possible content of the homepage is done.

Future plan

To achieve the mission-vision of the UPOU Digital Library System, the following shall be undertaken:

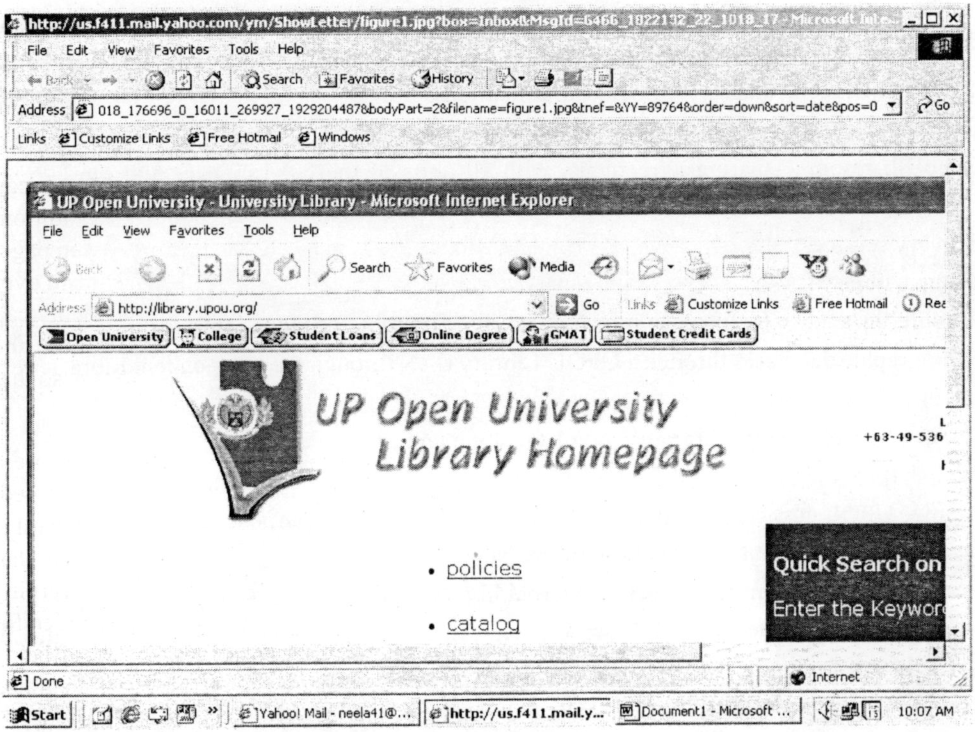

Figure 10.1: The UPOU library homepage

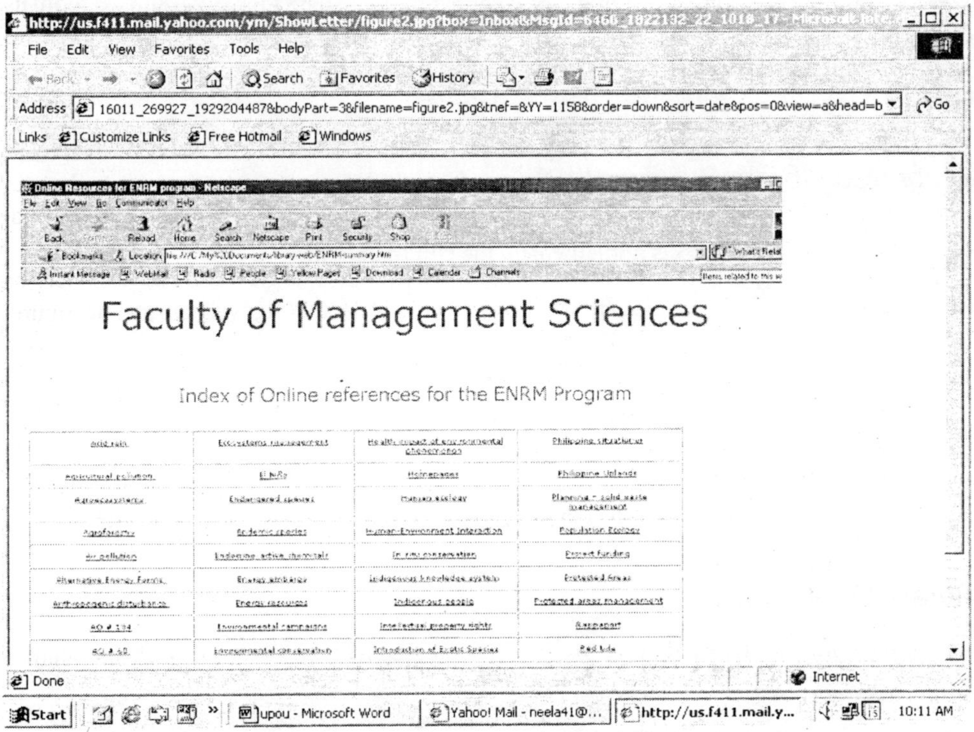

Figure 10.2: Index of online references for the ENRM program

- Build a core collection of print and non-print library materials (books, journals, course materials, reference materials, audio-visual materials, and CD-ROM) with the help of the UPOU faculty.
- Collect, document, and service UPOU publications.
- Create an electronic library catalog with on-line public access.
- Establish resource-sharing agreements with all units of the UP Libraries and the UPOU Learning Centers and other libraries to avail facilities reciprocal interlibrary loan and document delivery services.
- Set-up a library LAN.
- Provide an access to Internet information resources including e-journals, full-text and bibliographic databases through a UPOU Library LAN through the independent Library web server.
- Set up a Listserv for all librarians and/or faculty members.
- Publish (provide web access) the UPOU Library catalog on the Internet.
- Digitize UPOU curriculum materials and other publications for purposes of preservation, fast access, and for possible publication on the Net.
- Acquire and implement a networked internal library system.
- Launch and market the UPOU Library as a tele-center for distance education and educational technology information.
- Provide opportunities for library staff to acquire knowledge and skills required for the new information environment

There are six points to be considered in the development of distance library resources, namely: Integrated library system, library operations, Educational technology collection, Electronic digitization project, access and use of UP and other collection, and computer and network resources.

1. Integrated Library System (ILS)

Until such time as the UPOU ILS is implemented, the UPOU should:

- Provide access to the Union catalogue (when available) via the UPOU Web site and integrated library system.
- Investigate other investigate ways of providing access to the UPOU online catalogue during the interim period (such as Web interface to CDS-ISIS or groups of records exported or converted to Web pages).
- Consider providing copies of the UPOU CDS-ISIS catalogue via CD-ROM to the Learning Centers, particularly once collections to support the programs are well established.

2. Library Operations

Reorganize the library system and move towards a web based management. The web application should include:

- Library policies and services.
- Information about special events such as trial online databases for evaluation.
- "Feedback" and "online library help" email links (to be monitored regularly by the librarian. This would be useful means of soliciting feedback from faculty and others about trial online databases).
- Links to useful materials in appropriate subject areas. Either the librarian or faculty may identify these links, although the faculty should review the materials that are made available to students.
- Provision of online guides for using the catalogue, online databases and other services.

3. *Education Technology Collection (ETC)*

Develop a collection focusing on educational technology. Steps that may be followed could include:

- Identify current resources in education particularly educational technology, which are available online.
- Identify other educational programs that might potentially be interested, through a brief questionnaire or email message.
- Establish a mailing list of interested parties.
- Identify alternative products.
- Work with experts to determine cost of license for such a project.
- Identify funding for the project, at least in the short term. These might include outside sources, participating library budgets and if interest is sufficiently widespread, the UP administration.

However, as with many other activities, key components for the success of this collection for UPOU and others are communication and awareness.

4. *Electronic Digitization Project*

UPOU will move towards digitization of appropriate supporting materials for courses and programs. There are several programs that lend well to do this, as there are many materials already available in the Web that would support these programs. Examples are Environmental and Natural Resource Management (e.g. digital gallery of Philippines endangered species) or Master of Public Health (e.g digital gallery of parasitologic diseases).

Crucial to the success of this goal are:

- Identification of appropriate materials for digitization.
- Identification of related online materials available on other Web sites.
- Provision of appropriate access through a 'course' Web page. The Library could maintain this page. It would provide access to the digitized materials and to related online materials available at other Web sites.

- Availability of sufficient network capability and workstations in at least one UPOU Learning Center or local Network café.
- Dedication, enthusiasm and close collaboration among those responsible for producing the regular course content and the digitized content.

5. Access and Use of UP and Other Collections

It is highly desirable that UPOU students have access to as wide a variety of materials possible. Many students and Learning Centers are located near or on other UP campuses or near other resources. Some flexible arrangements could be made to ensure the safety of the UP Libraries' books but also provide the necessary access to information. For example, it is worth attempting to expand the right to borrow materials to the Learning Centers Coordinators. Using the catalogue, faculty or other appropriate individuals could identify books available locally to which would be of interest to students. The Learning Center Coordinator could then obtain them for the period of the students' visit. Students could consult the materials within the Learning Center, and photocopy (within the copyright law) sections of interest. These materials would supplement those provided through UPOU. It should be noted that UPOU materials may well be of interest to other UP students and UPOU would need to provide reciprocal access to materials.

6. Computer and Network Resources

Sufficient network bandwidth and workstation capacity are absolutely crucial to the full realization of many of the UPOU library projects. In particular to utilize a suitable ISP would cost UPOU a quite large amount per year. While this may be a prohibitive sum, the current network arrangement will significantly hamper the UPOU's ability to achieve its stated goals. This is a more pressing priority than the purchase of an integrated library system at that time, given UPOU information priorities and some alternatives for provision of access to information about the collection.

Outreach services

As mentioned earlier, UPOU students are located strategically all over the country. It is quite hard for the main library to give library services directly to the students. Thus, the UPOU library provides a copy of the reference materials and required books / textbooks of the specific program offered in all learning centers. However due to financial constraints, these library materials are for room use only since only one copy is provided per learning center. The library is finding other means to reach the distance learners and better serve their information and bibliographic needs.

Future plans

In the year 2001, the UP System to which UP Open University is a constituent university, initiated a project proposal entitled "UP Library Modernization Plan: the Development of Electronic Libraries". The goal of the modernization plan is to transform the UP libraries into electronic libraries. The plan involves two phases: a) conversion of bibliographic records into electronic format and establishment of online public access catalog and union catalog and b) implementation of automated circulation system, which is best done after conversion is completed. With this new support, the UPOU can now implement the above mention points to achieve the mission-vision of the UP library. . Acquisition of hardware and software that would facilitate access for distance learners is in process. UPOU is also trying to enter into a consortia with other non-UP libraries so that distance learners located near these libraries can have more access to the information they required. A proposal to connect all the learning centers, creation of policies for borrowing, library orientation and visits to learning center sites, is also being studied.

Conclusion

Library resources and services in institution of higher education must meet the needs of all their faculty, students and academic support staff, wherever these individuals are located, whether on a main campus, off campus, in distance education or extended campus programs, or in the absence of the campus at all; in courses taken for credit or non-credit; in continuing education programs; in courses attended in person or by means of electronic transmission; or any other means of distance education (ACRL Guidelines for distance learning library services, 2001). The UPO library is slowly but surely moving towards providing quality library resources and services to it distance learners as well as other possible clientele.

References

ACRL Guidelines for Distance Learning Library Services. Fall 2000 www.ala.org/acrl/guides/distlrng.html

David, L.T. (1999). *The U.P. Open University Library: Services for Distance Learners*. Report of the UPOU Consultant from the College of Science Library, UP Diliman, Quezon City.

Ferrel, N. (1983). Alaska's flying library, *Library Journal*, 108(6), 554-555.

Kaskus, M. and W. Aguilar. 1988. Providing library support to off-campus programs, CRL 49(1), 29-37

Stephens, K., L. Unwin and N. Bolton. (1997). The use of libraries by postgraduate distance learning students: a mismatch of expectations, *The Journal of Open and Distance Learning,* 12 (3): 25-33.

Strategic Plan 1999-2008. Harnessing technology to improve access to quality education. 1999.

UP Open University Primer. 1996.

UPOU General Brochure 2000. UPOU… in the New Millenium: harnessing Technology to improve access to quality education.

11

Library Services for Distance Education and Open Learning At Sukhothai Thammathirat Open University

Boonta Wissawapaisal

Introduction

Education is crucial to human development. The Royal Thai government set up a project to institute an open university in 1975. The project attempted to fulfill two important needs of the Thai people. The first was the need to provide equal access to higher education to people throughout Thailand. Secondly, the government sought to make the concept of lifelong education a practical reality. The distance education system was viewed as a practical method to supplement the conventional university system. The Sukhothai Thammathirat was established three years later as an open university using a distance education system to serve these two needs. The Sukhothai Thammathirat Open University (STOU) is playing a leading role in the development of distance education. The University has been designated by UNESCO as the Lead Institution in the Consortium on Innovations in Distance Education for Asia and the Pacific. In 1992, STOU was awarded the Asian Management Award in Development Management, which recognized STOU's outstanding achievement in improving the quality of people's lives. In 1995, the University was granted the Award of Excellence, jointly by the Commonwealth of Learning (COL) and the International Council for Distance Education (ICDE), which recognized STOU's institutional achievement in distance education.

STOU is the first distance education institution in Thailand and in the Southeast Asia. The University was founded by Royal Charter on September 5, 1978 as a state university under the guidance of the Ministry of University Affairs. Till now, STOU has established 12 academic schools: Liberal Arts, Educational Studies, Management Science, Law, Economics, Health Science, Home Economics, Agricultural Extension and Cooperatives, Political Science, Communication Arts, Science and Technology, and Nursing. The enrollment of students in 2001 was about 211,200 students.

STOU provides both degree programs and non-degree programs: undergraduate degree programs, graduate degree programs, doctoral degree programmes (in cooperation with Charles Sturt University, Australia), certificate programmes, continuing education programmes and training programmes. The main educational materials for undergraduate students are textbooks and workbooks, while supporting media include audio cassettes, radio and television programmes, movies, videotapes and computer programmes. The University also provides tutorial and counseling sessions at regional and local study centers throughout the country. Independent study and research by the students is also encouraged. Additionally, a number of practical experience programmes are provided at the STOU Training Center or at specialized academic, professional or vocational institutions within the student's area. Graduate students study by themselves under the guidance of instructors. Many academic activities are arranged for them: orientation of new graduate students, academic seminars, intensive thesis courses, independent study courses and professional experience training.

Owing to the new era of the *National Education Act of B.E.2542* (1999) and the emergence of the information and knowledge age, STOU announced its intention to follow "*STOU Plan 2000*", its master plan for teaching and learning on March 14, 2001. STOU students can learn according to their needs, by using print-based or web-based media. For STOU library services, the plan will result in the development of services to support the theme "anyone, anywhere, anytime".

Library and information services

At the STOU library and information services are provided by the Office of the Documentation and Information (ODI). ODI works as the main or central library. It has many branches spreading out all over the country. The Library is an automated Library, which has been using the VTLS automated library system since 1994.

Visions and commitments of ODI

The principle of lifelong education is an important part of STOU's educational philosophy. STOU's mission includes improving the quality of life for the general population, providing opportunities for educational and professional advancement to working people, expanding educational opportunities at the university level and providing educational opportunities to the general public. To support the University's mission, ODI has outlined visions and commitments as follows:

Visions

The Office of Documentation and Information provides library and information services. It supports the University in a comprehensive and efficient manner, consistent with academic and technological progress, the distance education system. It serves as a center of life-long learning, with the aim of developing the nation's human resources.

Commitments

- Carry out its tasks in the development of information resources and information search tools, and provide comprehensive information services in terms of supporting both educational provision as well as academic and professional services for society.

- Increase the potential of library and information services through the use of new technology, as well as improving the library building and facilities for the convenience of users.
- Cooperation between the various library units within the University network and also with other academic libraries.

Library and information services system

ODI has arranged the library and information services system into three service levels covering most STOU students throughout the country: central services, regional services and provincial services.

Central services

Central Services are provided at the main library (ODI Building), which is located at the University main campus. Library system administration and technical services for all library services centers are the main library's responsibility.

Regional services

Regional Services are provided for STOU students and the general public at ten Regional Distance Education Centers (RDEC) (STOU's outside campus) located in Nakhon Si Thammarat, Phetchaburi, Nakhon Sawan, Ubon Ratchathani, Sukhothai, Udorn Thani, Lampang, Chantaburi, Yala and Nakhon Nayok. Regional Services are also provided at two Graduate Educational Resource Centers (GERC) (Collaboration with outside organization). The first one is located in the Rajamangalapisek Library in Prachuap Khirikhan Province, with the cooperation of the Department of Non-Formal Education. The second one is located in Tinnasulanon Library, with the cooperation of Mahawachirawut School in Songkhla province.

Provincial services

Provincial Services are provided at "STOU Corners" with the cooperation of various government organizations.

- 75 STOU Corners are located in 75 provincial public libraries with the cooperation of the Department of Non-Formal Education
- 4 STOU Corners are located in Bangkok with the cooperation of Bangkok Metropolitan Administration
- 1 STOU Corner is located in Tinnasulanon Library, Songkhla province with the cooperation of Mahawachirawut Secondary School
- 1 STOU Corner is located in Bang Kwang Central Prison, with the cooperation of the Department of Corrections, Ministry of Interior

The regional and provincial service centers are STOU branch libraries. Basic library services at the main library and regional libraries are reference and information service; loan service; inter-library loan service; information access and retrireview; photocopying service; orientation and library visit and user education. Regional services at the RDEC also include bookmobile services along with STOU educational services. They bring reading or portable book boxes to serve communities on certain occasions.

Library cooperation and networking

Library cooperation

Developing the nation's human resources is not a one-man task but is everybody's business. Library cooperation and networking are important tasks for teaching and learning, especially for life-long and distance learning. Cooperation with libraries and information services allows students in rural areas the opportunity to use STOU library resources while also benefiting regular students in rural institutions and the general public. The low income and disadvantaged groups who need to learn and utilize information can come and use these library and information centers. STOU educational materials (printed media) are regarded as good academic textbooks. Community libraries and information centers have found that the cooperation is very useful for their collections and information services.

Library networking

Library networking is another channel for providing opportunities to remote users to access library resources. Communications technology is developing rapidly. Academic libraries in Thailand have begun to realize that they need an automated library system and network links between academic libraries both nationally and internationally. THAILINET and PULINET were established with the cooperation of the Office of the Permanent Secretary of University Affairs and with the support of the Bureau of the Budget. The Project was launched in 1995 and has finally developed into the ThaiLIS project (Thai Library Integrated System), managed by its committee. ODI and many other public university libraries have received many benefits from the project. Public university libraries received a budget from the government sufficient to acquire library automation systems, Internet linking (UniNet) and access to electronic reference databases (ABI/Inform, ERIC, DAO, Medline, IEEE). STOU library and information services can now work more efficiently and support outreach library services to help its target student groups as well as the general public.

Other outreach library services

ODI visions and commitments center around the notion of life-long learning. According to the commitments, ODI provides library and information services to communities. For instance, its activities include providing library and information services for prisoners, knowledge for kids project, and establishing libraries for the military and their families.

Providing library and information services for prisoners.

ODI has established an "STOU Corner" at Bang Kwang Prison for STOU students and other prisoners. ODI also makes book donations to them. Another cooperation with the Department of Corrections is personnel development. ODI has arranged a library training project for their personnel responsible for library services for prisons all over the country. These services open more opportunities to disadvantaged groups in the prisons.

Knowledge for Kids Project. ODI runs a portable library project named 'Knowledge for Kids Project'.

The Project has been in operation since 1987. The aim of the project is to promote reading habits among children. Portable book boxes and reading materials are acquired through by fund-raising, mostly from the donations of library users and are rotated among different primary schools within the University's neighborhood. The Project was originally operated by STOU main library and was subsequently moved to Regional Distance Education Centers. At present it is a part of mobile information services.

Library consulting and library establishing.

ODI takes a consulting role, and offers advice and assistance to other organizations with regard to library services. Many years ago, ODI was invited to help some army sub-organizations in planning and establishing libraries for STOU students who were soldiers or army staff or members of their families. ODI operated the following activities: physical planning of library space, acquiring reading materials and personnel training. The goals of the project reflect ODI's commitments, of which library cooperation is a crucial part.

Future development

According to "STOU Plan 2000" the educational reform acts and rapid advances in communications technology, ODI needs to develop its services and support to teaching and learning at STOU. Electronic documents, electronic reference database and computer facilities have to be acquired in order to complete distance learning systems. Information and resource sharing as well as library cooperation will be continued, so that students can get quicker and better access to meet their needs. Some students who cannot afford to have a computer or internet access at home can come to use the facilities at the regional centers and find the information they require. ODI will play an important role in promoting distance education not only for STOU students and STOU staff, but also through community libraries for the general public.

Conclusion

Life-long learning and distance learning have become popular concepts in the new information technology era among academic universities and other organizations which are concerned with education management. Owing to advances in a variety of information and communications technologies, distance and open education have been recognized as significant alternatives for learners. In order to make distance learning efficient, appropriate library and information services must be made available to distance learning students. Library cooperation and networking can serve this objective and help to promote equal learning opportunity and life-long learning for both distance students, who are the target group of library and information services as well as general public, who may wish to upgrade their status, knowledge, or the quality of their daily life. With cooperation and by reaching out to others we can have a society where life seems promising and hopeful for everybody.

References

Chutima, Sacchanand (1977). "Library Networks for Distance Education :Case Study of Sukhothai Thammathirat Open University (STOU), Thailand." Paper presented to the Poster Session, 63rd IFLA Conference, Copenhagen, Denmark, 1-6 September.

Sujin Butdisuwan (1999). "Community Libraries and Information Services in Thailand" in Libraries and Librarianship in Thailand : from Stone Inscription to Microchips. Bangkok : IFLA' 99 National Organizing Committee.

Sukhothai Thammathirat Open University (1996), 18th Anniversary of Sukhothai Thammathirat Open University. Nonthaburi: SukhothaiThammathirat Open University Press.

12

Efforts of the Indonesian Open Learning University Library: Making Library More Accessible to the Users

Effendi Wahyono

Introduction

The Indonesian Open Learning University (Universitas Terbuka - UT) was established on two issues: low capacity of the university, and low quality of the teachers. Based on the idea of increasing capacity of university with low cost and increase the quality of the teachers the government decided to establish a distance university with open system. The government hopes that UT can accommodate a large number of high school graduates and can increase the quality of the teachers which in turn can improve the quality of Indonesian Education.

For the easier operation, UT was designed as a university with networking system which covered all of state university in Indonesia. With this networking system, UT can use the facilities of the university, manpower or library facilities. UT utilizes the experts of the university to prepare learning material and tutorial, and the facility of Regional Center (UPBJJ) management in 32 cities (now 31). The libraries are used to facilitate the UT students.

UT cooperates with several institutions, such as PT. Pos Indonesia, PT. Telkom (National Telecommunication Institution) and National Library. Post Office was used as an administration and registration agent, distributing learning and examination material. PT. Telkom was used to make easier communication with the student and member of the network all over Indonesia. National Library in 26 provinces (named as regional library) provides services for the reference material to the students.

This networking made UT capable in holding educational program all over Indonesia. As a result UT got 400,000 students in 15 years and qualified as one of the mega top ten university category, which has 300,000 graduation.

Services of UT became more efficient, since the services were provided only by 630 administration staff and 789 academic staff for all students. These services should be supported by the technology of information and communication. So now UT is using Information and Communication Technology (ICT) to facilitate online registration service, tutorial and e-library activities. Problems faced in developing the ICT program are limitation of access to UT by the students, financial constraints or know-how about ICT, the habit of the students still being traditional. Since the government is supporting the development of the ICT as big program so as to face the global market, some of these problems are taken care of.

This chapter discusses the services of UT, especially library services, various problems that may come up and efforts on how to face it.

Geography of UT student

UT students are not restricted in one area only, but distributed all over Indonesia having 1.9 million square Km land and 7.9 million sq. mts. ocean. Administratively, the students of UT are distributed in 26 provinces which has 303 districts and 3.839 under districts. Apart from that, there are many UT students who stay outside Indonesia such as Germany, The Netherlands, South America, Japan and Saudi Arabia. Most of them are non-resident Indonesians.

With a wide access of the open system and flexibility, UT has given chances to Indonesian citizen to have better higher education. UT has so far had up to 400.000 students, i.e., 20 per cent of all education participants in the higher education in Indonesia.

Providing wide access can have huge impact in giving services to the students, in a situation where they are not living in one concentrated area. Most of the UT student live in four big provinces in Java. Geographically, Java island has better living condition compared to other islands, as the transportation and communication is much more easier. As a result around 60 percent of Indonesians live in Java. But UT provides same services to all the student in Java and outside Java.

Efforts to provide same services to all students faced many problems, especially in transportation and communication matter. Transportation of postal services to specific area outside Java needs around 20-30 days, whereas in Java only one week is required. Same is the case in the telecommunication front. National Radio (Radio Republik Indonesia - RRI) is the only one communication facility which has wide access. National Television (Televisi Republik Indonesia -TVRI), theoretically reaches to all over Indonesia, but some areas are deprived. Telephone is another alternative, but it is not yet popular in Indonesia, especially because many of those living in Java do not have the facility. Five private television stations can only be reached by part of people who live in Java.

Under such circumstances it becomes difficult for UT to provide quality services. Keeping this in view UT initially enrolled students who lived in provinces / cities. But later on, based on higher demand, UT finally started enrolling students living outside provinces / cities, even those who live in small islands in the middle of the sea, inside Kalimantan, and Irian Jaya. Following graph shows the distribution of students in provinces.

Chart 12.1: Student population based on Provinces*

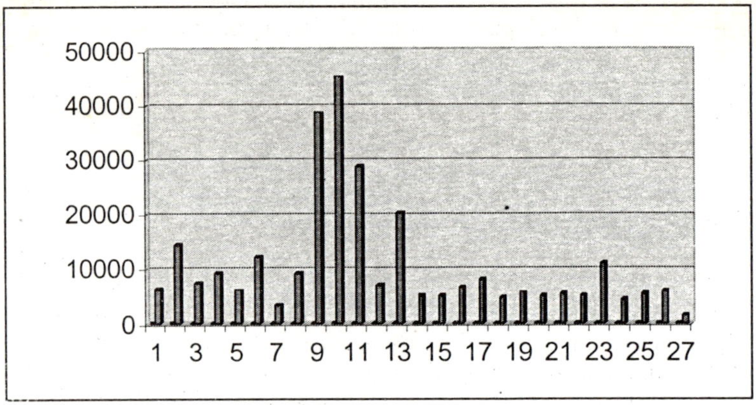

1. DI Aceh
2. North Sumatera
3. West Sumatera
4. Riau
5. Jambi
6. South Sumatera
7. Bengkulu
8. Lampung
9. DKI Jakarta
10. West Jawa
11. Midle Jawa
12. DI Yogyakarta
13. East Jawa
14. Bali
15. West Nusa Tenggara
16. East Nusa Tenggara
17. West Kalimantan
18. Midle Kalimantan
19. South Kalimantan
20. East Kalimantan
21. North Sulawesi
22. Midle Sulawesi
23. South Sulawesi
24. Souteast Sulawesi
25. Maluku
26. Irian Jaya
27. The others

---

*Vertical : Student population
Horizontal : Province

Chart 12.2: Student population at UPBJJ Pekan Baru (Riau)*

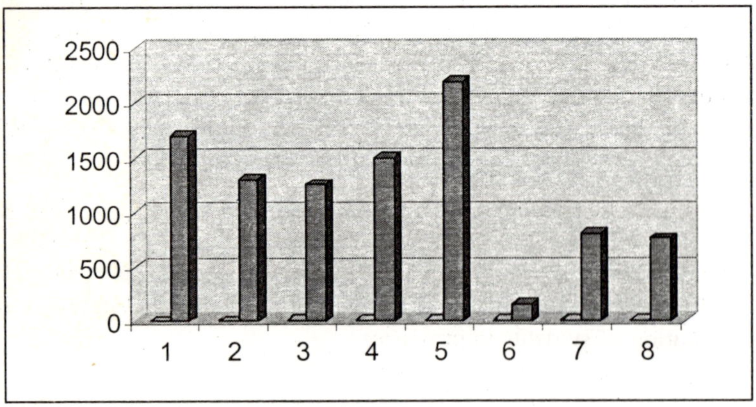

1. Indragiri Ulu
2. Indragiri Ilir
3. Kep. Riau
4. Kampar
5. Bengkalis
6. Kuantan Sing.
7. Pekan Baru
8. Batam

---

*Vertical : Student population
Horizontal : District

Chart 12.3: Student population at UPBJJ Banjarmasin (South Kalimantan)

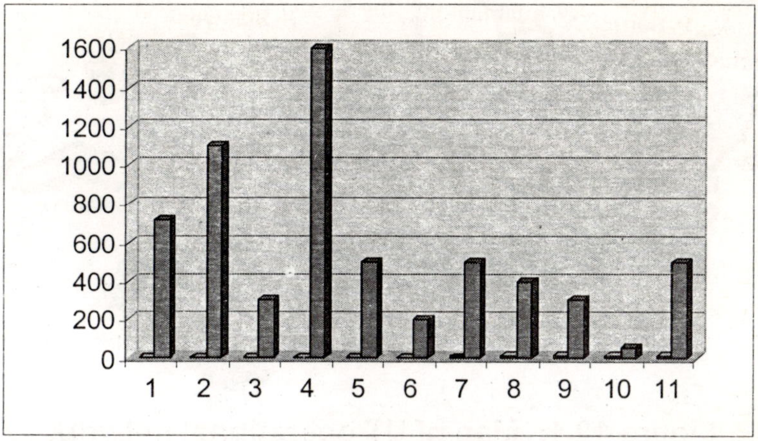

1. West Kota Waringin
2. East Kota Waringin
3. Katingan
4. Kapuas
5. South Barito
6. East Barito
7. North Barito
8. Gunung Mas
9. Muning Raya
10. Saruyan
11. Palangkaraya

---

*Vertical : Student population
Horizontal : District

The graphs are based on data from March 2001, which shows 355,000 students, 160 or 48 per cent domicile in Java. The rest live in other provinces. In each province, UT student lives in almost all regions including Mid Kalimantan and Pakan Baru (Riau). The graphs show that UT student living in outside provinces is larger than those who live inside provinces. Transportation from provinces to outside provinces or vice-versa outside Java usually is very difficult.

UT services can run smoothly, as UT has networking in all provinces in Indonesia (26) and additionally five cities outside provinces which have government university such as Bogor, Purwokerto, Surakarta, Malang and Jember. Those five cities in Java island, have better infrastructure which was made a central networking service for its government university. The central service of UT network in government universities can be utilized by UT to set up offices. The following map shows UT operational network spread throughout Indonesia.

UT library as an e-library

Geographic distribution of student population is the cause for the major problems faced in providing services to the students, especially the library services. UT would like government universities to provide library services to UT students and cooperate with regional library, so that the library can focus on developing services for the educational staff and subject matter experts.

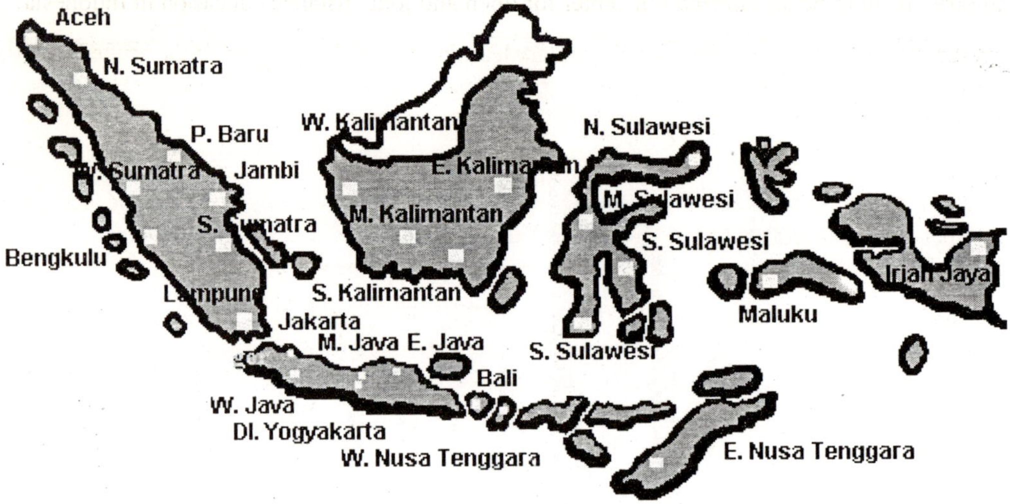

Figure 12.1: Map of UT operational network

Since 1996, UT library worked with State Universities Library Forum which has members from all state universities in Java. The purpose of this forum was to utilize library collection of all network members. All students from Network University could utilize the collection. This was very effective as pass card issued by the forum could be used to access all state university in Java. Unfortunately, this is being utilised only for reading at the site. This is not implemented for borrowing by cross system service among libraries.

UT tried all possible ways to optimize the library service for the last 17 years, but the students still got low service. Libraries of the Region state universities are already busy with their own students and are not so eager to serve UT students. The regional library collection is not sufficient to match with the needs of UT students as it was implemented to serve general public and not for UT students.

Keeping in view the past experiences it was felt necessary to utilize ICT for providing quality services to distance and remote areas instead of depending on the conventional systems of delivery.

As a result UT started to develop the e-library since 1997. Initially UT was using online catalogues, but limited budget stopped the activities in 1999-2000. It was again resumed in 2001. In 2000 the concentration was to build a new library building and move the collection to it. The library now emphasises on transferring the UT library into an e-library.

CDS/ISIS software developed by UNESCO is being used to develop the e-library. Unfortunately CDS/ISIS only can be used stand alone or Local Area Network (LAN), it can be used for internet facility. Another program is used to show it in the internet. At first, we used Access, and now we are trying to use Linux. Earlier data provided on internet was only bibliographic (catalogue), but now, abstracts of research results are also provided. UT library is transferring the research result of open learning and long distance from printed material to electronic format in the from of CD-ROM and in a database which can be accessed through internet. The full text (use WAIS supported by CDS/ISIS) of the research results can be accessed through internet. This matches with the library vision to be an information center for open and long distance education in Indonesia.

Presently, UT web site provides supplementary learning material in addition to the printed material for the students. The students can get the printed material by purchasing it at UPBJJ offices and freely access the supplementary material through the internet.

To give easy access to the users, UT library provides three modes of services. First, direct service to student (users) who come to library. Second, through intranet (LAN), and third through internet. The first and the second modes are utilized by UT staff and several students who live in Jakarta. The third, serves the UT students and public who cannot come directly to the library.

UT staff use UT LAN to get data or information through internet. Physical connection between UT LAN to internet is using Indonet service by telephone. UT uses dual-load balance technology to connect LAN and internet. Two telephone lines are used to connect modem with 56 kb / per sec speed capacity each. Unfortunately, telephone network in UT Campus neighborhood is not so good, so the maximum speed cannot be reached. That's why UT web site is difficult at times to access.

Ideally, internet connection by telephone should be changed by satellite, but till now, UT has not been able to rent a satellite which is very expensive. UT operational budget is only Rp 50,000,000,000, or around US$ 5,000,000. Renting satellite by the library is impossible as UT library budget is only US$ 20,000. UT has requested Directorate General of Higher Education (Direktorat Jenderal Pendidikan Tinggi - DIKTI) to utilize the satellite facility owned by DIKTI.

UT faces another problem that is student's ability to utilize information technology. Computer for most of UT student is still a luxurious good, as most of them come from mid low income class. Out of 210,000,000 Indonesian population, only 6,000,000 persons have telephone line at home. Government is planning to establish internet facilities throughout in Indonesia as a public facility and UT can utilize this infrastructure for its use.

If this materializes then there will be 3,839 public internet facilities. UT students can utilize this and can have access to UT library through internet. In private sector, many businessmen have invested their money to open public internet facilities. According to Indonesian Public Internet Facilities Association (APWI), there are 16,000 public internet facilities all over Indonesia. At present there are only 2,000,000 users or less than 1 percent from total Indonesian population using internet whereas in comparison in neighborhood countries such as Singapore, it is 42 per cent, South Korea 32 per cent, Taiwan 29 per cent and Malaysia 7 per cent.

With the development of public internet facilities, UT students may not worry about the expenses, and this will in turn will facilitate more users to utilize UT library services.

Conclusion

A large number of UT students make it difficult for UT to develop a library with conventional model. UT's library system must be developed to facilitate easy access to the students and e-library can be possible solution in this direction.

The e-library system can facilitate students to get information, not only bibliographic catalogue data but also abstract of research results, specific articles related to open and distance education. Student can visit UT web site as well as to get full text supplementary learning material.

Internet technology is still an expensive and exclusive thing, but it is hoped that it will be an open and big thing in the future. ICT application in UT is being integrated not only to provide library services but also to serve online registration, e-tutorial, UT information, exam result, and long distance examination.

References

Dharmayanti, Tri, dan Argadhata Sigit, (2001) "Geografi Mahasiswa Universitas Terbuka", paper presented in Seminar Potensi Warnet dalam Mendukung Pengembangan Pendidikan Terbuka dan Jarak Jauh), Jakarta: Universitas Terbuka.

Fahmi, Ismail, (1999) "ISIS-Network dan Otomasi Perpustakaan Menuju Digital Library", paper presented in Seminar Peran Teknologi Informasi sebagai Sumber Informasi dalam Menunjang Pendidikan dan Penelitian di Era Milenium, Bandung: ITB.

"From The Margins to The Mainstream: Developing Library Support for Distance Education", *Library Online* (An Occasional Newsletter of the University of Minnesota Libraries- Twin Cities May, 1997 Vol. 8, November 4). http://www.Lib.umn.edu/pubs/LibLine/Llvol8n.

Fulcher, Glenn and Debbie Lock,1999) Distance Education: The Future of Library and Information Services requirements, *Distance Education*, 20(2).

Hardhono, A. P. (2001) "Pemanfaatan Internet di Lingkungan Universitas Terbuka", paper presented in Seminar Potensi Warnet dalam mendukung Pengembangan Pendidikan Terbuka dan Jarak Jauh, Jakarta: Universitas Terbuka.

Rahardjo, Arlinah Imam, "Proyek Jaringan Virtual Perpustakaan Universitas Kristen di Indonesia: In CU-VL", (Workshop Pengelolaan Internet bagi Perpustakaan Perguruan Tinggi), Surabaya: Universitas Petra.

Universitas Terbuka (2001) "Statistik Mahasiswa Universitas Terbuka masa Registrasi 2000.2", Universitas Terbuka.

Subagjo (2001) "The Virtual UT", (Draft Proposal), Universitas Terbuka.

13

Open Univerity Sri Lanka Library System, Services and its Future Plans

K.H. Sellathurai

Introduction

The Open University of Sri Lanka (OUSL), established in 1980, introduced distance education using an integrated multimedia approach, incorporating structured self-study, tutorial support and guidance. The resulting package enabled learners to work at their own pace. The OUSL offered courses at certificate, diploma, degree and postgraduate levels.

With the literacy rate at over 90 per cent in Sri Lanka, it could be surmised that the OUSL was established for those who could not enter the traditional institutions of higher education as they were employed. The establishment of the OUSL thus offered an opportunity to those who wished to upgrade their education on a part-time basis.

Today, the OUSL has a main campus where the major resources of the library are concentrated. There are still only four Regional Centres, but the nine original Study Centres have now increased to sixteen, covering the greater part of the country. They basically aim to link the campus and the distant learner. The OUSL library thus faces the challenge of finding ways and means to provide students with the skills to use information resources, international databases and virtual libraries. Given the location of both distance learners and information resources, this is a challenge.

Virtual classrooms and virtual libraries are complementary necessities of distance learning. The delivery systems for distance education have evolved from print media to telecommunication and electronic media. Information is delivered to distance learners through interactive video via communication satellites, and through electronic mail, electronic bulletin boards, tele-conferencing and online databases. Korale (1996) remarked that:

All this means of funding for library services should be adequately provided, either by the university itself or through cost-sharing arrangements … If co-operative networking exists and compatible systems are in place, students will have access to other library catalogues as well.

OUSL programmes and student enrollment

There are three faculties, with eight programmes in Engineering, ten in Science and twenty-five in the Humanities and Social Sciences.

In Engineering, the Diploma in Electronic Engineering is in greatest demand, as there is a demand for Information Technology professionals, in the country. Computer awareness programmes have done a service for students to be computer literate, to meet the current needs in society. The science degrees have always been popular. We are the pioneers to offer a degree in Nursing in Sri Lanka. In the HSS (Humanities and Social Sciences), the Post Graduate Diploma in Education (PGDE) is very popular, because the graduate teachers need a diploma for their career development. Even in the regions, apart from the basic and advanced English courses, there is a demand for the PGDE.

Admissions to the Management Diploma and the Law degree courses are highly competitive, and there is an entrance level exam for these courses. The degree course in Social Science has been picking up. The HSS faculty have paved way to offer degree courses in Management and English.

There are about 18,000 students, of whom 10,000 have registered in the central campus, and more than 50 percent of them are below 25. This is because, ours being a small island, many students are within reach of the central campus, and school leavers also find it a means to further their educational advancement, whether employed or not.

Library collection and library facilities

The library is open 7 days a week from 9.a.m. to 7 p.m. except on special holidays, which occur 7 or 8 days in a year. The Audio-Visual Centre of the library, located within, also offers viewing facilities to students. Reference facilities are available to all students, and lending facilities to students from level 3 and above. Photocopying of library materials is also available at nominal rate.

The books are generally located in the central campus. Multiple copies of all course materials, books as well as audio-visuals are available in the Regional and Study Centres. The departments have identified a few textbooks as core books for each course. These core books are duplicated and are sent to the Regional and Study Centres, where necessary, as instructed by the divisional heads. Periodically, the past question papers, model papers and answers are also sent to the Regions and Study Centres. The departments also select books for teaching and reference purpose through their book allocation. The library utilises its own vote, for general reading, IT and special needs of the faculties and students.

Present collection

Main Campus - Library

The CampusLibrary has 58,000 textbooks, 4,288 reference books, 1,142 bound journals, 336 pamphlets, 102 CD-ROMs, 656 audios and 817 videos.

Centres

The Regional and Study Centres have 25.921 books, 146 journals and 47 locally acquired books.

Strengthening collection

A good collection of up-to-date Science and Technology books has been purchased through an ADB (Asian Development Bank) loan, and core books and other useful books have been duplicated at the Regions and Study Centres, where necessary. The UNESCO and World Bank projects supported, in for improving book collection in courses dealing with Education.

Problems pertaining to library materials and students' views

The ability to find what they want is better among the present generation of students, even though their reading habits are poor. They select what they want and get them photocopied. However, the demand for library materials among students in descending order is, course materials first, past question papers, core books, text books and finally audio-visuals.

Since most students have poor language ability in English, they either tend to limit their reading to the recommended books or their course materials. So there is always a demand for the core books. But generally there are not many duplicated copies of the core books. They have to be multiplied at the centres. This paucity can be remedied by further photocopying services.

- The user survey shows that about 50 per cent of the students depend on course materials and wish that the course materials should include all what is needed, including extracts from reference materials that are convenient for them to do their studies, without the bother of travelling to the study centres, often situated far away.
- 25 per cent of them prefer better photocopying facilities. They wish to have the relevant pages from the reference materials photocopied and made available as handouts, rather than their coming, searching and photocopying. But the Librarian holds the view that the students should be able to search for themselves at least from a given number of reference materials, and select what they want, so as to broaden their understanding of the subject, and improve their reading, as adults.
- 25 per cent of them feel that the number of copies of the core books available is not adequate, even though the lending facilities are available and core books are duplicated, as everyone would want to borrow the same books. These books may not be available sometimes, even for photocopying. Due to assignment deadlines, it is not feasible to reserve and await books. Today, time and information are considered as resources or commodities, and students are frustrated when they cannot find what they want. They also feel, that the fine is a barrier for many students to make use of the offer to borrow books. However the Library management views, that the fine is necessary to make the students return the books in time, as duplication of core books need to be carefully thought out, so as to strike a balance between the demand and constraints from funds available.
- Generally there are requests to make copies of cases in Law and of past papers.

In some cases, the regional centres are far from their residence, in the range of 50 km or above, and they are not able to go and do reference. Students feel that the communication between the staff is not always easy, so they prefer face-to-face classes, conducted in the regions. Unlike the students in the west, in developing countries students are shy to communicate and ask from the library staff or lecturers all what they really want.

- The use of other libraries, even for reference, is dependent on goodwill rather than on a formalised scheme. The provision of reference facilities to external users is still not a regular part of library services in Sri Lanka.
- Document supply, in general, takes longer, and the students are not confident that they would receive them in time, as we cannot rely on the postal system in our country. Facilities are not adequate in the regions, for making queries through e-mail, as in the main cities. However, even for students to go to the centre, to make their requests and get the necessary documents delivered to them, remains time consuming. The same is true for ILL requests, and hence they try to depend on the course materials.
- A few keen students feel that not enough periodicals are available. This is because the journals are costly and more money is spent on developing the book collection.

The recent past

Widened customer services

- Even though the students were allowed to refer books since the 1980s, during the last few years we have afforded lending facilities, after a deposit of Rs. 500/- for each book the student is allowed for a fortnight at a time, and a fine is imposed, in order to encourage the users to return the books in time. The students are given a maximum of two tickets.
- The In-House Statistics show that the usage of books has improved after lending facilities were offered to students.

Earlier, it was the course materials and past papers that were in great demand. But after the lending facility was given we have recorded an increase in the use of the core books and other text books. Other subject-related materials are being equally used, particularly in subjects like Computer Science, Engineering, Mathematics, Chemistry, Law, Management, Botany & Zoology. There is a notable demand for the computer- related books.

Videos are popular among the students. Students do look at the videos that are part of their course materials or accompanying materials, which are freely available at the centres. But there are not enough videos developed locally, suitable for the Engineering and Science students that would facilitate their study. Some of the OU-UK videos are available that would facilitate the students' awareness of the subjects.

Library promotion

- Library Brochure giving the library hours and services, is given to students. Also available at the counter.
- Guided tour to the library as part of the orientation programme, when each new batch is enrolled.
- Staff generally tries to answer any queries, either through e-mail, telephone or by post, without much delay.

- A video had been developed to keep the users informed about the library services. Another video deals with the Library OPAC CDS/ISIS software.
- Staff assistance in doing searches on OPAC, as and when needed.
- Free Internet access and access to the campus-wide LAN (Local Area Network).

Present scenario

LAN

- There is a campus-wide LAN, which connects all the departments, establishments and the administration since 1998. This paved the way for us to provide access to bibliographic information campus-wide, on WINISIS.
- This year the library purchased ALICE, an integrated Library Management System, from Softlink, South Asia, which will help the users not only to access the bibliographic data, but also the circulation information and to making reservations through LAN, as well as through Internet.

Internet

- Even outsiders can access the library bibliographic databases through INTERNET (Inter-related Networks or a Network of Networks).
- With the main campus the students are given free Internet access, for subject search, as a reference tool.

CD-ROM databases

The library subscribes for the electronic database, for ERIC, in CD-ROM format, which has been used by the staff as well as students, but only in the main campus.

Minding the communication gap

Hathaway (1999) notes that: 'The 'Gap' is the black hole between the tasks demand by the students curriculum and the provision of resources and services in the library/learning resource centres.... The lecturers and librarians failed to communicate concerning curriculum changes, and this led to students demanding resources that were not in stock". In addition, whatsoever measures are taken, it takes longer time to acquire books published abroad, than expected.

With a decrease in class contact time, and an increase in student - centered resource based learning, the student is expected to spend a higher proportion of time learning with resources. Even though the Distance Learning takes a lot of the 'student centered teaching and learning support', the reality in the developing countries is that the infrastructure is not adequate for the use of Information Technology, particularly in the regions. In order to promote their making use of these limited facilities, the students should be better trained to use library facilities available for distance learners.

It is worth mentioning here that demand for document delivery is not significant enough to make improvement. This is partly because the students do not know about the facilities in the library, and their right to demand for them. Some user education has to be promoted among the students, if necessary in a compulsory manner as some o. the universities in the West are doing. They should be educated to search for material within the library, or through Internet, from the additional references given in the department's web-sites, and to communicate with the course co-ordinators.

Hathaway (1999) writes, regarding developments in Information skills at Reading university, ...' The aim of the course is to help students achieve facility in their scientific writing and to become familiar with the use of information technology."

The course is a collaborative venture between library staff and academic colleagues to:

- reflect as closely as possible the different routes of access to information that students are likely to employ in a subject search;
- allow self-paced learning;
- increase attractiveness of the material to students;
- maintain choice between electronic media and paper formats;
- help the library staff to have better links and understanding about the curriculum, academic and the students at various level, in various parts of the country, to be responsive and serve them better.

University IT policy and library services

Main campus

IT Policy had been drawn to provide better access to students in using the computers and the number of hours a student should be given at different level

Developing the regions

a) by providing access to library bibliographic database, Island-wide.

b) Improving ILL, within OU (Regions & Study Centres)

The regions have to further the following facilities

Increasing internet access points

With the help of an organisation, interested in promoting distance learning, we intend providing many more Internet access points, for the benefit of students in the regions, as well as in the main campus. As a first step the regional centres will be given the LAN connection.

Lecturers contribution

In order to encourage the students to read outside their course materials, the lecturers are planning to provide news clips and information about relevant topics in support of the course contents available in the Internet, and extracts from particular books. These will be included in the lecturers web-page, in the Universitiy's web site. This is to provide Internet facilities, by giving them access to the University web site where the lecturers have additional notes clips, or guidance to improve their studies.

Factors preventing from improvement of services

- Poor reading habits
- Not many subject-oriented books are available in Sinhalese or Tamil, and poor students have no command of English.
- Lack of time for the Staff to do research or for students to do extra reading.
- ILL is not properly organised to share resources.
- Not all the academic and special libraries have OPAC, with a web-inquiry to the OPAC

Future activities / objectives

Our five year co-operate plan includes the following :

- User Survey, at different levels.
- Liaison with course teams to discuss the changes in presentation and how we should guide the students
- Develop a video on doing searches with the newly installed Library Management Software, ALICE for Windows (AFW).
- Provide face-to-face user training at residential schools, wherever feasible.
- Improving User Service by providing SDI (Selective Dissemination of Information) Service, Document Supply
- ILL, among the University as well as the Regional and Study Centres
- Widening Resource Access and Document Supply by:
    i) Having an Intranet linking all the academic and special libraries and Educational Institutions, so as to strengthen resource sharing within Sri Lanka.
    ii) More access points to Internet and to the LAN in the main campus and regions.
    iii) Scanning contents pages of journals and having them on the web, giving information of the availability of the articles from each library within the library co-operation scheme.
    iv) Photocopying and delivering other user requests through e-mail or post.
    v) Keeping the Library Bulletin Board lively, providing more information on user education and useful subject related web-sites as reference tools and improving current awareness services.
- Establishing links between Open Universities in the Asian region to share resources and to mutually access databases.

Conclusion

The OUSL as a whole, has acquired considerable experience in promoting Distance Education and has plan to further this concept, both in the area of coverage as well as depth of learning. The use of IT plays a key role in facilitating this. Even the library's present five year co-operate plan hope to have a greater distribution of students and facilities in the regions.

References

Korale, S.R. (1996) Library services for distance education : the Sri Lankan experience, *Information Development*,12(2), pp. 113-116.

Hathaway, Helen (1999) Developments in information skills at Reading University, *Relay: The Journal of the University College and Research Group* , 48, pp 11-12.

Downing, Richard (1999) Mind the gap: developing teacher /librarian partnerships for learning, *Relay: The Journal of the University College and Research Group*, 48, pp 9-10

Unwin, Lorina; Stephens, Kate & Bolton, Neil (1998) *The Role of the Library in Distance Learning*, London: Bowker Saur.

UKOU (1997) *Library Unit Plan 1998-2002*, Milton Keynes: The Open University.

14

Information Resource Centre: Mainstream for the Flow of Information for Lifelong Learning

Muhammad Saadat Ali

Introduction

Distance education is a slogan, a form of teaching in new shape, a system that implies commitment to shared educational beliefs. "The most widely agreed beliefs are about opening up learning opportunities to a wider range of people and enabling them to learn more congenially and productively. This involves reducing barriers to access and giving learners more control over their own learning" (Rowntree, 1992:13). "Open learning is not just about access alone, it is also about providing people with a fair chance of success" (Holt & Bonnici, 1988, quoted in Rowntree, 1992:14).

Trained and qualified teaching staff

"Good education demand good teachers. Over the course of twentieth century, as the teaching profession has grown, so have its standard risen" (Perraton, 1995:1). In this context and keeping Bangladesh and other Third World countries in consideration, it can be stated that most teachers who are engaged in teaching in distance education are not sufficiently trained, even in conventional education. To run open learning and distance education effectively and to achieve the targeted goal, distance education deserves specially qualified and trained teachers. But unfortunately, the developing countries are to depend on the teachers of conventional education the maximum of whom are less qualified, and many of them do not have sufficient training on teaching in the concerned educational system. Under the distance-education programme, the planners, designers, and directors of the concerned courses stay in the headquarters. They do not teach learners directly. The reality is that the teachers who are engaged in tutorial centres, who take classes and participate in interactions with learners, who exchange ideas and views, are not even properly acquainted with the systems and desired aims and objectives of open learning and distance education. It is also true for most tutors and coordinators. So, effective result from their teaching and from their service cannot be expected. As there is no alternative in hand and the whole system and structures cannot be changed in a day, all are to be dependent on existing situations. Necessary steps are to be taken to employ selected high-caliber teachers and make sufficient scope to train them in the concerned system and field. In this process, though it will take time, it is expected that, in the long run, the whole system, the whole student community, and ultimately the nation will be benefited, and the open-learning system will achieve the desired goals.

Quality education

Virtually, not only in the open learning, the conventional system of education deserves optimum standard of education, and to achieve this goal, not quantity but quality education is to be ensured. Therefore, it is to be considered that to make the open learning system effective and to achieve the desired goals, quality and trained teachers are very much essential and inevitable. So, there is no alternative of taking long-term programme and plan to do so.

In 1969, when an open university was established in Britain, they had to take necessary steps for teachers' training to have effective result and to achieve the desired goal of their plan and programmes.

Communication media

The major attraction of distance teaching is the use of communication media technology for catering millions of students irrespective of location of residence. Taking opportunities of media communication, a university can meet educational needs of all types of students of a country, although there may be some practical constraints. Easy use of communication media and their faster speed help quick dissemination of desired information. "In its initial years broadcasting contributed only ten percent of a student's time, printed text being the main medium of instruction" (Chander, 1991:53). During the early days of the Open University of the UK, there was tremendous and widened use of "audio and video cassettes, video discs, cable and satellite TV, telephone and telex, and micro computers" (Chander, 1991:53) in addition to traditional TV and radio. In the UK, all citizens have access to radio and TV today.

Cost effectiveness of media communication

The cost of media production is coming down whereas the cost of print is going up. This means that even institutions with low budgets can hope to produce and distribute some non-broadcast audio-visual media. The new types of media give students greater control over the learning process and interaction. While students cannot interrupt broadcasting for purposes of revision and integration, they can do so with the new media.

Role of electronic media in dissemination of information

Broadcasting by TV and radio is a popular means of communication in open learning/ distance education because of their worldwide accessibility. Although some restrictions are there, telephone is an effective means of communication. It can be applied only in a society wherein most people own this facility. "Telephone helps reduce the sense of isolation a distance student may feel; it can make the contact with the tutor speedier avoiding problems of travel and terrain. Teleconferencing has developed as an effective means of interaction which can be exploited for educational purposes. It is a sort of simultaneous telephone calls arranged for communication between teacher and several students. ...but not suitable medium for lecturing or for courses in which visuals are necessary. It is suitable for limited groups and for specialist needs in education"

(Chander, 1991:55-56).

In the last few years, distance-teaching institutions in the industrialized world have set up telephone conferences to link students and have taught them through computer networks. In the developing world, the universities of the South Pacific and of the West Indies have used satellite communication to reach students across their scattered territories (Perraton, 1995:3).

Media in open learning

The role of media in open learning and distance education is vital in imparting information and dissemination of knowledge to a large number of students in the widened field and of different disciplines. Therefore, the use of communication technologies, especially in modern days, becomes the integral part of open learning and distance education. It is also a widely accepted and recognized truth that there is a significant positive relationship between the revolutionary advances in communication and information technologies and the phenomenal growth of distance education.

Internet for open learners

Computer-based education and training might have to create scope and allow learners to have open access to Internet, so that they can make them able to use Internet at any time and at any place especially during their leisure time. Without Internet and online facilities, learners will straightway be unable to keep close contact with their teachers, programmes, latest developments and happenings in the courses of their concern. So, for the following reasons, learners will have to be given scope of easy use of Internet :

- to strengthen their ability to work on course/lessons at their convenient time and place;
- to avail of online facilities either to download a course material or components to be worked on; and
- to acquaint themselves with the latest news, course design, instructions, other related programmes, etc.

Open learning in Bangladesh

For obvious reasons, the overall situation of Bangladesh Open University (BOU) cannot be compared with other universities of this kind in other countries. BOU is the first university of its kind in Bangladesh. The need for an open university in Bangladesh was felt long ago. The history of distance education in this country dates back to 1956, when the Education Directorate was assigned with the responsibility for distribution of 200 radio receivers to educational institutions. This led to the creation of an Audio-Visual Cell and later the Audio Visual Education Centre (AVEC) in 1962. In 1978-1980, a pilot project titled School Broadcasting Programme (SBP) was taken up. In 1983, the SBP and the erstwhile AVEC were merged, and the National Institute of Educational Media and Technology (NIEMT) was established and developed.

In 1985, Bangladesh Institute of Distance Education (BIDE) was established, and NIEMT was incorporated in BIDE. Apart from producing and supplying audiovisual materials to educational institutions, BIDE organized a Bachelor of Education (BE. d) course, using the distant-teaching mode for untrained secondary school teachers. As per the Bangladesh Open University Act,

1992, the Government has merged BIDE with the Bangladesh Open University (BOU, 1997:2-3). Bangladesh joined the world body of open learning/distance education in 1981.

After the emergence of Bangladesh, the very concept of distance education was first conceived in 1974 in the report of Kudrat-e-Khuda Education Commission. Its relevant section says, "With the present education system there should be ample scope for part-time, drop-out and irregular students, so that they can receive higher education. All the irregular students should have been given scope to sit for the examination, in this case, evening course can be started. To achieve this goal, an Open University can be started like that of U.K." (Kudrat-e-Khuda Education Commission, 1974:88)

The aim of launching the distance-education programme was "to expand all levels of education, knowledge and science by a diversity of means, including the use of technology. It intends to provide opportunities of education to all classes of people and create efficient manpower by improving the quality of education." (BOU, 1999:1). By this time, Bangladesh has achieved a literacy rate of 48.7% (*Bangladesh Statistical Yearbook* 1999:493).

The BOU organizes its educational programme through 12 Regional Resource Centres (RRCs), 80 Local Centres (LCs), and more than 800 Tutorial Centres (TCs). Each regional and local centre is equipped with a PC, but each regional centre has TV, VCP, VCR, etc. By this time ideas are matured and programmes are chalked out, so that the RRCs are equipped with related necessary items for allowing modern facilities of the networking system in the long run and that enrolled students can use the library and multimedia facilities of the regional centres, although the local centres are yet to be equipped.

Quality of any education largely depends on the facilities offered to students. Among other things, access to information and information resources are very much important. Although there are limited and controlled library facilities in the regional centres, these are not sufficiently organized and are not also networked. The course participants do not get access to the central library of BOU from their own environment or from the access centre, as there is no online facility here and for the same reason all the RRCs and LCs are out of reach. But the BOU has plans to facilitate access of course participants to information resources from its headquarters in Gazipur, about 30 km from the capital city. This programme could not be implemented mainly due to financial constraints. To facilitate and ensure an effective and appropriate online distance learning, online access to information and information resources is essentially needed.

Prospect of open learning in Bangladesh

Open learning/distance education (OL/DE) is widening rapidly throughout the world. The teaching methodology is quite different from that of conventional teaching and education. In the OL/DE system, the scope is wider, and an expert teacher can teach millions of students with the help of electronic media. In the OL/DE system, both learners and participants have better scope of learning, viz. modular guidebooks, audio-video tapes, television, radio, teleconferencing facilities, Internet, and also direct interactions from tutors in the tutorial centres. So, in developing countries, like Bangladesh, OL/DE has a great potential; it is, thus, very much prospective and lucrative. In Bangladesh, distance learners come from different spheres of life—towns and rural areas. In other words, learners belong to three different levels: (i) economically sound and employed, (ii) under-employed and aspires to be more educated and more skilled, and (iii) jobless and economically poor rural people.

Although the teaching system in the BOU is technology-based, it still has several limitations or constraints. Some examples are: the rural areas do not have the facilities of digital phones and computer-networking system. The distance learners are required to be dependent on the RRCs of BOU. The LCs of BOU are also not yet properly set up and equipped.

In the conventional system of education, teacher-student interactions take place in classrooms only. But in open learning/distance education, it is done through tutorial centres and other media. The RRCs are also termed as community centres/relay stations for distance learners. These centres can relay all the programmes to the LCs, and after transmitting the programmes from the main campus, the RRCs can receive and store them in the resource centre/e-library. The distance learners visit the RRCs during their leisure time and use these programmes as and when required.

In Bangladesh, the LCs of BOU are located mainly in the rural areas where cable television facilities, dish antenna, and digital phones are not available, and there is no scope to establish an e-library which is very much essential for an online-teaching. So is the truth for RRCs also, because the distance learners depend on printed media only. On the other side, the RRCs are situated far away from the rural areas where the LCs are located. It is cumbersome and difficult for rural jobless learners to visit the RRCs and avail of facilities from these centres. If all the LCs could be developed with e-library facilities, it would be very much helpful for the rural jobless and economically downtrodden distance learners.

- Total enrollment in all programmes (upto June 2000): 2,43,782.
- Total Students number of students passed: 49,882.
- This statistics received from Examination Division on 15-7-2001.

In open learning/distance education, the role of e-library is always positive. In this system, all books, guides, and modular lessons prepared by expert teachers are put into the memory of computer and website in the Internet. During leisure time, learners use computers and access their desired and related topics and lessons.

Establishment of e-library in Bangladesh for the learners under the distance-education programme will be very much fruitful. Initially, it may be expensive, but in the long run it will indeed be cost-effective and useful like anything. In the existing system, quality education is always not ensured. But in OL/DE, which is based on media technology, each learner can get uniform education.

Growth of population is a threat to any developing country like Bangladesh. To meet the demand and to ensure education of an increasing number of population, the Government has to manage the situation and chalk out appropriate plans. Hence, it would be an absurdity to think that more educational institutions will be set up to meet this need. Rather it would be wise and realistic if mode of education is changed, and then only within the limited scope and resources, maximum result can be achieved.

Open learning is the only mode of education to tackle such a situation, create sufficient scope for the deprived, offer facilities, and overcome all the arising problems. The number of population in Bangladesh is still growing in an alarming rate, and in this circumstance, OL/DE must be implemented to meet the need of the society, and also to meet the increasing demand in the 21st century. Under this mode of education, a less number of expert teachers are needed, and in the age of technological development, only one expert teacher is sufficient to teach a subject for disseminating the contents for thousand learners.

Table 14.1 Enrollment and the status of success students since the launching of the distance education programme in Bangladesh Open University

Name of Programmes	Students enrolled									Total enrolled upto June 2000	Total passed upto June 2000	Remarks
	1992	1993	1994	1995	1996	1997	1998	1999	2000			Course yet to be completed
M.Ed	-	-	-	-	-	-	-	1106	1312	2418		-
B.Ed	5075	6121	5571	5575	5443	4761	4804	3506	2593	43449	24990	Course yet to be completed
C.Ed	-	-	-	-	-	-	1812	2098	2039	5949		Course yet to be completed
H.S.C	-	-	-	-	-	-	-	12006	25694	37700		Result of 1999 batch yet to be published
S.S.C				16168	14111	15803	16427	25114	24107	111730	21524	
B.A / B.S.S	-	-	-	-	-	-	-	-	7352	7352		Course yet to be completed
CELP			3039	3007	1767	922	1117	787	435	11991	2358	-
CALP	-	-	-	-	601	228	158	98	118	1203	302	-
BELT	-	-	-	-	-	1073	607	345		2025		Course yet to be completed
B.Ag. Ed	-	-	-	-	-	1735	1079	646	522	3982	371	
CPFP	-	-	-	-	-	-		44	30	74	66	
CLP	-	-	-	-	-	-		59	44	103	94	
DYD	-	-	-	-	-	-		150		150	37	
GDM	-	-	-	1375	3518	3470	1705	1239	711	12018	31	
CIM			-	294	242	320	204	207	83	1350		
MBA	-	-	-	-	-	-	196			196		Course yet to be completed
DCSA	-	-	-	-	-	-	720	624	748	2092	109	
Total:										**243782**	**49882**	

Role of IRC in open learning

The aim of Information Resource Centre (IRC) is to provide information and cater services to all. Its one of the main objectives is to ensure services and make liaison with learners, knowledge seekers, and other potential clienteles with that of its own information-dissemination programme. But when the open learning or distance education is concerned, as because, it is for the drop-outs, women, housewives, jobless, less-privileged, physically handicapped, financially unsound, unemployed and under-employed people, career developers, unskilled workers. They will have to consider more and more to create better scope for dissemination of information, appropriate technology for proper utilization, and provide facilities, so that the IRCs can attract open learners easily than other conventional libraries. The IRCs are also to keep into consideration why people are moving from conventional to flexible learning. Taking all these reasons into consideration, the following are to be analysed:

- IRCs are to be the centres of knowledge and learning for proper education.
- They will have to ensure the availability of all sorts of informative materials required by the learners and appropriate knowledge seekers.
- IRCs are to be able to cater more flexibly for a wide variety of learner needs and expectations.
- Resource-based learning provides an easier basis to learn and earn knowledge. IRCs should ensure this type of facilities and services.
- Distance learners are considered to be irregular students, jobless people, or engaged in different professions, unemployed or under-employed people, rural people, women, less privileged, or financially unsound people. So, they should be given better scope and facilities and multiple choice of learning, and vis-a-vis significant help should be extended to them.

Keeping the BOU and its learners into consideration, it is essential that the traditional library system is converted to become an e-library system. For the last few years, the price of IT equipment has gone down. So, the developing countries, like Bangladesh, can smoothly go for the introduction of electronic and media technologies for OL/DE. Librarian or information resource manager should remember that their learners are mainly aged workers, service holders, women, housewives, physically handicapped people, and jobless urban and rural people. Sitting at home or at any suitable place, or in the working station if one can make linkage with the learning process, i.e. online system of learning, will greatly be benefited. In this process, learners will have access to the facilities, resource materials, lecture notes, suggestions of teachers, and other relevant materials. In this course of action, place and time are not at all barriers. In the online process, satellite-based television, CD-ROM, Internet, website, and multi-media facilities can be used. During leisure, students and learners will take advantage and opportunities to use different media for their linkage and learning. Therefore, for obvious reasons, distance learning is quickly becoming 'Internet learning' in the most popular form of non-traditional education delivery.

Librarians and the Internet in open learning

It is believed that the 21st century will be the age of electronics and media technology. By this time, this concept is widely recognized and accepted to the information seekers. Virtually, academic librarians are on the front lines of making new technologies accessible and useful to scholars, teachers, and students. But the pedagogical responsibility of a librarian is to ensure essential flow of information and relevant services to all information seekers, especially to students. In other words, computer and the Internet are recognized as useful tools—and only tools. If one can use them successfully, one can complete an assignment on the desired topic, gather knowledge on the desired subject, and develop skills on desired discipline.

It, however, obviously depends on how skillfully a librarian has designed his/her information management system, and on the other hand, the students or the concerned people do operate it. Thus, the use of computers and access to the Internet are always given importance in open learning and distance education.

"The implications for education and training are immense. Learning can be independent of time and place, and available at all stages of person's life. The learning context will be technologically rich. Learners will have access not only to a wide range of media, but also to a wide range of sources of education.

The challenge for educators is how to utilize this power, so that education and training meet the needs of individuals and society at large" (Bates, 1997:229).

Technology and open learning in the 21st century

Although it is the age of electronic media, print items still play a great role in the dissemination of information and also in distance teaching. The print items are the only items with which students and learners can interact repeatedly and conveniently within their available time. In the past days of open learning/distance education, all concerned had to depend on printed materials (books, modules, etc.) only. Later, one-way communication was introduced—radio and audio-cassettes were used as additional tools for education. With the technological advancement, two-way communication, i.e. telephone teaching and audio-graphics, computer-based learning and use of multimedia, computer-mediated communication, etc. gradually replaced the previous conventional and early systems and tools. In true sense, "developments in multimedia that give teachers and learners the tools to reconstruct and personalize knowledge, the development of computer-mediated communications, and the eventual integration of multimedia with electronic networks suggest the essential function of computers in education in moving away from the notion of the computer as substitute teacher toward that of a 'true' technology, a set of tools to be used by teachers and learners, to facilitate the task of learning and understanding" (Bates, 1997:227).

Conclusion

Although, with the facilities of the electronic age and modern communication technologies, most distance learners of urban area are heavily dependent on online services, the utility of the old print-based education and face-to-face tutoring cannot be denied. Despite this, online systems carry more learning advantage for students, and, therefore, are set to gradually replace the paper-based delivery of learning material and face-to-face tutorial to other old systems and services. It is true that the advantage of online education over print-based distance education lie in the following:

- Quick and loss less home-delivery of learning materials.
- Quick tutor feedback on assignments.
- Quick and much expanded and two-tier interactivity: student-student and tutor- student.
- Quick updating of learning materials.

- Quick acquaintance with latest information regarding open learning and distance education.
- An overall time saving learning system.

The key to the widening participation also depends on affordability. Reduction of tuition fees, extending helps for less-privileged groups, allowing interest-free loan to the poor, and extending financial supports to the students taking assistance schemes in hand are also important factors in open learning to be considered in the perspective of developing countries. The education policy of the Government of Bangladesh should, thus, focus each of the above characteristics, so that target groups could avail advantages of it.

All these also demand organization of efficient and effective electronic information resources centres to facilitate provision of the needed support and flow of information for lifelong learning by those who could not avail of normal education due to constraints beyond their control.

References

BOU (1999) *Bangladesh Open University at a Glance*. Dhaka.
BOU (1997) *Bangladesh Open University Project Proforma*, Dhaka.
Bates, A.W. (Tony). (1997) *Technology, Open Learning and Distance Education*, London: Routledge.
Chander, J. Jose (1991) *Management of Distance Education*. New Delhi : Sterling Publishers.
Perraton, Hilary (ed) (1995) *Distance Education for Teacher Training*. London : Routlege.
Report of Kudrat-e-Khuda Education Commission, 1974:88.
Rowntree, Derek. (1992) *Exploring Open and Distance Learning*, London : Kogan Page.

SECTION 4

OUTREACH LIBRARY SERVICES IN UK AND USA

15

Going the Distance: Solutions and Issues of Providing International Students with Library Services

Mou Chakraborty and Johanna Tuñón

Introduction

The issue of how to provide international students with quality library services is becoming more critical as an increasing number of international site - based programmes and online programmes are offered to students around the world.

This becomes even more challenging when one must deal with document delivery solutions for students overseas. Nova Southeastern University (NSU) provides library services to site-based classes for six graduate programmes in ten countries in Latin America and Europe and three doctoral programmes offering online degree programmes. It is necessary to identify the challenges faced by the Distance and Instructional Library Services (DILS) at NSU in supporting the library needs of graduate students doing scholarly research. Valuable insights into solutions are provided for supporting library services for graduate students that work and the challenges that still need to be addressed. The question of whether it is possible for libraries to ensure that international students who are in distance graduate programs can be provided with equal or equivalent library service solutions to those offered to on-campus students and distance students who live within the United States is examined. The solutions cover an array of topics and have been tried at the Nova Southeastern University: NSU tried developing formal library resource centers as "branch libraries." NSU negotiated formal library agreements with local academic libraries. The library has also explored a variety of arrangement with document delivery suppliers including host agreements with two major research institutions - Wayne State University and the University of Michigan - for document delivery of journal articles and the provision of document delivery services using the British Library. In addition, the main library, at the Library, Research and Information Technology Center (LRITC) sends materials from its own collection via courier services such as DHL to ensure faster turnaround time.

LRITC is exploring several technological solutions for providing online document delivery to students using Prospero and ILLiad. In the area of public services, the library provides students with access to subscription to more than two hundred online databases and students have remote access to numerous full text journal articles and electronic books. The library has experimented with providing students with help by answering questions synchronously and asynchronously. The library provides students with either online or site-based training in how to do online research and locate full-text resources. To provide Distance and Instructional Services, librarians travel extensively to different clusters in the United States as well as overseas for timely and effective bibliographic instruction. The library also provides international students with online tutorials and subject specific web pages for further assistance as well as an in-depth printed manual that is handed out to the students during the sessions. The problems raised by telecommunications infrastructures in both developing countries and Europe are also addressed. On a different note, issues created by offering international students instruction in a language other than English are discussed and the problems faced for rendering library services to these students are examined. Last but not the least, issues relating to the understanding of cultural and political factors are also addressed.

The library at Nova Southeastern University (NSU) has never fit the traditional image of an academic library. For thirty years, first the Einstein Library and more recently the LRITC has been supporting the needs of distance students at NSU. The library has pioneered the provision of document delivery, online access, reference, and bibliographic instruction for distance students. It strives to achieve the 'Guidelines' delineated by the ACRL (Association of College and Research Libraries) to provide the graduate students with equal or equivalent distance library services (See the Association of College and Research Libraries Guidelines for Distance Learning Library Services at http://www.ala.org/acrl/guides/distlrng.htm. There are challenges enough for providing library services to distance students within US but the problems are compounded if the students are geographically dispersed around the globe. This chapter considers the challenges and considerations experienced by the library on providing quality library services to the international students.

NSU has extensive experience with delivering graduate programs at international sites. NSU currently offers graduate site-based programs in the Bahamas, Brazil, Canada, China, Dominican Republic, France, Germany, Greece, Jamaica, Panama, and Venezuela and the university has plans to open new sites in Krakow, Poland, Eleuthera, an island in the Bahamas, and Mandeville in the central part of Jamaica during the first few months of 2002. NSU offers a variety of site-based masters and doctoral programs in business and education as well as online graduate degree programs in business, education, computer science, and social sciences, to the university's international students.

Document delivery

Distance learners depend largely on document delivery to fulfil their research needs. The traditional methods have been via mail, fax, courier service or getting the material from commercial vendors. With the dramatic technological advancements, document delivery has employed novel ways of storing, retrieving and transmitting information in the fastest possible way. However, the problem arises when one is faced with providing international students with document delivery services equivalent to services provided to distance students within the United States. At NSU, the library provides distance students with resources that meet students' research needs rather than negotiating contracts with local libraries where site-based classes are offered. In order to accomplish this goal, the library provides all distance students with free document delivery for up to 25 documents per week. These include free photocopying and mailing or faxing of journal articles as well as the mailing of books and free microfiche documents in the public domain.

Doctoral students are also provided with two free copies of non-NSU dissertations that cannot be obtained in a digital format.

Delivering library materials to distance students across international boundaries present special challenges. Postal delays and bottlenecks in customs cause major frustrations to students waiting for the materials. NSU uses DHL and FedEx to speed up the delivery of books overseas and provide the books with more security, but this solution is expensive. The other problem is that books obtained through interlibrary loan and document delivery services cannot be mailed to distance students.

In order to address this issue, NSU's main library explored using the British Library as a document delivery supplier for students for the European sites. The British Library has a very impressive department known as the Document Supply Centre (BLDSC) that provides a rapid document delivery service to individuals and organizations worldwide. (See http://www.bl.uk/services/bsds/dsc.) Because copyright fees are more expensive in the United States, NSU's library is exploring the possibility of getting document delivery for new sites in England, France, and Greece through local partnerships.

On a different note, the library has begun exploring new technologies for delivering research materials online that would be timely and less costly. Because of copyright considerations, the library rejected the idea of scanning documents and sending them to students as attachments. Instead, the library looked for technology solutions that permitted the library to scan documents but house the documents on the university's server to facilitate students to retrieve the documents from the NSU site. The library is currently using Prospero, a freeware program designed to complement ARIEL. Prospero delivers ARIEL documents to end-users by posting them on a Web server. Documents are scanned into PDF (Portable Document Format) files and uploaded to Web sites. The Prospero software generates email for participating students with the URL where the document resided and a PIN number for accessing the site. Students can access the document using Adobe Acrobat. Students in some countries, however, have problems obtaining printing cartridges at reasonable prices and prefer not to do their own printing. Other problems include the fact that Internet connect time can be very costly and unreliable for countries, and some students still lack the technology skills and equipment to access these documents. As a result, the library still provides traditional document delivery via mail or DHL to students who prefer this option.

A second solution has also begun being tested during the 2001/2002 academic year. ILLiad is an automated interlibrary loan resource sharing management software from OCLC that automates manual tasks performed by the inter - library loan staff with software modules that scans and posts documents for document delivery. As a member of the Southeast Florida Library Information Network (SEFLIN), the NSU Libraries was selected as one of the ILLiad testing sites, but at present, the software has not been yet installed and implemented. So the relative merits of the two software packages cannot be addressed now.

Access to online resources

Online databases provide a great solution for document delivery for international students. The main library provides NSU students with access to over 200 online databases. Students are able to access full-text online journal articles, dissertations, and reference resources including online encyclopedias. The problem with online databases is that the level of online coverage varies substantially between the various disciplines. Business students can find as much as 75 percent of what they need online, but students in the social sciences can only find about 25 - 30 percent of the indexed materials full text online.

Distance students express high level of satisfaction when they are instructed to the access and use of these full-text databases. On the other hand, some students are unaware of the availability of the full-text articles or are unwilling to print the documents themselves because of the cost and/or availability of printing cartridges as mentioned previously. The quality of Internet services available in a number of countries can also present problems when telecommunication systems are not reliable or fast enough.

Formal agreements with local libraries

Formal agreements with local libraries have been a traditional solution for providing library services to students at distance sites and NSU has certainly explored this option. The library has negotiated with a number of formal library agreements with local academic libraries in Panama, Jamaica, the Bahamas, Venezuela, the Dominican Republic, France, and Greece with less than satisfactory results. The libraries at local sites in developing countries are inadequate by U.S. standards, and many of the libraries have library collections that do not support NSU's academic programs. Some local libraries also demand exorbitant fees for formal agreements. More often, however, most academic institutions see NSU as competitors and are not willing to negotiate library agreements.

Building local research resources

NSU tried starting branch libraries in Panama, Jamaica, and the Bahamas. The library set up research rooms, hired professional librarians, and arranged for a budget of approximately $40,000 per site for print resources. These branch libraries were not "silver bullets" that solved library access problems. Business students were less and less interested in print resources when they could access an increasing number of full text resources online. The other problem was that local research rooms were not a workable solution for online students around the world.

Reference and bibliographic instruction services

Students who cannot walk into the bricks and mortar library in Fort Lauderdale, Florida, must also be provided with reference services and library training. NSU provides email reference to international students, but this asynchronous service has its drawbacks. The Reference Desk is staffed 13 hours a day. What this often means, however, is that students in Europe, Asia, and Africa often have to wait for responses to their queries until the following day.

NSU provides excellent bibliographic instructional services for the distance students. Because NSU delivers distance education in a variety of formats and a variety of different program designs, no one solution has worked for the whole university. As a result, there have been a number of solutions: MBA students, for example, get training via online tutorials that are integrated into the curriculum (Tuñón, 1999). Several doctoral programs including students in the Doctorate of Business Administration, the Humanities and Social Sciences, and Computer and Information Sciences come to campus for orientation at beginning of their programs. Still other programs that have students meet at sites, librarians have to go to the sites to provide the training. If the students meet at sites and there is no opportunity to provide training on campus, librarians are sent to the sites even if this entails international travel. As a result, librarians have travelled to Greece, France, Sweden, Panama, Jamaica, the Bahamas, Venezuela, Puerto Rico, and the Dominican Republic to provide library training.

However, the bigger challenge is how to provide library training to international students who take classes online and do not meet at specific sites. If the students receive their instruction in some type of online or asynchronous format, the library provides the training using those technologies (Pival & Tuñón, 2000). The European Consortium of Independent Schools (ECIS) program is a good case in point. This online program for European educators who provide English-based education in Europe is starting in April 2002. The students will not meet as a group until the end of the program. As a result, the library is collaborating with the program administrators to develop online library materials and activities that will be integrated into the first two semesters of the course.

Providing library services in the languages of instruction

A number of academic institutions are beginning to offer distance programs in other languages, but they are not always attempting to provide students with reference, bibliographic instruction or document delivery in the languages of instruction ("Distance learning abroad", 2000). Fortunately for the library, NSU requires that students can read English so that the library can use materials written in English to support students' research. On several occasions, the library contracted with librarians to provide the bibliographic instruction in Spanish or Portuguese. As more institutions begin offering instruction in other languages, libraries will have to find ways to better support these new student groups.

Cultural and political sensibilities

There are discrepancies in the practice and application of library services to distance learners. Slade and Kascus (1998) identify four models of library services to distance students: (1) online collections and resources at the remote sites, (2) cooperative agreement and resource sharing among libraries, (3) document delivery from the parent institution and (4) remote access to online resources. These models are not mutually exclusive and many institutions, like NSU, have adopted a combination of the different models.

It is not unusual that students around globe perceive libraries and library services differently. Computers, online databases, easy access to the materials are some of the services that the students in the US and other western countries take it for granted. Language and differing cultural experiences often pose problems as well. International students enrolled in an online course from a foreign university realize that the library procedures, resources, and systems differ from what they are familiar with in their native country. Moreover, the educational systems of other countries may view the role of the library differently. Students in some countries do not always have extensive experience doing library research to write research papers or locate information in traditional print formats, much less online. Even international students who have taken online classes from a number of institutions have often experienced very limited library support services. It is not because the libraries at the institutions are unaware of or unwilling to provide the services, but more so because of the political and the socio-economic infrastructure. As a result, students do not always fully comprehend how libraries and online resources can help them.

The student perceptions present problems. In some parts of the world, in previous years, distance education was viewed as a remedial education for students to obtain a degree when it was not otherwise possible in a regular educational system. However, this notion is changing rapidly and the dramatic advancement of technology has made distance education a viable and a popular alternative. The students enrolled in distance courses are often older and may feel left out in some sense being away from a physical campus. They often lack the self-confidence to approach the librarian and use the library effectively. This is a significant problem for even traditional libraries, but the problem is compounded when the students' library happens to be located in another country. The problem escalates when trying to communicate and reassure students who are uncomfortable with the library and using library services when there are language and cultural barriers as well.

In order to address these issues, NSU has employed or contracted bilingual librarians when possible. The library, for example, has sent Spanish-speaking librarians to do the library training sessions in Venezuela, Panama, and the Dominican Republic. The library was prepared to contract to send a Portuguese-speaking librarian to Brazil, as well, but the site never got started. It is true that one-shot training sessions in Spanish or Portuguese are not enough to overcome all student fears and apprehensions, but it can go a long way in mitigating some of these problems.

Conclusions

The goal of providing international students with the same kinds of library services as those offered to distance students is a laudable goal that all libraries should work toward, but the harsh reality is that it is a goal that is not easily attained in spite of the fact that online journal articles, e-books, and other resources have made the jobs of libraries much easier. If libraries believe that all students on or off campus, in the United States and abroad, are entitled to equal or equivalent access to library resources and services, however, than there is much more work that needs to be done to improve the level of these resources and services for international students especially, in the instructional arena. Technological advances have made synchronous and asynchronous teaching a viable option but as far as the quality is concerned, from the student feedback that we receive, much is to be desired. If libraries are to truly "go the distance" for their international students, new avenues will continuously need to be explored to find better solutions for document delivery, reference services, and bibliographic instruction for the students who live abroad.

References

Association of College and Research Libraries. (2001). Association of College and Research Libraries guidelines for distance learning library services. Retrieved November 27, 2001, from the American Library Association Web site: http://www.ala.org/acrl/guides/distlrng.html

Distance learning abroad: Challenges and solutions to D.L. library services to foreign countries. (2000, July 9). Panel discussion for LITA Distance Learning Interest Group, International Relations Committee, American Library Association Annual Conference, Chicago.

Pival, P. & Tuñón, J. (2000). Innovative methods for providing instruction to distance students using technology. In P. S. Thomas (Compiler) *The Ninth Off-Campus Library Services Conference Proceedings* (pp. 221-230). Mount Pleasant, MI: Central Michigan University Press.

Tuñón, J. (1999, June 7). Asynchronous/distance instruction: A case study of the MBA at NSU. Special Library Association Conference in Minneapolis, MN, on June 7, 1999.

Slade, A. & Kascus, M. (1998). An international comparison of library services for distance learning. In P. S. Thomas & M. Jones (Comps.) ***The Eighth Off-Campus Library Services Conference Proceedings***, Providence, RI, April 22-24, 1998 (pp. 280-281). Mount Pleasant, MI: Central Michigan University

16

International Centre for Distance Learning (ICDL) and Services to Distance Learners

Nazira Ismail-Kaye

Introduction

The International Centre for Distance Learning (ICDL) is an international centre for research, teaching, consultancy, information and publishing activities based in the UK Open University's Institute of Educational Technology (IET). It received world class rating in the 1992 and 1996 from Higher Education Funding Council for England (HEFCE) Research Assessment Exercises. ICDL promotes international research and collaboration by providing information from its library and databases. An essential knowledge resource built up over 15 years is its distance education library and databases.

ICDL has in the past received funding from the United Nations University and from 1989 to 1997 it was funded by the Overseas Development Administration (now known as Department for International Development) of the UK government to provide an information service to the Commonwealth of Learning. At present, it is partly funded through external projects and partly by the UK Open University.

Databases

ICDL databases are accessible over the World Wide Web free of charge (http://icdl.open.ac.uk). The three databases consist of:

- Providers/institutions offering distance learning programmes around the world. This includes a brief description of the institution including the full address, a list of the courses it offers and admission details.
- Details of information on distance learning courses in the UK. Information includes a brief description of the course, entry requirements, duration of the course, methods of assessment, key media of learning and language of instruction.
- Bibliographic references, including abstracts, to the literature of distance education. These include books, journals, journal articles, conference proceedings, research reports, and many other documents relating to open and distance learning around the world.

The databases can be browsed using the ICDL subject classification list or can be searched using a keyword, author or title.

In addition, the web site also provides information on distance education associations/councils, forthcoming events, journals, both online and print, and projects in which ICDL is involved.

Requests from organisations and individuals

Various kinds and types of requests are received from organisations and individuals. The most predominant of these are individuals requesting information on courses they wish to study. Regrettably, we are not in a position to deal with individual enquiries because we do not have the necessary human and financial resources to cope with the several hundred enquiries we receive; instead we ask them to conduct their own searches using the database. However, we occasionally conduct searches for those who do not have online access and results are mailed to them.

We also receive enquiries from researchers and postgraduate students from other institutions and organisations who have accessed the database and request for publications. Wherever possible we try and provide photocopies of articles, conference papers, book chapters protecting copyright law. ICDL being a self-financing unit, we get filled Photocopy Declaration Form and collect charges for providing photocopy services.

Requests from organisations are normally handled on a contractual basis. ICDL is actively engaged in internal, national and international research. Current projects include:

- The Marchmont Project (http://www.marchmont.ac.uk) - An ADAPT-funded project working in collaboration with the University of Exeter and Knowledge Media Institute, Open University. The website includes facilities for information capture, search, retrieve, view, interaction, debate and idea sharing as well as modelling and intelligent knowledge extraction.
- Hobsons Publishing plc (http://www.hobsons.co.uk) - in collaboration we have produced Distance and Supported Open Learning in UK - printed information on distance learning to those who can not have access to WWW.
- World Bank Group (http://www1.worldbank.org/disted/) - This website provides a coherent and comprehensive guide to distance education. Phase 1 of this project was completed in 1999 and Phase 2 began in 2001. It is being coordinated by the Commonwealth of Learning and apart from ICDL, the other partners are Centre for Research in Distance and Adult Learning (CRIDAL), Open University of Hong Kong; Indonesian Distance Learning Network; Universidad Estatal a Distancia, Costa Rica; and the South African Institute for Distance Education (SAIDE). The purpose of Phase 2 is to revise and extend the online database – an authoritative source containing 400 selected and edited items on all aspects of setting up and running distance education programmes, It is intended to be a resource for policymakers, practitioners and participants in World Bank projects. During Phase 2, plans will be developed for extending the network of regional partners and achieving a sustainable future.

Services to distance learners

Since 1997 the Open University has been offering a Master of Arts in Open and Distance Education through its Institute of Educational Technology. All courses for the MA Programme are offered online using the World Wide Web and interaction is through the First Class conferencing system. The MA Programme is available to students residing anywhere in the world with the exception of Australia.

Because of its unique collection of documents on open and distance education, ICDL is ideally placed to provide a service to the students of the MA Programme. To this end, an online conference called 'Ask ICDL' within the First Class environment has been set up for participants to share and exchange information on open and distance education, for example, details of new publications, conferences, web sites with information relevant to open and distance education (ODE). If they have any general questions about ODE or if they require information on a particular aspect of ODE, for example, use of a particular technology in ODE or in a particular discipline, a message is posted in this conference and ICDL tries to help by pointing to relevant resources. Through 'Ask ICDL' students can request for photocopies of ten articles and/or book chapters a year for each course from the ICDL Library. The advantage of setting up this conference is that it provides quick – response to queries that are generally handled within 24 hours but more importantly, other students of the MA Programme, irrespective of which course of the MA they are studying, can also respond to queries if they know the answer. In that respect, interaction in 'Ask ICDL' is not just between student and ICDL but also between students. Equally, students also keep ICDL informed of any information they have come across that ICDL is not aware of. So the sharing of information occurs among all the parties involved.

We try to deal with requests for photocopies of documents on a first come first served basis. However, requests from students residing abroad get dealt with first because it takes longer time for documents to reach their destination through the postal system. Students, residing abroad, therefore, need to forward plan and wait for some time to receive the documents.

In addition, to the ICDL database and 'Ask ICDL' we have also developed a database of selected online resources called 'H80X Resources'. This database has information which can be accessed online, and which is relevant for the courses of the MA Programme, for example, listservs/ discussion lists, web sites with resources on distance education, online databases other than ICDL, online journals, conference papers/proceedings, book chapters and so on. We limit the number of items in this database to around 500 and these are constantly scanned to remove old items and add new ones. The database can be browsed using keywords or searched using free text search.

For ICDL, this is a unique experience as this has been the first time that ICDL has directly been involved in courses and with students. On a final note and as an example of student's appreciation of the service provided, I attach an email message received from a student of the MA Programme.

10 September 2001 15:11:57

From: Cathleen Gibson

Subject: Re(2): Request for input

To: Nazira Ismail-Kaye

Nazira ...let me hopefully add some more joy by thanking you very, very much for taking the time to provide these insights. It is extremely relevant and helpful to my EC project. I am using a real case study that is considering cmc integration for faculty development. I was able to attend some of their faculty development training workshops. The best presentation was by the Health Science Librarian who is directly involved in the informaticscomponent of the programme curriculum. I had the pleasure of interviewing her afterwards for my project. I was sharing with her how information management skills are integrated in the H80* courses and the value of your services re the H80* resources/Ask ICDL conference. At some point would you mind if I shared your e-mail response with her?

I think programmes are beginning to see the value of integrating library services more into courses. Lucky for us the OU is one of the champions.

Thanks again for your professional insights - continued success in your role.

Cheers,

Cathleen

17

Open University – Open Libr@ry: How the Open University Library in the UK Supports its Students

Gill Needham

The UK Open University

The Open University is the largest distance teaching university in the United Kingdom. It has been in existence for more than 30 years and currently has 185,000 registered students (both undergraduate and postgraduate). Since its establishment in 1969 around 250,000 students have graduated. The University's main headquarters are at Milton Keynes, about 80 kilometres north of London and the thirteen regional centres are situated in key locations throughout the UK.

The university offers more than 200 courses through its 9 faculties. The courses are developed by multi-disciplinary course teams. The delivery method is 'supported open learning' which means that the majority of students study alone in their own home but with support from a tutor. The university employs 7,000 part time lecturers as tutors. They provide telephone and email support, mark assignments and run optional face to face tutorials using more than 300 study centres as venues. A typical OU course is delivered through various media. Students receive printed and audio visual materials sent by post that may be accompanied by TV and radio broadcasts. Increasingly courses now have an on-line component, with some courses delivered entirely on-line. They are extremely popular. A first level course entitled 'You, Your Computer and the Net' delivered entirely on-line attracted 15,000 students last year. More than 80,000 students now study on-line.

The University has used the First Class conferencing system to create a virtual university community – not only for teaching and learning but also to provide virtual common rooms, bars, cafés and student societies, all moderated by the Open University Students Association.

The Open University library

One of the underlying principles of the Open University since its inception has been equity of access for all students. There are no entry requirements and students should be able to study in any location. Until recently this meant that the majority of courses were designed to be self contained. Students were not required to read anything more than the course materials supplied and in some cases one textbook they were expected to purchase. They did not therefore need to visit libraries to support their studies. The role of the Library on the Milton Keynes campus therefore, was primarily to support the 1,000 academics in their course development and their research and to provide services to the 500 full time research students, but not to support Open University students. Where some of the smaller postgraduate courses did require students to carry out library research, the subject specialists in the OU Library would provide guides for using libraries and databases to be included in course materials. It was hoped that students would be able to use the library facilities of universities in their local area. In the 1990s a number of significant changes took place. Higher Education policy in the UK began to emphasise 'skills for lifelong learning'. It would no longer be deemed acceptable for students to graduate without having learned to use libraries and other information sources. At the same time students themselves began to recognize that using libraries is an important part of 'being a student'. The most important factor, however, has been the opportunity offered by technology and, in particular, a steep increase in the proportion of OU students having access to the Internet.

Against this backdrop, in 1995/6 a new Director of Library Services was appointed. She was given a new remit – to develop a library service to support OU students directly. Planning a service from scratch for so large a user group was a considerable challenge. The service would have to depend largely on the use of network technology. The Library, because of its unusual role and history, had little experience in this area. A major culture change was required.

Funding was obtained from the University to appoint a new group of staff – a learner support team – to develop and provide the services to students. Four staff were appointed initially in 1997, followed by a post of Learner Support Coordinator whose role was to develop an overall strategy.

The learner support strategy

The number of potential users and their geographical distribution meant that the new service would have to depend heavily on the creative use of technology. The first task however was to carry out a systematic investigation of user needs. Very little was known about the information needs and expectations of Open University students.

The Students and Libraries Project (Bremner, 2000) was a Delphi survey which aimed to discover the information needs of OU students. In 1999, 1,500 students were surveyed from all courses, at all levels. The first finding of the survey was that far more students were using resources not provided by OU course materials than had been expected. Three fifths of both undergraduates and postgraduates were using other information gathered from various sources including bookshops, public and academic libraries, the Internet, television, and newspapers and magazines they bought themselves.

When asked about the type of information they had used OU students indicated that books were the items most frequently used, followed by newspaper articles, encyclopaedias, Internet (Web) sites and journal articles. Internet sites were being consulted far more frequently than traditional sources of academic research material, such as journal articles.

Over half of the students who had used other information were obtaining it via public libraries and a third of the students in the survey overall had used the public library to obtain materials, or as a quiet place to study. Only 15 percent of OU students had used academic libraries, partly because they were unaware that the majority of UK academic libraries can be used for reference purposes by students at other institutions.

The survey also showed that over half of the students in the sample had access to the Internet at home. Finally, the students were asked in the survey to suggest ten services they would particularly appreciate. This generated a "top twenty" of information services that OU students most required. Two thirds of students wanted online access to the OU Library, and over 60 percent wanted lists of relevant web sites for each OU course. This was followed by requests for lists of libraries open to OU students and postal loan of books and articles from the OU Library.

The results of this survey, together with the experience of offering some pilot electronic services to small postgraduate courses and evaluating their use helped to inform the development of a five year Learner Support Strategy. This Strategy was important in providing a framework for the development of the new service. The Strategy's primary objectives were as follows:

- To investigate OU students' needs.
- To help students access local library resources.
- To provide access to relevant content.
- To help students to develop skills.
- To provide support and guidance to students.

Objective 1: To investigate OU students' needs

The Students and Libraries survey reported above is now repeated every two years. This will enable the Library to monitor the impact of developing services and to keep in touch with trends and changing requirements. Opportunities are also taken wherever possible to obtain feedback from students about current services – these include feedback forms on the web, focus groups at student events and the inclusion of questions about library use in regular OU student surveys.

Objective 2: To help students access local library resources

Although every effort is made to provide all possible services electronically, it is recognised that some students will need to use a 'physical' library. To this end the Learner Support team have set up and maintain a database of academic libraries in the UK detailing the access and levels of service they will offer to OU students living in the area. The information is updated twice a year. Students can search at their town library or a specific library or they can select a region on a clickable map. They will find information about services and costs and also links to the web sites of the individual libraries. Information about public libraries and national libraries is also provided and work is in hand to see how this might be integrated with the database of academic libraries.

Objective 3: To provide access to relevant content

The Library has developed Open Libr@ry – an extensive electronic library tailored to the needs of OU students. Open Libr@ry is essentially a gateway to a vast amount of web-based information (some subscription-based, some freely available) selected to meet the needs of the range of courses provided by the OU. Selection of relevant material is facilitated by the role of the Library's subject specialist teams. These teams work closely with the course teams in their faculties to provide advice and support and to ensure that resources and services are appropriate to the needs of their students. The content of Open Libr@ry includes:

- 5,000 full text electronic journals
- 75 bibliographic databases
- Newspaper indexes
- Reference materials
- ROUTES (Resources for Open University Teachers and Students) – a database of web resources selected for specific OU courses by the Library's subject specialists together with the academic course teams.
- Information about libraries (including the Access to Libraries database described above).

A new project is underway to personalize the Open Libr@ry website as 'My Open Libr@ry' so that individual users will have their own personal library space where they can tailor the menu of resources to reflect their needs and interests. The project will also investigate the possibility of users storing their references in this personal library space and receiving tailored current awareness messages.

Objective 4: To help students to develop skills

Many OU students have not had the opportunity to develop skills in information literacy. The UK government higher education policy places considerable emphasis on students' developing transferable skills, and information literacy is an important set of skills for lifelong learning. The OU Library has a programme of work to help students develop these skills and has recently set up an Information Literacy Unit within the Library. The programme can be summarised as follows:

Working to embed information literacy into all OU courses

It is recognised that the most effective way of improving information literacy is to embed the skills across the curriculum. The Library's subject specialists and Learner Support librarians advise course teams on including activities in their courses which require students to develop and use information skills. In some cases they will write the materials and activities on behalf of the course teams. For postgraduate courses, library staff have written detailed 'Guides to finding and using information' – some are printed, others web-based.

Face to face training programme

While it is not feasible to offer face to face training for OU students, it is important that academic staff are kept up to date with information services and resources. Library staff run a regular programme of information literacy training sessions at the Library for people working on the campus in Milton Keynes and also at the regional centres.

SAFARI

SAFARI stands for Skills in Accessing, Finding and Reviewing Information. It is a web-based interactive tutorial being developed by Library staff for OU students. It is hoped that it will supersede written 'Guides to Information' which become out of date very quickly. SAFARI is a generic tutorial which should be relevant to students on any course – it has subject specific content also. It consists of seven sections as follows:

- Understanding information (a general introduction)
- Unpicking information (how information is generated, and how it is categorised)
- Planning a search for information (search strategy, choosing sources)
- Carrying out a search for information (use of library catalogues, bibliographic databases and the World Wide Web)
- Evaluating information (what is information quality? How to appraise information)
- Organising and presenting information (filing systems, personal bibliographic software, 'bookmarks', citations, references and bibliographies)
- Sharing information and keeping up to date (conferences and discussion lists, current awareness).

Students may work through SAFARI from beginning to end, or pick out sections relevant to their needs. Although it will be freely available on the World Wide Web to any user, OU students will be able to log in so that their responses will be saved and can be retrieved at any time. A number of OU courses are planning to link into sections of SAFARI at relevant points, thus embedding the skills in context. SAFARI has been developed by librarians with academic staff acting as critical readers. Current OU students have developmentally tested the material and reactions have been generally favourable. It should be available on the Web before the end of the year.

Information literacy assessment

Library staff have been working with the University's Key Skills Project. The Key Skills Project aims to help students develop their key skills and have these acknowledged. Assessment units have been produced for Information Technology, Communications, 'Improving own Learning' and now Information Literacy. These are like courses but are content free – the idea being that students who feel that they have developed these skills during their study can submit evidence in the form of specially designed assignments, have these assessed and then receive appropriate accreditation.

A new short course in Information Literacy

The most recent project undertaken by the Library's Information Literacy Unit is the development of a stand-alone, web-based short course. The title of the course is 'Making sense of information in the connected age'. This course is being developed with support from the OU's Faculty of Education and Language Studies. It will be a first level course (first year undergraduate) and will involve around 100 study hours to complete. Like SAFARI it will be delivered entirely on-line, but will also include readings and assessment. The course will be offered twice a year. The duration of the course is 12 weeks. By the end of 2003 more than 1000 students are expected to be enrolled. The course team is working closely with a national task force on Information Literacy set up by the Standing Conference of National and University Librarians (SCONUL).

Objective 5: To provide support and guidance to students

The Library now employs 10 Learner Support staff (5 professional librarians and 5 assistants) who provide a helpdesk for enquiries from students. Students can contact them by telephone, letter, email, web form or First Class conferencing. They help students to access the resources provided via Open Libr@ry, deal with problems and advise on all aspects of finding and using information. The Learner Support staff are attached to subject teams, so students can choose to contact a named member of the team supporting their Faculty. They also have the back-up of the subject specialist librarians who can deal with particularly complex specialised enquiries.

An analysis of the email enquiries received by the Learner Support team in 1999 showed that 50 percent were sent by students 'out of hours'. This is not surprising as 70 percent of OU students are in full time employment so they study in the evenings and at weekends. It means that, unfortunately for the students, they may wait from Friday evening to Monday morning for a response and they are unable to get help with even the simplest of enquiries when it is most required. A pressing need was therefore identified for some kind of 24 hour service. There appeared to be three possible approaches to this:

- *A 24x7 or 24 hour staffed helpdesk*: This would be prohibitively expensive and not cost effective.
- *A shared service with libraries in other time zones*: This appeared initially attractive but too many of the enquiries received are specific to the resources and services of the Open Libr@ry for it to be effective.
- *An automated solution*: Since more than half of enquiries received are 'routine' or 'repeated' and even more are questions which could be answered by information which isreadily available on the Open Lib@ry site, it seemed that this could be a possibility. It would not be conceivable for such a system to deal with all enquiries out of hours, but it could help considerably by answering the straightforward ones.

To this end, funding was obtained from the University for an 18 month research project – OPAL (Online Personal Academic Librarian) which aims to investigate and experiment with technical solutions to providing an automated service. The Library is working with the OU's Knowledge Media Institute and with two partner institutions – University of Leicester and Birkbeck College. At the time of writing the project team have developed an Operational Requirement (informed by a focus group of librarians from libraries around the UK), carried out an extensive review of technical solutions and similar projects worldwide and run an experiment with 60 OU students to investigate user perceptions of different forms of enquiry system. Work is in progress to develop a prototype OPAL system using a content management system called Zope and this will be tested on OU students and students in the two partner institutions.

Two smaller but related projects are planned for 2001/2. Like OPAL these are both intended to improve the interface between Open Libr@ry and its users. The first project is to develop a virtual induction tour of Open Libr@ry. This should parallel the library induction session provided to all new students attending a campus university. The second project will experiment with the use of 'chat' software to support students who might need help while they are using the Open Libr@ry web site. They will be offered the option (within Library opening hours only) of chatting on-line with a member of the Learner Support team. The project will evaluate the acceptability of this approach to students and the impact it has on the service as a whole.

Conclusion

The task of developing a library service for OU students has been a challenging one. The service is still in its infancy but considerable progress has been made in three years. The organizational and cultural implications of this development should not be forgotten. The encouragement of students to use resources outside their course materials was initially threatening to many academics. There was considerable, initial resistance to the development of electronic library services on the grounds of 'equity of access', although this argument has diminished with increasing Internet access in students' homes, workplaces and public libraries. Library staff have, from necessity, developed considerable skills in negotiation and change management. The new role has also changed the Library itself beyond recognition. A staff of 35 in 1996 had grown to 85 in 2001 and at present there are 90 staff. Longer-serving staff have had to adjust to an unprecedented rate of change. The staffing structure has been strained by the speed of development and is about to be replaced by one more appropriate to the Library's current business.

It is difficult to predict the extent to which demand from students will develop in the future. The majority of courses (particularly at 1st and 2nd levels) still do not require them to be on-line or to use library resources but this is expected to change. The University's Learning and Teaching Strategy has instructed all courses to include an on-line element by 2003. Library staff are working now with course teams to embed information literacy into courses which will start in 2003 and 2004. It is hoped that the developments described in this paper will mean that the Library will be more than ready to meet any level of demand.

Reference

Bremner, A. (2000) Open University Students and Libraries Project 1999. *Library and Information Research News*, 24(76), p.26-38.

APPENDIX

Indian Library Association

(Sectional Committee on Distance Education)

Guidelines for Library Services to Distance Learners

(Approved by the Council of Indian Library Association on its meeting held on 28th July, 2001)

Introduction

Distance Education has become very popular in the Indian sub-continent. At present there are nine state open universities, one national Open University, and about sixty-four Correspondence Course Institutes/Distance Education Directorates operating in regular universities of the country. The range of courses/programmes on offer varies from academic to professional and vocational to technical in nature. All disciplines including science, technology, agriculture, medicine, nursing etc. have distance education programmes. The learners are also heterogeneous as the diversity of the programmes on offer. More and more individuals are joining these programmes, as distance learning provides flexibility in terms of time, place and pace of learning. In other words, it facilitates learning while earning. Mostly the learners receive packets of printed learning materials presumably self sufficient in nature for self study and learn. These learning materials, though many a times designed very carefully by a team of experts in the field/subject, can't be termed sufficient for effective learning equitable to face-to-face teaching and learning. In face-to-face teaching and learning systems, the learners after having attended the classroom teaching undergo a variety of learning tasks including consultation and use of library materials. In distance education, the print materials have just replaced the classroom teacher allowing the learners to be independent self-learners. Therefore, for a complete learning experience, the distance learners need to make use of resources other than printed materials provided by the educational institution. The situation calls for a critical reflection on the place of library in distance education. Various scholars have emphasized that:

- The library has a prominent role to play in facilitating learning.
- Libraries in Open and Distance Learning Institutions have hierarchical systems: Central library at the Headquarters and Regional and /or Study center libraries at the grass-root level.
- There are different formats of resources available for the use of the learners.
- Users need material, facilities and information services.
- All kinds of libraries, public, academic and special, have to make combined efforts to meet the diverse requirements of the widespread learners.

- The use of modern technology has a special role in providing effective library services.

In order for effective use of library resources and development of information literacy skills to play a significant role in student learning, distance education programme designers must consider and give special place to library services at the course/programme design stage itself. Therefore, the "Guidelines" call for a paradigm shift in provision of course materials as "sufficient" to "basic minimum" for distance learning.

Mission

To ensure the provision of equitable library services to distance learners by assisting in the development and improvement of library services for new and existing distance learning programmes.

Scope

The guidelines are generic in nature and are applicable to Open Universities, Correspondence Course Institutes/Distance Education Directorates, Open Schools, and other Private Distance Education Providers using print, multimedia, teleconference, and web-based or any other course delivery methods. These are applicable to all credit and non-credit based certificate, diploma, degree, post-graduate degree, postgraduate diploma, and research degree programmes.

Target groups

The guidelines are aimed at administrators of distance learning providers, distance learning programme coordinators/managers, library professionals in charge of managing distance learning services and other support staff responsible for effective implementation of the distance learning programme. As a secondary target group, the guidelines may also benefit various accreditation bodies in the country.

Definitions

Chief Professional Librarian: A professionally qualified librarian, who has been designated by the Distance Education Provider to look after the library system.
Distance Learners: Students enrolled in a distance learning programme.
Distance Learning Programme Coordinator: An academic in charge of conceptualization, organization, preparation and delivery of a distance learning programme.
Distance Learning Provider: The organization usually responsible for offering and funding courses and programmes through distance mode.
Professionally Qualified Librarian: A person holding at least a Bachelor's degree in Library and Information Science from a recognized institution.

1. Philosophy

1.1 Access to library resources is essential for quality education regardless of where the learner and programmes are located.

1.2 All registered distance learners and course tutors are entitled to library services equitable to those provided for learners in face-to-face educational institutions.

1.3 With distance learners being disadvantaged in terms of library access, special services need to be designed for them. In other words, traditional library service designed for on-campus users will not meet the requirements of distance learners.

1.4 Effective library support requires advance planning by the distance learning programme coordinator in consultation with the library professionals of the institutions. In other words, the programme/course design committees should have at least one library professional.

1.5 Since resources are scarce, partnerships, networking, and resource sharing are essential ingredients of effective library resources for distance learners. For this the distance education provider may use MOU with local institutions and/or technology based networking systems.

1.6 It is for the Library and Information Science professionals to create awareness and demand for library and information services in the distance learning mode.

2. Management

2.1 The head of the distance education provider should ensure through a designated Chief Professional Librarian, the adherence of national and international standards in library services, and provide for appropriate fund, staff, and other resources as may be required.

2.2 The Chief Professional librarian should demonstrate leadership in developing relationships and methodologies (including partnerships, networking and access to remote databases) to address the library needs of the institution's distance learning programmes.

2.3 The distance learners being geographically dispersed, access structures of the libraries should be in accordance with the institutional support structure (e.g. IGNOU has a three tier structure with Headquarters at New Delhi, Regional Centres, and Study Centres across the country).

2.4 The library services should be planned and monitored by a Library Committee in the institution. The Committee should include amongst other members, representative of partner institutions, regional and local libraries, and learners.

2.5 The Chief Professional Librarian should prepare all such reports required for decision-making by the Library Committee.

3. Finance

3.1 The distance learning provider should make available adequate funding to ensure that its distance learners receive quality library services.

3.2 The library budget should take into consideration the following factors:

- The number of programmes on offer;
- The size of the distance learning programmes in terms of number of learners and access centers activated for the programme;
- The type and number of library service planned for the programme.

3.3 Funding for library services should generally come from the institute's operating budget. However, specific library services may be offered as fee-based services. In addition, a specific percentage of student fee collected should be given to the library budget. As such there should be three major sources of finance for the libraries as suggested under:

(i) 6-10 % of the institute's operating budget;

(ii) 2% of the fee collected from the learners; and

(iii) Fee collected from specific services.

4. Personnel

4.1 Personnel involved in providing library services to distance learners should be professionally qualified.

4.2 The distance learning provider should designate a Chief Professional Librarian for coordination of the different library access points and for the overall management of the system to work under the advice of the Library Committee.

4.3 Each library access point should have professionally qualified personnel as full-time or part-time staff in accordance with the institutional policy of staffing support services to support the Chief professional Librarian for achieving the goals and objectives of the institute.

4.4 As distance library services require specialized skills, personnel with specialized skills in non-print media, networking and online services (including databases handling) should be recruited and/or specialized training be provided to the employees on a regular basis.

5. Facilities

5.1 The distance learning provider should provide adequate space, equipments and communication links to enable the designated staff to operate effectively as service units. Examples of suitable arrangements include but are not limited to:

- Space for reading room(s);
- Space for holding library materials;
- Space for office staff;
- File storage cabinets;
- Dedicated telephone line for learner queries;
- Access to fax, Internet, Photocopier;
- Access to packaging and mailing services;
- Access to audio, video, and multimedia equipments;
- Access to appropriate computer facilities.

6. Resources

6.1 Library resources should include materials in all kinds of formats (Physical and electronic). However, they all should meet the requirements of learners, faculty, and other support staff.

6.2 Multiple copies of specific library items should be made available.

6.3 Master copy of all non-print media should be preserved carefully.

7. Services

7.1 In order to meet the information needs of the distance learners, faculty and other support staff, a wide range of services may be necessary. The kinds of services that may include, but are not limited to:

- Reference service either in person, by telephone, or fax, or through e-mail;
- Bibliographic services (Manual and/or computerized) to faculty;
- Borrowing of copies of library materials;

- Obtaining specific copies of articles for course work in compliance with copyright regulations;
- Preparation of "Readings of Articles" in print and/or online on specific topics after copyright clearance;
- Access, from remote locations, to the Website and OPAC of the library and other library networks (eg. DELNET, INFLIBNET);
- Access to online journals, databases located at different serves through student password;
- Access to interlibrary loan services;
- Mobile library services for remote areas;
- Access to Book Bank or recommended "Set of Books";
- Access to reading rooms; and
- Establishment of Learning Resource Centres at Public and Private Libraries through MOUs.

7.2 Some of the library service may be fee-based as per the institutional policy.

7.3 The services should be available during all working hours for optimum access by the users. Efforts should be made for providing services during holidays.

8. Documentation and research

8.1 Library policies should be printed and made available to all patrons.

8.2 Library statistics (including use of the services and about collection) should be prepared regularly.

8.3 User guides, membership forms, and other user related documents should be made available easily.

8.4 All the addresses of the key library professionals along with their duties and responsibilities should be printed in the user guide/manual.

8.5 Evaluative research studies should be conducted at regular intervals to measure the effectiveness of existing library services and design new library services. Internal staff may do the evaluation or external agencies specialized for such activities may be asked to do the job on turnkey basis.

9. Publicity

9.1 Access to library facilities, resources, and services should be clearly advertised and promoted in the programme guide.

9.2 Library timings should be clearly mentioned in the signboards and other documents of the institution.

10. Library education

10.1 To enable the initiation of an academic professional specialization in distance learning library services, Universities should include in their Master's curriculum, an optional special paper on Distance Librarianship.

10.2 Continuing professional development programmes of short duration on all areas of Distance Librarianship should be conducted at regular intervals by professional associations and library schools.

Implementation

To implement the guidelines in its spirit at the national level, the Indian Library Association may consider entering into Memorandum of Understanding with the Distance Education Council, which is the national body for coordination and monitoring of Distance Education in India.

Members of the Committee

Dr. Neela Jagannathan — Chairperson
Librarian & Information Officer
Indira Gandhi National Open University,
Maidan Garhi
New Delhi 110 068

Dr. Ashu Shokeen — Member
Reader in Library and Information Science
Kurukshetra University
Kurukshetra 136119

Dr. Uma Knajilal — Member
Reader in Library and Information Science
Indira Gandhi National Open University,
Maidan Garhi
New Delhi 110 068

Dr. Dinesh K. Gupta — Member
Lecturer in Library and Information Science
Kota Open University
Rawatbhata Road, Akhelgarh
Kota 324 010

Dr. G. Sujata — Member
Deputy Librarian
Dr. B.R. Ambedkar Open University,
Prof. G. Ram Reddy Marg
Road no. 46. Jubilee Hills
Hyderabad 500 033

Ms. Sushma Paudwal — Member
Deputy Librarian
SNDT Women's University Branch Library
Sir Vithaldas Vidya Vihar
Juhu Road, Santacruz (West)
Mumbai 400 049

Dr. Sanjaya Mishra — Convener
Senior Lecturer in Distance Education
Indira Gandhi National Open University,
Maidan Garhi
New Delhi 110 068

About the Editors

Neela Jagannathan holds M.A., MLIS and Ph.D degrees from the University of Bombay. She had worked at various academic and special libraries before joining the B.R. Ambedkar Open University, Hyderabad (1984 to 1987). Since 1987, she has held the posts of Deputy Librarian and Librarian at the Indira Gandhi National Open University, New Delhi. She has published several papers in Indian and foreign journals, attended various national and international conferences and produced a number of educational study materials for distance learners in a varied range of media formats. She has moderated the Virtual Conference on "Library / Information Systems and Student Support" from November 10-December 6, 1998 organised by the Commonwealth of Learning, Vancouver, Canada. She has organized national and international conferences and travelled widely in India and abroad. She is the recipient of "Best Librarian" award from the Federation of Publishers and Booksellers of India.

Neela was the Joint-Director of the project and is the co-author of *'Directory of Women Studies Organisations in India'* published by the Association of Indian Universities and the Commonwealth of Learning. She has jointly edited a book entitled *'Speaking for Ourselves: Women and Distance Education in India'* with Asha Kanwar and co-edited *'Library Services to Distance Learners in the Commonwealth: A Reader'* with Elizabeth F. Watson, Librarian of Learning Resource Centre, Barbados, published by the Commonwealth of Learning, Vancouver, Canada in 1997. Neela has co-edited two volumes entitled '*50 years of Library and Information Services in India*' and '*Library and Information Services in India: States and Union Territories: On the Eve of New Millennium 2001*' with M.K.Jain and others.

She has been a member of the Editorial Board of '*Asian Libraries*', the Library and Information Management journal for Asia and the Pacific published by MCB University Press, Bradford, UK; '*The New Review of Libraries and Lifelong Learning*' published by Trylor Graham, Cambridge, UK and the '*Journal of Library and Information Services in Distance Learning*' to be published by the Haworth Information Press, New York, USA.

She has served as member of the Program Advisory, Board of the Off-Campus Library Services Conference (OCLS) sponsored by the Central Michigan University from 1993-95.

Contact Address: University Librarian and Information Officer, Indira Gandhi National Open University, Maidan Garhi, New Delhi 110 068, India. Tel: 91 011 26962797, Fax: 91 011 26862312; neela41@yahoo.com

Santosh Panda holds Ph.D. in Education (Kurukshetra U.) and Cert. in Educational Television (BBC, UK), and is Professor of Distance Education & Coordinator of Staff Development, at Staff Training & Research Institute of Distance Education (STRIDE), Indira Gandhi National Open University, India. Previously he has worked as Director of STRIDE (1997-2000); Director of Research, Association of Indian Universities (1994-97); Associate Professor and Lecturer in DE at IGNOU (1987-1994); and Lecturer, Faculty of Education, and Project Officer in the Center for Adult & Continuing Education, Kurukshetra University (a dual-mode institution) (1984-87).

Santosh is a Member of the Research Council, and the International Division Task Group at

IGNOU, and Convener of the IGNOU-Government of India Task Group on Training; External Expert, President's Research Grant Committee, Open University of Hong Kong; Member, Commonwealth of Learning-International Research Foundation for Open Learning 'International Steering Team for Research Training in DE'; Member of Advisory Committee, International Center for Training in Open Schooling, National Open School, supported by the Commonwealth of Learning and UNESCO; Member, Advisory Committee, Virtual Distance Learning, University of London External Programme. Dr. Panda largely devotes his time leading and consulting professional development activities for curriculum development, instructional design, learner support, student evaluation, quality assurance, and research and development within distance education, and also for higher education, teacher education and open schooling, both in the 10 open universities and 104 dual-mode universities in India and distance teaching institutions overseas. Has consulted for World Bank, Commonwealth of Learning, UNESCO, UNDP, Government of Nigeria; and currently teaches two masters courses at a distance - '*Communication Technology for Distance Education*', and '*Distance Education: Economic Perspectives*' offered in 14 countries internationally.

He has interest in and researches on planning and management of distance education (including research policy, student attrition and completion/recruitment and retention, human resource development and management, funding policy); instructional design and course development; teacher education, and continuing professional development for new technologies and effective student learning; and telelearning. Has published internationally in these areas (including book chapters for publishers like Routledge, Kogan Page, Commonwealth of Learning, Commonwealth Secretariat), and is currently involved in six referred international journals: founder editor of *Staff and Educational Development International*, co-editor of *Global E-Journal of Open, Flexible & Distance Education* and *Indian Journal of Open Learning,* and editorial board member of *Canadian Journal of Distance Education*, *Educational Technology and Society*, and *OSAC Journal of Open Schooling*. His recent book *Planning and Management in Distance Education* has been published by RoutledgeFalmer, New York and London. In 2003, he is a Fulbright Visiting Professor at the University of New Mexico, USA presenting, teaching and researching on 'online constructivist continuing professional development'.

Contact Address: Staff Training & Research Institute of Distance Education, Indira Gandhi National Open University, New Delhi 110068, India. Fax: +91-11-26857073; spanda@ignou.ac.in; pandasantosh@hotmail.com (http://www.spanda.org).

Uma Kanjilal has an M.A. (Economics), Masters and Ph. D. in Library and Information Science and P.G. Diploma in Distance Education. She joined Indira Gandhi National Open University in 1989 as Lecturer in the Faculty of Library and Information Science. Presently she is working as Reader in the Faculty. She has been actively involved in the planning, preparation and implementation of the BLIS and MLIS Programmes of the University from the beginning. Her specializations include Library and Information Management; Classification and Cataloguing; Multimedia and Web interface Designing and Teaching. Prior to joining IGNOU she worked as Research Assistant in National Manpower Information System Project, Department of Industrial Management Engineering., IIT Kanpur (1984-85); Cataloguer in the ILA Project at Indira Gandhi National Centre for arts, New Delhi (1987-88); and Senior Library Assistant, Indira Gandhi National Centre for Arts, New Delhi (1988-89).

Uma was awarded Fulbright Professional Fellowship in Information Science and Technology for

1999-2000. During the fellowship she was placed in the Graduate School of Library and Information Science, University of Illinois, Urbana Champaign, USA and was involved in development of web and multimedia based courseware on "Total Quality Management in Libraries and Information Centers". Presently she is involved in a major project funded by the Department of Scientific and Industrial Research (DSIR), Government of India on "Web Enhanced Training Programme on ISIS (Windows interface)". She is also coordinating a Certificate Programme on ICT Applications in Libraries to be launched by IGNOU in a year's time. She has a number of papers to her credit in national and international publications and papers presented in national and international conferences. She has also authored a book titled "*Far and Wide: Information Technology and Libraries for Distance Learners*".

Contact Address: Library and Information Science, School of Social Sciences, Indira Gandhi National Open University, Maidan Garhi, New Delhi 110 068, India. uma_kanjilal@hotmail.com

About the Contributors

Andrew McDonald is the Director of Information Services and Professor of Information Management and Strategy at the University of Sunderland. He has lead the development of integrated learning services, new services for distance and lifelong learners, extensive electronic services, cross-sector partnerships and innovative buildings.

National work includes the Joint Funding Council's Space Management Group and the Department of Culture, Media and Sport's Steering Committee on Empowering the Learning Community. He sits on the Chartered Institute of Library and Information Professional's Council and chairs its International Panel. He also chairs the Society of College, National and University Libraries Advisory Committee on Buildings.

Publications, conference papers and research interests span lifelong learning, digital libraries, strategic planning, quality management, information skills, and library planning and design.

International work embraces the International Federation of Library Association's National Forum and its Build Committee. He has directed several international seminars for The British Council and has undertaken consultancy work all over the world.

Contact Address: Director of Information Services, University of Sunderland, Langham Tower, Ryhope Road, Sunderland, UK SR 27EE, Andrew.mcdonald@sunderland.ac.uk

Annie Chan is the Assistant Librarian II (Systems) serving in the Technical Services at the Open University of Hong Kong. She received her Bachelor of Arts Degree (Hons) from the University of Hong Kong and the Master of Librarianship from University of Wales, Aberyswyth in Great Britain. During her years of service at the Open University of Hong Kong, she has helped in the daily administration and operation of the DYNIX Library System. She has also participated in the implementation and operation of the systems of the Electronic Library Project.

Contact Address: Assistant Librarian II, The Open University of Hong Kong Library, 30 Good Shepherd Street, Homantin, Hong Kong. Tel: 852 2768-6783 Fax: 852 2789-33530; ymchan@ouhk.edu.hk

Anthony W. Ferguson has obtained BA in Asian Studies and Political Science in 1968 from Brigham Young University; MA in Political Science in 1971, MLS in 1972 from University of Washington, Ed.D. in 2001 from Columbia University Teachers College, his dissertation is on: library and informational needs of Television University students in China.

He is the University Librarian, University of Hong Kong, 2001. Prior to this, he worked as the Associate University Librarian, Columbia University from 1985-2001; Assistant Library Director, Texas A & M University, 1984-1985; Head Collection Development Department, Asian Studies Librarian, Brigham Young University, 1972-1984.

He has been the collection assessment and development consultant and columnist for "Against the Grain" (Backtalk); HE has participated in various conferences worldwide and is currently the chair of Pacific Rim Digital Library Alliance Steering Committee and vice chair of the Joint University Librarians Advisory Committee (Hong Kong).

Contact Address: University Librarian, University of Hong Kong, 23 Shawan Drive, Pine Court Block 1, Flat 18B. Pokfulam, Hong Kong, SAR.; Tel: 852 2859 2200; (Fax) 852 2858 9420;

Ferguson@hkucc.hku.hk

Audrey G. Anday graduated from the University of the Philippines (UP) at Los Baños with a degree in Bachelor of Science in Applied Mathematics in 1997. After a year, she took up her postgraduate studies, Master of Library and Information Science (MLIS), in UP Diliman. She passed the Philippine Board Examination for Librarians in November 2001 and took her oath to the profession in December 2001. She is currently Information Officer I of the University of the Philippines Open University (UPOU) Library and performs all the library activities in the UPOU Library. She has been connected with the UP Open University for more than 3 years now.

She is the member of the Philippine Librarians' Association Incorporated (PLAI) and UP Library Science Alumni Association (UPLSAA).

Contact Address: Information Officer 1, UP Open University, UPOU Bldg., College, Los Banos, 4031, Laguna, Phillippines. Tel: +6349 5366001 to 06 loc 721 Fax: +6349 5366015; au_anday@yahoo.com

Bhupender Kumar Singh is working as the Asst Librarian & in-charge of the Central library, Kota Open University, Kota, Rajasthan, India. He has obtained M.A. in Geography, MLIS & Ph.D. in Library & Inf. sc. from Banaras Hindu University, Varanasi and PGDDE (Post Graduate Diploma in Distance Education) from IGNOU, New Delhi. He has contributed about 18 (Eighteen) papers in professional Journals and books and attended several National & International conferences, seminars & workshops. His areas of study are user studies, application of information technology and distance librarianship. He is the life member of ILA, IASLIC, UPLA, RLA.

Contact Address: Assistant Librarian and Officer-in-charge, Central Library, Kota Open University, Kota; Tel: 0744 470595; Fax: 0744 470451; bksingh5@yahoo.com

Boonta Wissawapaisal is the Director of the Office of Documentation and Information, Sukhothai Thammathirat Open University since 2000. Boonta Wissawapaisal served for many years as a library administrator in the role of deputy director of the STOU Library or the Office of Documentation and Information. She is a senior librarian who has been involved in library planning and developing, particularly in the development and installation of automated library systems. Prior to working with the STOU Library, she worked with the National Institute of Development Administration Library of Thailand for nearly ten years.

Boonta's specialization is in cataloging and classification systems and library management. She is also responsible for the preparation and editing of STOU textbooks as well as a tutorial instructor of courses in library and information science, both in graduate and undergraduate levels.

Boonta has been involved in outreach library services. She works as an advisor for building library collections and library services in local communities and other organizations. She is a member of the Thai Library Association and other library clubs and served as chairperson of the Public Relation Section, Library Standard Section, and other executive library professional boards under the Thai Library Association.

Boonta received a master degree and graduate diploma from Chulalongkorn University, Thailand. She was awarded a Thai Library Association Plaque of honor in recognition of her outstanding professional career in the year 2000.

Contact Address: Director of the Office of Documentation and Information, Sukhothai Thammathirat Open University, Pakkred, Nonthaburi 11120, Thailand Tel: 662 503-3601, 662 5302121-

4 Ext.7001; Fax: 662 503-3600; dilawboo@stou.ac.th

Effendi Wahyono, born in Tegal, Meddle Jawa, Indonesia on May 21 1960, has master's degree in social history from the University of Indonesia. Since 1985 till now, he has been working as academic staff (lecturer) at the Faculty of Social and Political Science, The Indonesian Open Learning University (Universitas Terbuka-UT). In addition, he also became an editor for Journal of Indonesian Studies at Research Department. Since 1996 he has been the head of the library at the Indonesian Open Learning University. He has participated in seminars on digital library in Indonesia seminar on Indonesian Culture at SOAS London in 1990, and sandwich program for one year at State University Leiden, Netherland, 1990.

Contact Address: Head of Library, Indonesian Open Learning University, Kompleks Universitas Terbuka, Block B, No.8, Jabon Mekar, Parung, Bogor, West Java, Indonesia. Tel: 62-21-7490941 Fax: 62-21-7490947; Effendi@ka.ut.ac.idd

Gill Needham is Learner Support Services Manager at the Library of the Open University in the UK. She has taken in a leading role in developing the Library's services to its 180,000 distance learners, including an electronic library 'Open Library' a helpdesk and the Information Literacy Unit that delivers materials like the on-line tutorial, SAFARI. She is course chair for the Open University's short course in Information Literacy (MOSAIC - Making Sense of Information in the Connected Age) and is one of the authors for a second level course in the OU's School of Health & Social Welfare called Knowledge, Information & Care. Before joining the Open University in 1998, Gill worked for 15 years in the National Health Service as an information specialist and researcher. She has published articles and book chapters on health information and evidence based practice.

Contact Address: Learner Support manager, Open University Library, UKOU, Walton Hall, Milton Keynes, MK7 6AA, UK. Tel+44 1908 858369 Fax:+44 1908 8653571; G.Needham@open.ac.uk

Harvey Gover is a specialist in branch campus library services for land grant university systems. Harvey is tenured on the library faculty of the Washington State University Libraries and currently serves as Assistant Campus Librarian and Head of Reference for Washington State University at Tri-Cities, in Richland, Washington, one of three branch campuses in the Washington State University (WSU) system.

Earlier, Harvey was Public Services Librarian at Tarleton State University, a branch of the Texas A&M University System. Harvey has taught as an adjunct academic faculty member both at Tarleton and WSU Tri-Cities. Also served as an adjunct library faculty member for the Tri-Cities Learning Center of City University, an international, exclusively distance learning institution based in the greater Seattle area. Harvey previously served as Chair of the Editorial Board for Alki; the Journal of the Washington Library Association.

In 1999-2000, Harvey was Chair of the Distance Learning Section (DLS) of the Association of College and Research Libraries (ACRL), a division of the American Library Association (ALA); finalizing a major reorganization with establishment of new interest area committees, including appointments of more than eighty individual committee members and chairs; designed and organized the tenth Anniversary program, invited and introduced the speakers, and served as moderator.

Harvey is internationally recognized for his work on the 1998 *ACRL Guidelines for Distance Learning Library Services*, and is the principal author of the current *Guidelines*, which were revised while he was Chair of the DLS Guidelines Committee, and worked closely with the Committee, as well, on a 2000 minor revision, designed to make the *Guidelines* more outcomes oriented.

A native Texan, Harvey holds his BA from Baylor University, MLIS from the University of Texas at Austin, and an MAT in Public Administration from Tarleton State University of the Texas A&M System.

Contact Address: Assistant Campus Librarian and Head of Reference for Washington State University at Tri-Cities, 2710 University Drive, Richland, Washington 99352-1671. Tel: 509-372-7204; hgover@tricity.wsu.edu

Johanna Tunon is Head of Distance and Instructional Library Services at the Nova Southeastern University. Her department handles the bibliographic instruction for students on campus, online, and at distance sites. She also handles the accreditation and licensure issues for the library. She has an MLS from Texas Woman's University and an EdD in Instructional Technology and Distance Education from Nova Southeastern University. Her Presentations include sessions at the Off-Campus Library Services Conference and American Library Association Conference as well as at a variety of regional conferences including SOLINET, SLA, SEFLIN, the Michigan Library Association, and the Florida Library Association. She co-edited two reference books, Plays for Children and Young Adults: An Evaluative Index and Guide (1991) and North American Romance Writers (1999). She has also written and published a number of published articles and is currently working on a chapter of annotations on the topic of information literacy and distance education for the fourth edition of Alexander Slade's Library Services for Open and Distance Learning: The Third Annotated Bibliography.

Contact Address: Head of Distance and Instructional Library Services, Library, Research & information Technology Center, Nova Southeastern University, 3100 Ray Ferrero Jr. Blvd. Ft. Lauderdale, FL-33314, USA; Tel: 954 262-4608; tunon@nova.edu

Kirupa H. Sellathruai is at present the Senior Assistant Librarian (SAL) at the Open University of Sri Lanka. Born in Jaffna, Sri Lanka, she obtained her MLS in 1999 from the University of Colombo, earlier in 1993 she completed Masters in Business Information Systems (MBIS) or M.Sc. from the University of East London and in 1978, she did B.Sc. from the University of Jaffna. She has been in the library field since 1993. Prior to this, she had taught Mathematics and Science in schools in Sri Lanka & Nigeria.

At present her responsibilities cover the automated library information management system in addition to normal library duties as SAL. She also lectures to Diploma students taking courses conducted by the Sri Lanka Library Association, mainly in Information Technology & other related subjects.

Contact Address: Senior Assistant Librarian, P.O.Box, Library, Open University of Sri Lanka, Nawala, Nugegoda, Sri Lanka, Tel: 094-1-805476 Fax: 094-1-436858; khsel@ou.ac.lk

Madhukar Shewale, B.Sc. (Chem), MLISC. is presently working as Assistant Librarian in Yashwantrao Chavan Maharashtra Open University, Nashik (Maharashtra State) - India. He is also actively engaged in co-ordination of Library and Information science programmes - BLIS and MLIS of the University. He visited the Open University of Hong Kong during 1998 and presented a paper in the pre-conference seminar. i.e. 'Asian Librarian's Roundtable'. Four articles have been published in the National level journals. He coordinated 'INFLIBNET Regional Training for

Library Automation' in November 2001 for the state of Maharashtra.

Contact Address: Assistant Librarian, YCM Open University, Nashik 422 222, Maharashtra; Tel: 0253 231714, 231715; Fax: 0253 231716; m-shewale@yahoo.com

Mou Chakraborty is the Distance & Instructional Technology librarian at Nova Southeastern University. She has an MA in English from University of Calcutta, India and an MLS from University of Missouri-Columbia, USA. Her primary job responsibility is teaching on-campus and at distance sites, and via compressed video. She also provides general reference assistance. She is a liaison for several academic departments communicating with the faculty for collection development and bibliographic instruction.

She had been a medical librarian before joining NSU at several prestigious academic institutions. She has extensive teaching experience and enjoys developing web pages. As a librarian-faculty she has developed a course and has also co-taught graduate level drug information courses. She was a recipient of a faculty development grant to develop a Problem-Based Learning Center. She was also the primary liaison for a Nursing Davis Grant to evaluate the nursing collection and collaborate collectively with other area colleges. She has presented paper at several conferences and her recent poster session at ALA was nominated as a sample poster for future ALA conferences.

Contact Address: Distance / Instructional Technology Librarian, Research & Information Technology Center, Nova Southeastern University, USA; Tel: 954 262-4647 1-800-541-6682 x4647 Fax: 954 262-6830; mou@nova.edu

Muhammad Saadat Ali was born in the Narsingdi district on September 14, 1950. He did his Master Degree in Library and Information Science in 1973 from the University of Dhaka. He started his career as Librarian in Army Central Library on August 4, 1976. On March 9,1998, he joined the Bangladesh Open University as Deputy Librarian. On March 12, he was assigned the duty of Librarian in-Charge. He is trained in distance-education librarianship in the U.K. He participated in AAOU librarians' Roundtable and Conference (Hong Kong : 1998), ICDE seminar (Hong Kong:1999) and AAOU seminar (New Delhi:2002). He is an author of 32 books on library and information science and other disciplines. He is a life-member of Library Association of Bangladesh, and Bangla Academy, member of the Asiatic Society of Bangladesh and donor member of the Dihi Union Public Library, Jessore.

Contact Address: Librarian in-charge, Bangladesh Open University, Gazipur 1705, Bangladesh. Tel: 8802-9800801-3/350 Fax: 8802-9800822; saadat@buo.bangla.net

Nazira Ismail works as Data and Communications Officer in the International Centre for Distance Learning at the Open University, UK. She has 17 years' experience in the collection and dissemination of information on open and distance learning and in developing the ICDL database on CD-ROM and Internet.

She has attended several conferences all over the world and demonstrated ICDL databse. She also supports the MA in Open and Distance Education as a resource provider.

Contact Address: Data and Communication Officer, ICDL, The Open University, Walton Hall, Milton Keynes, MK7 6AA, UK. Tel: +44 1908 653537/652717 Fax:+44 1908 654173; n.ismail-kaye@open.ac.uk

Neela Jagannathan *(see in 'About the Editors')*

Olugbemiro Jegede is currently the National Coordinator of the National Open and Distance Learning Programmes and the Director-General of the National Open University of Nigeria. Until September 2001 when he began setting of the National Open University of Nigeria, he was Chair, Professor and foundation Director, Centre for Research in Distance & Adult Learning (CRIDAL) of The Open University of Hong Kong. Prior to this he was the foundation Head of the Research and Evaluation Unit, Distance Education Centre, University of Southern Queensland, Toowoomba, Australia where he worked for six years. He holds the degrees of B.Sc.Ed and M.Ed from Ahmadu Bello University, Nigeria and a Ph.D from the University of Wales, U.K.

Professor Jegede is also a Chartered Biologist of the London Institute of Biologists, a Fellow of the Science Teachers Association of Nigeria, a recipient of the University of Southern Queensland 1995 Award for Excellence in Research, and a member of the New York Academy of Sciences. He was the foundation Professor and Dean of Education at the University of Abuja, Nigeria. Prior to this he was Associate Professor of Science Education and held the positions of Assistant Dean, Faculty of Education, and Head of Science Education at Ahmadu Bello University where he worked for 17 years. He was a Visiting Fellow at Curtin University of Technology, West Australia from 1998-1999, and a JSPS Fellow at Ibaraki University, Japan, in 1998. His areas of interest include applied cognitive science, science education, computer mediated communications, Instructional design, foundational issues in distance and open education research methodology, adult education and cultural studies in education.

Professor Jegede has over 150 publications including six books, chapter contributions to books, refereed journal articles, and refereed conference proceedings. He is Editor-in-Chief of the Electronic Journal of Instructional Science and Technology, and member of the Editorial Board of several international journals which include "Distance Education - An International Journal," "Journal of Computers in Science and Mathematics Teaching," "Journal of Research in Science Teaching" and "Journal of Science Teachers Association of Nigeria."

Contact Address: National Coordinator of the National Open and Distance Learning Programmes and the Director-General of the National Open University of Nigeria.

Sanjaya Mishra Phd is Senior Lecturer of Distance Education at the Staff Training and Research Institute of Distance Education at Indira Gandhi National Open University, New Delhi.

Contact Address: STRIDE, Indira Gandhi National Open University, Maidan Garhi, New Delhi 110068 India, sanjayamishra@hotmail.com

Uma Kanjilal *(see in 'About the Editors')*

V. K. J. Jeevan received M.Sc. and MLIS degrees from Banaras Hindu University, Varanasi; M.Tech in Computer Science from IIT Kharagpur; and has over eight years of professional experience. He had also qualified the UGC NET for Junior Research Fellow & Lectureship as well as had undergone an yearlong training in 'Information Technology Applications' at the National Centre for Science Information, Indian Institute of Science, Bangalore. He was at the Nuclear Science Centre, New Delhi and is presently working as Assistant Librarian at the Central Library of Indian Institute of Technology, Kharagpur. He received the Young Information Scientist Award by the Society for Information Science (SIS), New Delhi in 2000 and the Second Best Article Award in the National Paper contest conducted by Raja Rammohun Roy Library Foundation,

Department of Culture, Government of India in 2001. He is specializing in computerized information services, library databases, innovative librarianship, resource sharing, library education and library jobs. He has published over seven papers in International Journals, fifteen papers in Indian Journals, three papers in Proceedings of National Conference, and nineteen papers in Proceedings of National Conferences. Jointly with Prof. S Parthan, he has edited the 'Proceedings of the National Conference on Information Management in e-Libraries', Feb 26-27, 2002 organized by the Central Library, IIT, Kharagpur. He has been acting as the Moderator of INDIA-LIS, a listserv owned by IFLA and operated from INIST, France. He is currently an Executive Committee Member of the Society for Information Science (SIS), New Delhi.

Contact Address: Assistant Librarian, Indian Institute of Technology, Kharagpur; West Bengal, 721 302 vkjj@rediffmail.com

Index